POPE PIUS XII LIB., ST. JOSEPH COLLEGE

3 2528 01316 6

S0-CKV-007

Caring for
Children

Challenge to America

Caring for Children

Challenge to America

Edited by

Jeffrey S. Lande
Sandra Scarr
University of Virginia
Nina Gunzenhauser

LEA LAWRENCE ERLBAUM ASSOCIATES, PUBLISHERS
1989 Hillsdale, New Jersey   Hove and London

Copyright © 1989 by Lawrence Erlbaum Associates, Inc.
    All rights reserved. No part of the book may be reproduced in
    any form, by photostat, microform, retrieval system, or any other
    means, without the prior written permission of the publisher.

Lawrence Erlbaum Associates, Inc., Publishers
365 Broadway
Hillsdale, New Jersey 07642

Library of Congress Cataloging-in-Publication Data

Caring for children.

    Papers and comments at the conference held in
Charlottesville, Va., on Nov. 6 and 7, 1987, and
sponsored by the Center for Advanced Studies,
University of Virginia.
    Bibliography: p.
    Includes indexes.
    1. Child care services–United States–Congresses.
2. Child development–United States–Congresses.
3. Child welfare–United States–Congresses.
I. Lande, Jeffrey S.   II. Scarr, Sandra.
III. Gunzenhauser, Nina.   IV. University of Virginia.
Center for Advanced Studies.
HQ778.7.U6C37   1989   362.7'12   89-1152
ISBN 0-8058-0255-X
ISBN 0-8058-0256-8 (pbk.)

Printed in the United States of America
10 9 8 7 6 5 4 3 2 1

Contents

12

Insuring Child Care's Future: The Continuing Crisis
Sharon Kalemkiarian

13

No Room at the Inn: The Crisis in Child Care Supply
Karen Hill-Scott

14

**Cultural Context for Child Care in the Black
Community**
Janice Hale-Benson

15

Aims, Policies, and Standards of For-Profit Child Care
Ann Muscari

16

Issues and Obstacles in the Training of Caregivers
Jeffrey Arnett

17

**Future Directions and Need for Child Care
in the United States**
Deborah A. Phillips

18

General Discussion

References

Author Index

Subject Index

Preface

That experts and laypersons alike debate the virtues and vices of child care bespeaks the grave disquiet that we as a nation feel about mothers who work and about children whose care is delegated, part-time, to others. Child care is as essential a part of contemporary family life as the automobile and the refrigerator, because in the vast majority of today's families both parents are employed. Yet most families find it far easier to purchase quality cars and refrigerators than to buy good care for their children. Not only is there a critical shortage of high-quality child care in this country, but there is such ambivalence about providing child care that we have a shameful national dilemma. The dilemma is very simple: Although nearly 60% of American mothers of infants are now in the labor force, voices are still raised to oppose public support for quality child care on the basis that mothers ought to stay home. If mothers "choose" to work, day care problems are considered their private dilemmas.

Because of the real decline in family income from 1975 to the present, mothers in most nuclear families find it essential to work to support the family at a level above poverty. Similarly, divorced, single, and widowed mothers must work to avoid poverty. This reality has not yet silenced the useless national debate about *whether* child care. Given our nation's falling wages and increasing maternal employment, the debate must be rephrased into *whither* child care.

At the conference on "The Future of Child Care in the United States," held in Charlottesville, Virginia, on November 6 and 7, 1987, we heard many papers and comments and much lively discussion on complex issues surrounding working families, child development, and child care today.

Speakers were invited to illuminate and debate the many troublesome aspects of these issues from their diverse backgrounds and points of view.

Susanne Martinez, Helen Blank, Karen Hill-Scott, and Deborah Phillips presented policy issues at federal, state, and local levels and research on child care policies. Related concerns with standards for and regulation of child care were represented by Earline Kendall, Sharon Kalemkiarian, Barbara Willer, and David Lopez. Diverse issues in programming for early education and care were represented by Janice Hale-Benson, Ann Muscari, and Jeffrey Arnett. Developmental research and women's and family issues were debated by Jay Belsky, Sheila Kamerman, Michael Lamb, Steven Suomi, and Sandra Scarr. From the presentations and discussions at this conference, we achieved a closer look at the facts about children's, parents', and care providers' experiences in our current child care system, their discomforts and their satisfactions, and we oriented our developmental and family research findings to the most pressing issues:

For children, the most pressing issue is *quality* of care—care that will encourage and support all aspects of child development.

For parents, the most pressing issues are *affordability* and *availability* of consistent and dependable child care.

For child care providers, the most pressing issues are *staff wages* and *working conditions* and *public support for a system of high-quality care* that will meet the diverse needs of the working poor, minority families, middle-income families, and even Yuppy parents who want "the best" that money can buy.

For policymakers at federal and state levels, the most pressing issues are how to *fund* a system of quality child care, *regulate* those aspects of quality that can be legislated and enforced, and *coordinate* efforts with the private sector and at all levels of government.

It was quickly evident that not all the urgent needs of children, parents, care providers, and policymakers are necessarily compatible. Certainly, such different needs are not addressed easily by the same policies and practices. For example, if children need high quality care to thrive, how will parents afford it, or even find it, unless policymakers devise and support greater public spending on child care? But how will federal and state governments justify to taxpayers greater expenditures on child care if child care is seen as primarily a private family matter? How will child care providers upgrade their professional staffs and services when parents cannot afford to pay more for child care?

The chapters in this volume represent the most contemporary points in those debates, and the discussions, summarized at the end of each chapter, further clarify the issues. There were points of disagreement about the effects on infants of full-time care in the first year of life; about the role of federal and state governments in the provision of child care; about caregiver training, professionalization, low wages, and turnover; about the regulation of infant and toddler care; about the roles of for-profit and non-profit child care; and about women's rights and children's needs.

But there was also enormous agreement, which surprised and even exhilarated us, about the degree to which our diverse approaches and theoretical commitments led us to the same conclusions. In the last analysis, the warmth and generosity of the participants and the unanimous commitment to improving child care in America led to consensus on the most crucial point: We must all work together to build a child care system in America that can meet the diverse needs of working families and their children.

ACKNOWLEDGMENTS

The editors of this volume wish to acknowledge the assistance of Shelby Miller of the Ford Foundation, Jane Dustan of the Foundation for Child Development, and W. Dexter Whitehead, Director of the Center for Advanced Studies, University of Virginia, who sponsored the conference "The Future of Child Care in the United States" and provided funding for it.

1

Child Care and the Family:
Complements and Interactions

Sandra Scarr
Jeffrey Lande
University of Virginia
Kathleen McCartney
University of New Hampshire

Since the end of World War II, the percentage of women in the work force has increased dramatically in all Western nations. Although such increases are manifested in all age groups, they are most pronounced among women with children under 5 years of age (Hofferth & Phillips, in press; Kamerman, 1983). In the United States, the percentage of working mothers of infants and preschoolers has increased from 32% in 1970 to more than 50% in 1985 and is expected to approach 60% by 1990 (Hoffman, 1984). The most dramatic increases in maternal employment have occurred for married women with infants under 12 months; their rate of employment has increased more than 10% from 1975 to 1985 and now exceeds 50% (Kamerman, this volume).

In Bermuda in the last 20 years, the percentage of mothers in the labor force has been much higher than that of mothers in the United States. By 1980, 83% of mothers in Bermuda were employed, and 82% of Bermudian children were in child care by age 4 (Bermuda Bureau of Census, 1983). By age 2, 75% of Bermudian children are in nonmaternal care, most of them for more than 20 hours per week (Scarr & McCartney, 1988).

As the rate of maternal employment increases, so does concern over the possible effects of nonmaternal care. The traditional belief in many Western societies is that women must stay home with their children in order to be good mothers and to promote their children's emotional and intellectual development. Among psychologists, this belief has been supported, in part, by human (Barglow, Vaughn, & Molitar, in preparation; Bowlby, 1969; Schwarz, Krolick, & Strickland, 1973) and nonhuman primate (Harlow, Harlow, Dodsworth, & Arling, 1966) research findings, where repeated mother-child separations have been reported to have detrimental effects on an offspring's intellectual and socioemotional development. The belief in maternal care has also been supported by nonscientific cultural beliefs about women's place in society (see Scarr, 1984).

Even in scientific studies, however, cognitive deficits are not an inevitable consequence of nonmaternal child care. Several studies have reported that high-quality nonmaternal child care has beneficial effects for the intellectual development of children (Caldwell & Freyer, 1982; Caldwell, Wright, Honig, & Tannenbaum, 1970; Keister, 1970; McCartney, Scarr, Phillips, & Grajek, 1985; Ramey, Bryant, & Suarez, in press; Ramey & Farran, 1983). Many of these effects held for both lower and middle-class children. In general, however, nonmaternal care has been found to have neither beneficial nor detrimental effects on early intellectual development (Belsky & Steinberg, 1978; Fowler, 1974; Kagan, Kearsley, & Zelazo, 1978; Scarr, 1984).

By contrast, several differences have consistently been observed in the social behaviors of children receiving nonmaternal care and those reared primarily by their mothers. Children, particularly boys, receiving nonmaternal child care in child care centers have been negatively labeled as more peer oriented (Cochran, 1977; Finkelstein, Dent, Gallagher, & Ramey, 1978) and aggressive (Finkelstein & Wilson, 1977; Haskins, 1985; Schwarz, Strickland, & Krolick, 1974) or more positively labeled as assertive and independent (Clarke-Stewart & Fein, 1983). It should be noted, however, that by training child care providers to use behavioral management techniques Finkelstein and Wilson (1977) were able to reduce the frequency of aggressive behaviors in children receiving nonmaternal care to the same level as that of children who did not regularly receive nonmaternal care. Thus, "aggressive" behavior among preschool children in center-based care clearly depends on socialization practices that can be changed.

The question of whether deficits in the parent-child attachment develop, however, is a subject of continuing debate. Some investigators have reported a higher proportion of insecure attachment as assessed by the Strange Situation (Ainsworth & Bell, 1970) among infants enrolled in nonmaternal child care than in the general population (Belsky, this volume, 1986, 1988; Blehar, 1974; Schwartz, 1983). Other investigators have reported that nonnmaternal child care does not affect the nature or strength of children's attachments to their parents (Broberg, Hwang, Lamb, & Ketter-

linus, this volume; Cochran, 1977; Kagan, Kearsley, & Zelazo, 1978; Mc-
Cartney, in press; Moskowitz, Schwarz, & Corsini, 1977; Phillips, Mc-
Cartney, Scarr, & Howes, 1987; Rubenstein & Howes, 1979; Thompson, in
press).

Conflicting reports may be due in part to lack of generality of many of
the child care studies conducted in the 1970s. Much of this child care research was conducted in high-quality, university-based child care centers
with low child/caregiver ratios, which were atypical of group care available in most communities. Moreover, most young children were and are in
family day care, which has seldom been studied. *Family day care* refers to
nonmaternal care provided either in the child's home or in a home other
than that of the child, whereas *group care* refers to center-based child care.

Research has shown that caregiver/child ratios are an important component in assessing the quality of nonmaternal child care arrangements
(Brunner, 1980; Field, 1980; Francis & Self, 1982; Howes, 1983; Howes &
Rubenstein, 1985; Reuter & Yunik, 1973; Ruopp, Travers, Glantz, & Coelen,
1979; Smith & Connolly, 1981). Lower caregiver/child ratios are predictive
of emotional distress (Howes, 1983; Howes & Rubinstein, 1985; Ruopp et
al., 1979), less verbal communication and imitation (Francis & Self, 1982;
Howes & Rubenstein, 1985; Smith & Connolly, 1981), and less prosocial behavior (Ruopp et al., 1979) in infants. For infants, these deleterious effects
were found in nonmaternal child care arrangements where the
caregiver/child ratio was 1:6 or more. Brunner (1980), Field (1980), and
Reuter and Yunik (1973) noted, however, that the appropriate ratio for toddlers includes more children per caregiver than for infants. Toddlers displayed the best outcomes in arrangements where the caregiver/child ratio
was between 1:8 and 1:12. The researchers speculated that this finding was
due to the fact that toddlers interact and learn from peers much more than
infants do.

Andersson's (1987) Swedish child care study examined another
dimension of the consequences that child care may have on development.
His research indicates that children from nuclear families, with both
parents present, are developmentally more advantaged than children from
single-parent families, and that high-quality child care in Sweden is not an
advantage or disadvantage to children from two-parent families. However,
interactions between child care and family structure may be the underlying cause for many of the reported differences between single-parent and
nuclear families. At age 8, children from mother-headed families who had
spent a great deal of time in early group care scored as well as, if not higher
than, children from nuclear families on measures of cognitive and social
competence. Children from mother-headed families without early group

care experience, however, received the lowest scores of any group on cognitive and social measures.

The present investigation focused on the magnitude and continuity of effects of different types of child care on intellectual and socioemotional development. Specifically, the intent was to examine whether group and/or family day care had detrimental or beneficial effects on children's development and if any such effects were mediated by family types (e.g., nuclear families, mother-headed families, extended nuclear families, or extended mother-headed families).

In such a study of existing community child care, one must take into account the qualities that are represented by each kind of care. From previous studies, we knew that infant care in Bermuda is extremely varied and that existing regulations permit as many as eight babies per (untrained) caregiver. We also knew that most family day care providers do not accept such a large number of infants in their homes; rather, they tend to have small numbers of mixed-age children. Mothers at home, of course, rarely have more than two preschool children, because Bermudian families are small. Group care of children over the age of 2 is the most frequent type of care and is based on typical nursery school educational models. On the basis of this knowledge, we drew up the following hypotheses:

1. Infant group care, as it exists in Bermuda, would be less supportive of all aspects of infant development than either home care or family day care; at age 2, children who had extensive group care would score lower on developmental tests and ratings.

2. Neither group care nor family day care would have detrimental consequences on child development at age 4.

3. Higher adult/child ratios would be predictive of higher socioemotional and cognitive scores at age 2, but not at age 4.

4. Children reared in nuclear families would have higher socioemotional and cognitive scores than children in either mother-headed or extended families.

5. Time in nonmaternal child care would offset some of the negative consequences of being reared in single-parent families.

METHODS

Subjects

Participants were selected from Scarr and McCartney's (1988) sample of 127 families with 2-year-olds who were living in Bermuda from 1979 to 1983. To minimize variance due to cultural differences, only Black Bermudians were included in this report. Subjects were 100 Black Bermudian families with 2-year-olds (51 boys and 49 girls). Fifty-seven were nuclear families (mother, father, and child); 13 were extended nuclear families (mother, father, child, and at least one other adult in the household); 10 were mother-headed households (mother and child); and the remaining 20 were extended single-mother families (mother, child, and relatives of the mother, usually the mother's own parents or siblings).

As shown in Table 1.1, Bermudian families are small; the mean family size, including both children and adults, was 3.7, and the adult/child

TABLE 1.1
Descriptive Statistics of Measures of Family and Maternal Characteristics and Day Care Experience

Measure	Mean	sd	Range
Family size	3.68	2.39	2–13
Family income	9.84	4.43	1–20
Birth order	1.48	.70	1–4
Adult/child ratio	2.01	1.61	.33–9
Amount of time mother works	1.43	.87	0–3
0 = not employed			
1 = < 40 hours/week			
2 = 40 hours/week			
3 = > 40/hours/week			
Maternal occupation (NORC rating)	40.68	13.20	14–72
Maternal education (in years)	11.80	3.04	3–19
Mother's positive control			
When child is 2 years old	−.18	1.76	−4–2
When child is 4 years old	−.15	1.77	−5–3
Maternal WAIS vocabulary score	9.04	3.11	3–16
Hours in group care			
0–2 years	719.7	1,219.40	0–3,966
2–4 years	1,825.8	1,409.00	0–4,125
Hours in family day care			
0–2 years	1,104.4	1,372.00	0–4,116
2–4 years	779.6	1,243.7	0–4,020

ratio within a household was 2:1. Sixty percent of the target children were firstborn, and 27% were second-born; only 13% of the children were third- or later-born. Mothers had a mean occupational prestige rating of 40.68 as assessed by the NORC Survey Scale,[1] which is close to the average obtained in studies of young women workers in the United States (Scarr & McAvay, 1985). Twenty-one percent of the mothers were not employed, and 67% worked full time, or 40 hours per week. Mothers had an average of 12 years of education, and their mean WAIS Vocabulary Subtest score was 9.04.[2] It should be noted that for a Black sample, the achievements of these mothers are considerably higher than those of Black women in the United States (see, e.g., Scarr & Weinberg, 1976).

More than 75% of the target children were enrolled in some form of child care, at least part time, prior to age 2. The child care situations described in this study include group care in centers, family day care in other homes (occasionally including family day care in the child's own home), and maternal care in the child's own home. Because we could not observe in all the settings in which the children's care took place, we questioned parents carefully about the child's setting. The major differences in these settings were differences in adult/child ratios, both when the children were under 2 and when they were 4 years of age. Group care in centers afforded fewer adults per child—an average of 1:5.49 in the day care centers, compared with 1:2.20 in family day care and 2:1 in the child's own home. In group care centers, caregiver/child ratios were just one of many highly correlated aspects of quality, but one that was useful as an index (Phillips, Scarr, & McCartney, 1987).

Procedure

At age 2, the children's intellectual abilities were assessed with the Stanford-Binet Test of Intelligence (Terman & Merrill, 1972) and/or the Bayley Scales of Infant Development (Bayley, 1969). Children were given both the Bayley Scales and the Stanford-Binet when neither a ceiling score on the Bayley Scales nor a basal score on the Stanford-Binet was obtained. Scores were interpolated by using the basal mental age on the Bayley, adding months of credit on the Stanford-Binet, and entering the mental age into the Stanford-Binet Manual. Scores of children who required the use of both tests appropriately fell between those of children who were assessed exclusively with the Bayley and those who could be assessed with the Stanford-Binet. At age 4, all children were assessed using the Stanford-Binet. The internal consistencies of the Bayley Scales and the Stanford-Binet were .88 and .79, respectively.

Children's motivation to learn and to cooperate with adults was assessed at both 2 years and 4 years with a maternal teaching task, modeled on that constructed by Hess, Shipman, Brophy, and Bear (1968). Mothers of 2-year-olds were asked to teach their children to sort a set of four small toys by color and type. When the children were 4, mothers taught them to sort a set of six small toys, again by color and type. In addition to recording a child's performance, the experimenters rated the child's cooperation, enthusiasm, and resistance. Average interrater agreement ranged from .61 to .68. Experimenters also rated the "positiveness" of the mother's control during the teaching task on a 4-point scale. Average interrater agreement ranged from .72 to .74.

Children's motivation to learn and to cooperate with adults was also measured with the Cain-Levine Social Competence Scale (Cain, Levine, & Elzey, 1963). Items from the Cain-Levine were divided into two sets, one for adaptive skills, such as brushing teeth, wiping up spills, and tying shoes, and a second for everyday communication skills, such as understanding instructions and answering the telephone. This division produced separate scores for adaptive and communicative abilities. The internal consistency for the Cain-Levine was .93.

Children's personality was assessed through both maternal and examiner ratings on the Childhood Personality Scale (CPS; Cohen, Dibble, & Grawe, 1977), which was developed for use with children in the first 6 years of life. Scarr and McCartney (in press) reported that the CPS was best represented by a five-factor solution, labeled as *apathy, attention, expressiveness, hyperactivity,* and *introversion.* Internal consistencies on the scales ranged from .87 to .95 at both age 2 and age 4. Interrater agreement was as follows: apathy .47, attention .54, expressiveness .78, hyperactivity .64, and introversion .59.

Mothers also completed a history of child care questionnaire (Scarr & McCartney, in press). This assessed the amount of time that children spent at each month of age in nonmaternal child care by type of care (e.g., group or family day care) and other characteristics of care, such as number of hours, caregiver/child ratios, and the like.

Data Analysis

Because our primary interest was to assess the extent to which child care and family characteristics affected children's outcomes, multiple regressions were used. In the first set of analyses, each outcome measure was regressed on 10 predictor variables that were hypothesized to affect children's cognitive and socioemotional outcomes. These variables, as shown in Table 1.2, were selected because it was hypothesized that

TABLE 1.2
Predictor Variables in the First Set of Regressions

Variable	Assessment Instrument
Child's gender	Family Background Questionnaire
Child's birth order	Family Background Questionnaire
Family structure	Family Background Questionnaire
Family income	Family Background Questionnaire
Adult/child ratio	Family Background Questionnaire
Amount of time mother works	Family Background Questionnaire
Time spent in family day care	History of Day Care Questionnaire
Time spent in group day care	History of Day Care Questionnaire
Mother's positive control	Maternal Teaching Task
Mother's vocabulary score	Wechsler Adult Intelligence Scale

children's gender, maternal characteristics, time spent in nonmaternal care, and family characteristics would be significant influences on child development. Possible interactions were examined in another set of analyses by regressing outcome variables on family structure, time spent in child care by type of care, and the interactions between child care and family structure. Interaction terms were obtained by computing the product of the variables' scores (Cohen & Cohen, 1983). In the final set of analyses, each outcome measure was regressed on those variables and interaction terms that had accounted for at least 1% of that outcome's total variance in prior analyses. Pearson Product Moment Correlations were computed to assess the stability of measures as well as relationships between variables.

RESULTS

Stability of Measures

As expected, the correlation of Stanford-Binet or Bayley scores at 2 years with Stanford-Binet scores at 3.5 to 4 years was high ($r = .75$). Other reasonably stable measures included the adaptive and communications skills scales from the Cain-Levine and four scales from the CPS: Attention, Expressiveness, Hyperactivity, and Introversion. These correlations ranged from .28 to .49, as shown in Table 1.3.

Correlations between predictor measures ranged from -.40 to .65, as shown in Table 1.4. When predictors to be used in the same equation are moderately to highly correlated, inferences about causality are clouded. For

TABLE 1.3
Correlations Between Child Outcomes at Age 2 and Age 4

IQ	.75*
Cain–Levine Adaptive Skills (CL-AS)	.36*
Cain–Levine Communication Skills (CL-C)	.48*
CPS Apathy	.13
CPS Attention score (Att.)	.46*
CPS Expressiveness score (Exp.)	.28*
CPS Introversion score (Int.)	.40*
CPS Hyperactivity score (Hyp.)	.49*

*$p < .01$

example, in this sample, birth order and adult/child ratios were correlated .65; that is, firstborn children were likely to come from families with more adults per child than later-born children. Thus, the meaning of birth order and adult/child ratios in children's outcomes is confounded. Similarly, children who had many hours of group care under the age of 2 were also likely to have more hours of group care between the ages of 2 and 4 ($r = .52$), and mothers with higher WAIS vocabulary scores were more likely to have higher family income ($r = .50$), occupational status ($r = .47$), and educational levels ($r = .51$). Such is the world of correlated events (Scarr, 1985).

Fortunately, in this sample the important predictor variables of child care types and family characteristics were not confounded to any great degree, as no correlation between child care and family variables was above .25, with the understandable exception of family income, which was higher in families where both parents work and more child care is used. Table 1.4 shows those relationships.

Predictions of Child Outcomes

Regression equations were calculated for each outcome variable at ages 2 and 4. Results are shown in Tables 1.5 through 1.11. In each table, the beta coefficients are those in the best-weighted or final equation. The stepwise R^2s are the increase in R^2 attributed to adding the variable to a stepwise equation, and the rs are the zero-order correlations of the predictor with the outcome variable. Results are mentioned if the betas equal or exceed .15 and if the overall equation is statistically reliable at a level of p .05.

The first results concern intellectual development. Higher family incomes proved to be the best predictor of higher child IQ at age 2. The equation, shown in Table 1.5, that predicted higher child IQs was: higher family income, higher maternal WAIS vocabulary scores, more positive mater-

TABLE 1.4
Correlations Between Predictor Variables

	BO	FI	AC	TMW	G1	G2	F1	F2	MPC	WVS	MH	EMH	EN
Child's gender (CG)	-.01	-.01	-.04	.18	.12	.27	.03	.00	-.00	<.15	.00	.01	.12
Birth order (BO)		.00	.65	-.13	.02	-.05	-.08	-.02	.02	.03	-.13	-.17	.10
Family income (FI)			.15	.14	-.01	.09	.28	.08	.23	.50	-.17	-.35	-.06
Adult/child ratio (AC)				.01	-.02	-.07	.09	.03	.01	-.15	.14	.19	.24
Amount of time mother works (TMW)					.21	.23	.40	.25	-.14	-.02	.08	-.08	.01
Time in group care (0-2 Years) (G1)						.52	-.29	-.17	-.18	-.09	.11	.06	.03
Time in group care (2-4 Years) (G2)							.00	-.40	-.14	-.08	.02	.14	.09
Time in family day care (0-2 Years) (F1)								.42	.05	.17	.03	-.16	-.13
Time in family day care (2-4 Years) (F2)									.04	.19	-.10	-.04	-.13
Mother's positive control (MPC)										.35	-.17	-.11	-.05
Mother's WAIS vocabulary score (WVS)											-.22	-.17	-.09
Mother-headed household (MH)												-.18	-.10
Extended mother-headed household (EMH)													-.14
Extended nuclear family (EN)													

TABLE 1.5
Prediction of Children's Stanford–Binet IQ (Nuclear family = contrast group)

	Age 2			Age 4		
	Beta	r	Stepwise R^2	Beta	r	Stepwise R^2
Mother's WAIS vocabulary score	.21	.46	.21	.41	.50	.25
Mother's positive control	.18	.42	.26	.27	.35	.30
Amount of time mother works	−.18	.20	.30			
0 = not employed						
1 = <40 hours/week						
2 = 40 hours/week						
3 = >40 hours/week						
Family income	.24	.38	.34			
Child's gender	−.15	−.28	.36	−.22	−.30	.35
0 = females						
1 = males						
Time in group care (0–2 years)	−.13	−.26	.37			
	$F = 7.14$	$p < .000$		$F = 13.47$	$p < .000$	

nal control techniques, less maternal working time, and being female. At age 4, however, family income was no longer a significant predictor of a child's IQ. The equation that best predicted higher IQ at age 4 included higher maternal WAIS vocabulary scores, maternal positive control techniques, and being female. Neither at age 2 nor at age 4 were child care variables significant predictors of children's intellectual development, as assessed by IQ scores.

Lower adaptive skills at age 2 were predicted by coming from a mother-headed or extended nuclear household, spending many hours in group or family day care, or being male. But being in group care had a positive effect on the adaptive skills of children from single-parent homes. At age 4, lower adaptive scores were predicted by a different set of variables: children whose mothers used negative control and teaching techniques, with lower family income, and children who were male had lower adaptive skills scores. Neither the amount nor the type of child care predicted adaptive skills at age 4; nor were there interactions between child care and family characteristics. These results are shown in Table 1.6.

As shown in Table 1.7, children with lower communication scores at age 2 came from mother-headed households, spent more time in group care, had mothers who used more negative control techniques, came from families with lower adult/child ratios (confounded with birth order). But children from mother-headed households who had more group care ex-

TABLE 1.6
Prediction of Children's Cain–Levine Adaptive Skills Scores
(Nuclear family = contrast group)

	Age 2 Beta	Age 2 r	Age 2 Stepwise R^2	Age 4 Beta	Age 4 r	Age 4 Stepwise R^2
Child's gender	−.19	−.25	.06	−.16	−.15	.21
0 = female						
1 = male						
Mother's positive control				.22	.33	.11
Family income				.21	.13	.14
Amount of time mother works				−.13	−.20	.17
Mother's teaching style				.19	.16	.19
Time in family day care (0–2 years)	−.22	−.17	.09			
Extended nuclear family households	−.18	−.17	.12			
Mother-headed households	−.33	−.17	.15			
Time in group care (0–2 years)	−.18	−.11	.17			
Adult/child ratio	.13	.06	.18			
Mother's WAIS vocabulary score	−.11	−.03	.19			
Time in group care	−.11	−.03	.19			
×	.16	.00	.20			
Mother-headed households						
	$F = 2.24$ $p < .05$			$F = 3.71$ $p < .01$		

TABLE 1.7
Prediction of Children's Cain–Levine Communication Score
(Nuclear family = contrast group)

	Age 2 Beta	Age 2 r	Age 2 Stepwise R^2	Age 4 Beta	Age 4 r	Age 4 Stepwise R^2
Mother's positive control	.25	.35	.12			
Time in group care (0–2 years)	−.30	−.31	.18			
Adult/child ratio	.19	.06	.24			
Mother-headed households	−.38	−.23	.21	−.41	−.34	.23
Mother's WAIS vocabulary score				.27	.41	.17
Extended nuclear family households				−.08	−.13	.25
Birth order				.25	.15	.26
Family income				.14	.30	.27
Extended mother-headed households				.12	.04	.28
Time in group care (2–4 years)				.13	−.10	.29
Child's gender	−.11	−.23	.26			
0 = female						
1 = male						
Time in group care 0–2 years						
×	.26	−.08	.30			
Mother-headed households						
Time in group care 2–4 years						
×				.26	−.10	.32
Mother-headed households						
Birth order						
×				−.32	−.10	.33
Time in group care 2–4 years						
	$F = 5.05$ $p < .00$			$F = 5.38$ $p < .00$		

perience had better communication skills than similar children with less group care experience. Thus, although group care may be a disadvantage for many children in the first 2 years of life, it was an advantage for 2-year-old children from mother-headed households.

Lower communication scores at age 4 were still predicted for children from single-mother households, but children from mother-headed households were still scoring higher if they had more rather than less group care between the ages of 2 and 4. Group care, which was a substantial negative effect for infants, except those from mother-headed households, had become a mildly positive effect for the entire sample (beta = .13) and remained a considerable positive effect for 4-year-olds from mother-headed households. Earlier-born children (mostly firstborn in this sample), especially those with more group care from 2 to 4 years of age, and children with mothers with higher WAIS vocabulary scores had better communication scores at age 4. Child care variables were not main effects on children's communication skills at age 4.

Table 1.8 shows that children with lower attention ratings were more likely to come from mother-headed households, to have spent more time

TABLE 1.8
Prediction of Children's Attention Scores (CPS)
(Nuclear family = contrast group)

	Age 2			Age 4		
	Beta	*r*	*Stepwise* R^2	*Beta*	*r*	*Stepwise* R^2
Child's gender	−.18	−.23	.05			
0 = female						
1 = male						
Mother-headed households	−.37	−.22	.10			
Mother's positive control				.27	.36	.13
Mother's WAIS vocabulary score				.23	.30	.17
Birth order				.28	.16	.19
Adult/child ratio				−.21	.04	.21
Extended nuclear family households	−.12	−.18	.13	−.14	−.15	.23
Time in group care (0–2 years)	−.25	−.18	.14			
Time in family day care (0–2 years)	−.12	−.06	.16			
Amount of time mother works	−.13	−.04	.17			
Time in group care 0–2 years × Mother-headed households	.32	.07	.26			
Amount of time mother works × Time in family day care 0–2 years	−.12	−.06	.27			
Time in group care 0–2 years × Extended nuclear family households	−.15	−.23	.28			
	$F = 2.68$ $p < .01$			$F = 4.27$ $p < .01$		

in group care in the first 2 years of life, and to be males. However, children from mother-headed households who had spent more time in group care were rated as more attentive than those who had spent less time in group care. One marginal result occurs in this and no other equation: Children from extended nuclear families who have spent more time in group care were rated as less attentive than other children from such families.

As in the results for IQ, adaptive skills, and communication scores, family variables became much more important than child care history in predicting attention scores at age 4. At age 4, the equation that best predicted higher attention scores was: being later-born, having a mother who used positive control techniques and who had a higher WAIS vocabulary score (the two are correlated .35), and having fewer adults per child in the household (or being later-born). No child care variable predicted attention scores at age 4.

At age 2, higher introversion scores (being less sociable, more shy) were more likely for children from families with higher incomes and from mothers who used less positive control techniques. Children from any kind of household other than a nuclear family were also likely to be more intro-verted. At age 4, however, children's introversion scores were not reliably predicted by any of the family or child care variables measured. Child care variables were unrelated to introversion at either 2 or 4 years of age. Table 1.9 gives these results.

TABLE 1.9
Prediction of Children's Introversion Score (CPS)
(Nuclear family = contrast group)

	Age 2			Age 4		
	Beta	r	Stepwise R^2	Beta	r	Stepwise R^2
Mother's positive control	− .22	− .21	.04			
Family income	.35	.12	.08			
Extended mother-headed households	.33	.11	.13			
Birth order	.22	.18	.16			
Extended nuclear family households	.18	.21	.18			
Mother-headed households	.17	.03	.20			
	$F = 3.08$	$p < .01$		F = not significant		

Table 1.10 shows that children's lower emotional expressiveness scores at age 2 were best predicted by more hours in group care and by having a mother with lower WAIS vocabulary score. At age 4, however, lower ex-

TABLE 1.10
Prediction of Children's Expressiveness Score (CPS)
(Nuclear family = contrast group)

| | Age 2 | | | Age 4 | | |
	Beta	*r*	*Stepwise R²*	*Beta*	*r*	*Stepwise R²*
Time in group care (0–2 years)	−.25	−.30	.07			
Mother-headed households				−.28	−.31	.09
Extended nuclear family households				−.15	−.12	.12
Mother's WAIS vocabulary score	.24	.18	.10	.11	.19	.13
Family income	−.13	−.03	.11			
Birth order	−.11	−.09	.12	.12	.14	.14
Amount of time mother works	−.11	−.17	.14			
	$F = 2.30$	$p < .05$		$F = 3.05$	$p < .05$	

pressiveness scores were best predicted by being reared in a mother-headed household. At neither age were child care variables or their interactions with family variables predictors of children's emotional expressiveness.

The set of variables that provided the best prediction of higher hyperactivity scores at age 2 is shown in Table 1.11. Children who were rated by mothers and examiners as being overly active were more likely to be firstborns, to come from mother-headed households, to have mothers who used punitive control techniques, to have many adults in the household, and to be males. In addition, boys from mother-headed households were likely to be rated as more hyperactive than other boys or than girls from similar homes. At 4 years of age, the only predictors of hyperactivity were being male and having a mother who used more punitive control techniques. Of course, at both 2 and 4, the relationship between hyperactivity and punitive maternal control is not necessarily unidirectional or causal: Children who are more hyperactive are more likely to evoke such parenting (Scarr, 1985). Child care variables were not implicated in hyperactivity rating at either age 2 or age 4.

Regressing apathy ratings at age 2 on the entire set of predictor variables and interaction terms failed to yield any statistically reliable regression equation. Apathy ratings at age 4 were reliably predicted only by lower maternal WAIS vocabulary scores and more family day care, rather than by amount of group care or maternal care from age 2 to age 4 ($F = 3.12$, $p < .05$; beta = -.29).

TABLE 1.11
Prediction of Children's Hyperactivity Scores (CPS)
(Nuclear family = contrast group)

	Age 2			Age 4		
	Beta	*r*	*Stepwise R²*	*Beta*	*r*	*Stepwise R²*
Mother's positive control	− .43	− .42	.18	− .27	− .29	.07
Child's gender	.20	.37	.25	.30	.31	.17
0 = female						
1 = male						
Birth order	− .45	− .15	.28			
Adult/child ratio	.39	.07	.30			
Mother-headed households	− .46	− .01	.33			
Family income	− .13	− .23	.35			
Child's gender × Mother-headed households	.26	.22	.38			
	$F = 6.29$	$p < .00$		$F = 7.89$	$p < .00$	

CONCLUSIONS

Consistent with prior research, the best predictors of children's socioemotional and intellectual development were the child's gender and measures of maternal and family characteristics. At both age 2 and age 4, boys lag behind girls in many developmental areas. Our results replicate those of many other studies. We also replicated the finding of many other studies showing that children with mothers who have lower vocabulary scores and lower family incomes tended to score lower on developmental tests and ratings. The interpretation of these results is muddied by the fact that the two predictors are moderately intercorrelated and correlated with other family variables, including maternal discipline and control techniques (Scarr, 1985; Scarr & McCartney, 1988).

At age 2, children from mother-headed households often received worse ratings of adaptive skills, communication, attention, introversion, and hyperactivity than children from other types of households. These differential effects, however, were observed at age 4 only for communication and expressiveness. The mediators between single-mother households and child development have not been well explored in this or other studies, although in this study, unlike most others, single-mother households were not notably poorer nor lower in occupational status than other households

1. Child Care and the Family

(see Table 1.4). Thus, it seems that variables other than income and its correlated lifestyle must explain the differences in children's outcomes.

A crucial distinction in this study was made between single mothers living alone in mother-headed households and others living with their extended families. Children of single mothers living in extended families showed only one difference (higher ratings of introversion at age 2) from children in nuclear families. Children in mother-headed households were the ones at risk.

Both group care and family structure affected child development more at age 2 than at age 4. At age 2, children with the most infant group care had lower adaptive skills, communication scores, and ratings of attention and expressiveness than children with as much infant care in family day care homes or in maternal care. At age 4, however, there were no effects of group care in infancy (under the age of 2) and only positive effects of group care between the ages of 2 and 4 on communication skills. Family day care between the ages of birth and 2 showed no effects, compared with maternal care, and between the ages of 2 and 4 a negative effect on ratings of children's apathy, compared with group care and maternal care.

The developmental deficits observed in 2-year-olds who had large amounts of group care prior to age 2 may be explained by the fact that the group care we studied afforded fewer adults per child—an average of 1:5.49 in the day care centers, compared with 1:2.2 in family day care and 2:1 in the home. Because of the poorer caregiver/child ratios, infants in group care did not receive as much attention and stimulation as they would have in other settings. These findings reflect the need for lower child/caregiver ratios for infants and toddlers rather than providing any statement that group care per se is less desirable than maternal or family day care.

One of the most interesting results was that group care can interact positively with family structure, at least in infancy. At age 2, children of mother-headed families who had experienced more infant group care had higher adaptive skills, communication scores, and attention ratings than other children from mother-headed households. At age 4, however, this effect is noted only for communication scores. This finding is consistent with Andersson's (1987) findings in Sweden that high-quality group care can offset the potentially deleterious effects noted in single-mother households, even when those mothers are not poor. In the United States, Ramey and his associates (Ramey, Bryant, & Suarez, in press) found that children from poor families with single mothers benefitted considerably from early, high-quality care.

The beneficial effects of infant group care may rest on a need for stimulation and attention. Infants in mother-headed households may receive less attention and stimulation than their peers in group care simply because there is only one caregiver in the household. By attending group care, infants receive additional attention and stimulation. An alternative, or complementary, hypothesis for explaining why child care may offset the deleterious effects of mother-headed families involves parental stress. Hauenstein, Scarr, and Abidin (1987) found in another sample that single mothers in Bermuda with children under 2 years had higher levels of perceived stress than mothers who had at least one other adult living in the same household. It is possible that group care may reduce mothers' stress by relieving them of a portion of their daily responsibilities.

It is important to note that by the age of 4 the effects of family composition and child care arrangements have largely disappeared. The effects noted for mother-headed households apply at age 4 only to communication scores. There were no effects of amount or type of child care on children's development except that children receiving the most family day care between years 2 and 4 were more apathetic than other children. Preschoolers enrolled in family day care have less opportunity to interact with same-age peers, and thus their higher levels of apathy may reflect a socialization problem. Children in group care tended to have higher communication scores at age 4, which may result from greater opportunities to communicate with other adults and peers than children at home or in family day care have.

In sum, of the five hypotheses tested, all were supported, at least in part, by the data. Increased time spent in group care under the age of 2 resulted in lower scores on measures of socioemotional and cognitive development than either home care or family day care (hypothesis 1). Although group care resulted in lower scores on measures of intellectual and socioemotional development at age 2, such detriments were seen at age 4 only for family day care on one measure of apathy and for group care on no measure (hypothesis 2). Higher adult/child ratios in child care were predictive of better development of children at 2 but not at 4. Higher adult/child ratios in the family were confounded in the small Bermuda families with children's birth orders, such that the results are difficult to interpret (hypothesis 3). Children reared in nuclear families did not have consistently higher scores than children in other family structures except those from mother-headed households, who had the lowest scores on several measures of socioemotional and intellectual development at age 2, but even this was much less evident at age 4 (hypothesis 4). Evidently the circumstances of children in extended families in Bermuda, whether nuclear or single-mother, are such that the children are not seriously disadvantaged in comparison with children from nuclear families. Children reared in mother-headed families who had spent large amounts of time in infant group care had higher developmental scores than other children from similar families, thus suggesting beneficial effects of child care from children from such families (hypothesis 5).

The major lessons to be learned from this study are that the effects of child care on children's development are mediated by (a) the quality of the care, such as the ratio of adults to children and many other correlated qualities of care; (b) family characteristics, such as how much the family can offer the child in stimulation and opportunities that are appropriate to the child's level of development; (c) the developmental level of the child, in that appropriate care for infants is not necessarily what will best promote toddlers' or preschoolers' development; and (d) interactions between what the child needs, what the family can offer, and what the child care arrangement can offer to support the family's functioning. Investigators must carefully differentiate the kinds and qualities of care and the family circumstances of children receiving the care and must resist the temptation to draw sweeping conclusions about day care in general. Child care arrangements do not compete with family effects; rather, they are more likely to complement and interact with them.

DISCUSSION

Dr. Scarr was asked to comment further on the impact of the family situation on the effects of child care. There has been little research on how family situations actually interact with child care situations to produce outcomes, she noted, and it is an area that should be looked at more carefully. What is striking in the study reported here is that some of the characteristics usually associated with single mothers, such as low family income, do not account for the differences. It was not a poverty issue with these single mothers, or the fact that the mother was alone and struggling with all the responsibilities of a child and a household, with no support or help, although that must play a role. Research is needed into the differences that make some kinds of care advantageous to children from single-mother families. One can guess that contact with more than one adult and with other children will turn out to be important, but we do not know. We need research that will illuminate just what kinds of care will supplement and support families.

During the discussion period the participants explored various aspects of quality of child care, particularly for infants, and their relationship to child outcomes. An earlier Bermuda study (McCartney, 1984) looked at the overall quality in the nine centers caring for infants. The various dimensions of quality were not analyzed individually but were found to be highly correlated. In research ratings and assessments of social interactions between caregivers and children, quality was an important predictor of intellectual, language, and social development.

Adult/child ratios and the stability of the relationship with the caregiver were of particular interest. In the Bermuda studies the biggest difference between center care on the one hand and family day care or home care was adult/child ratio. In centers, caregivers cared for anywhere from four to eight infants under 2. The number of different caregivers each child had known was not studied, but the different kinds of care experienced by individual children—typically family day care and then center care, or family day care, a period at home with mother, and then a center—were known, and the number of changes appeared not to be related to 4-year-old outcomes. The turnover rate among staff members of each center was also known. It was not a powerful predictor of outcomes, but it was a negative predictor in some cases, where it showed even more persistent effects than adult/child ratios.

The patterning of arrangements and consistency over a child's life is an area that researchers are only beginning to look at, Dr. Scarr noted, and it may turn out to be one of the most important aspects of quality. Dr. Kamerman pointed out that although it is assumed that children are in just one type of care at one point in time, they actually may experience different kinds of care within the course of 1 week or even 1 day, and little is known about the consequences of such arrangements.

Closely related to the issue of quality is the subject of funding. Given limited funds for child care, where should the money go? At what ages do children need the highest quality care? Dr. Scarr's view is that development in the first year of life is so protected by biological design that it is very hard to get it permanently off course. Anything but a really abusive or neglectful environment probably does not have long-term or permanently damaging effects, whereas unsupportive conditions for 3- or 4-year-olds may have much more damaging or far-reaching effects. That does not mean that care for infants should not be high quality; it is expensive care because the ratio of caregivers to infants needs to be higher. But resources for high levels of training and educational programming are best spent on preschoolers. Dr. Kendall felt that if it came down to a choice between expensive care for infants and expensive care for toddlers, she would opt for spending more money on toddlers. "Something significant happens around age 2," she pointed out, and eight toddlers would be harder to care for than eight infants.

Several public policy issues came out of the discussion of quality. Dr. Kamerman stated that from this point of view probably the most important issue for researchers is what constitutes good-enough care. "As much as all of us are interested in the highest quality of care possible for our children," she said, "we cannot even provide that as parents, let alone go out into the real world and find it in other kinds of care." We need to know what kind of care, for what children, under what circumstances, is minimally adequate in order to avoid any kind of damage. From there we can talk about the cost of such care and how to provide it.

Adult/child ratios were also seen as relating to public policy. The cost of obtaining infant care is high because infants require high adult/child ratios. How long, then, should a child be considered an infant? If infancy is considered to extend to 2 years, parents are having to pay for high-cost care for a long period of time after the end of their parental leave, which usually lasts only a matter of weeks. There is a wide variation in how states define infancy, what ratios they set, and what staff training they require, and yet at this time we really do not have the detailed research to describe what kinds of care make what kinds of difference at what times in children's lives.

Dr. Kamerman cautioned that parental leave should not be considered as an alternative to child care services for infants. Some kind of leave at the time of childbirth is absolutely essential, but even if legislation were passed that provided paid leave for a time after the birth of a child, there are still going to be children under the age of 1 whose mothers are in the work force. Both leave policies and child care services need to be provided, not one or the other.

NOTES

[1] The NORC Survey Scale (National Opinion Research Council, 1978) is a standardized scale of occupational prestige based on a multidimensional scaling of the social and economic components of each occupation. The scale ranges from fabric mill employees on the low end to physicians and veterinarians on the high end.

[2] Mothers' WAIS Vocabulary Subtest score (Wechsler, 1955) was used as a measure of IQ because it correlates highly with overall IQ ($r = .81$). The WAIS-R was not used because it was not available at the beginning of this study. A family background questionnaire was constructed to assess family structure and demographic characteristics, such as parents' education levels and occupational prestige as assessed by the NORC Survey Scale.

2

Infant-Parent Attachment and Day Care:
In Defense of the Strange Situation

Jay Belsky
The Pennsylvania State University

The emotional tie between infant and mother, conceptualized in terms of the attachment relationship, figures prominently in contemporary writings concerning infant socioemotional development. Bowlby's (1969, 1973), Ainsworth's (1973, 1982), and Sroufe's (1979; Sroufe & Waters, 1977) theoretical and empirical writings have done much to promulgate the position that the quality of this relationship, particularly in terms of the security it affords the developing child, is likely to be influenced by the nature and quality of care the child receives and to contribute in important ways to the child's future development.

Central to attachment theory is the notion that the developmental experiences with the primary caregiver contribute to the infant's sense of the world as a predictable, responsive, and caring place and thereby to the child's own developing sense of self and of what to expect in relationships with others (Ainsworth, 1973; Ainsworth, Blehar, Walters, & Wall, 1978; Bowlby, 1969, 1973; Sroufe, 1979; Sroufe & Fleeson, 1986). When a mother perceives, accurately interprets, and responds in a prompt and appropriate manner to her infant's communications, a secure attachment relationship is presumed to be fostered. In such a relationship, the infant develops a sense of trust and assurance in the mother's availability and responsiveness, so that the mother functions as a "secure base" from which the infant can confidently explore the environment and relate to others. Conversely,

23

the caregiver who is consistently unresponsive or who is inconsistent in responding to the infant's signals is presumed to cultivate anxious or insecure attachment relationships by providing an unpredictable and uncontrollable environment. In such an anxious relationship, the infant is unable to develop a complete sense of trust and confidence in the mother's physical and emotional availability; the mother, in turn, does not function as a secure base, and as a result the infant approaches the environment with different expectations from those of his or her securely attached agemates.

THE MEASUREMENT OF ATTACHMENT
AND DAY CARE RESEARCH

One of the basic challenges that has confronted developmental psychologists, and particularly the proponents of attachment theory, is the measurement of individual differences in the security of the infant-mother attachment bond and the testing of predictions derived from the theory. In the early 1970s Ainsworth and her colleagues (Ainsworth & Wittig, 1969; Ainsworth et al., 1978) developed a laboratory procedure designed to expose the 1-year-old child to a series of developmentally normative stresses in order to measure variation in the extent to which the infant uses the mother as a secure base. The procedure consists of a series of 3-minute episodes in which the infant is placed with the mother in an unfamiliar and barely furnished laboratory room and then introduced to an unfamiliar adult before being separated from and reunited with the mother on two separate occasions. The infant's behavior in this (aptly named) Strange Situation, specifically the way in which he or she explores the room in the mother's presence, responds to the stranger, copes with separation, and reacts upon the mother's return, provides the basis for appraising attachment security; special emphasis is placed on the infant's reunion behavior.

Infants classified as secure in their relationships with their mothers seek proximity and contact with their mothers and find comfort and solace in that contact when distressed; when not overtly distressed, secure infants greet the parent in an unambiguous manner, often by means of a broad smile or other way of establishing psychological contact across a distance (such as babbling or showing a toy). Infants classified as insecure in their attachment relationship show a strong tendency to avoid physical and psychological contact with the returning parent (by averting gaze, refusing to acknowledge the parent's return, or aborting approaches to the parent) or to resist such contact after approaching and seeking contact. The former pattern of insecure behavior results in classification of the infant-mother relationship as insecure-avoidant, and the latter leads to an evaluation as insecure-resistant.

It is noteworthy that at the same time much basic research on attachment was being conducted, scientists concerned about the potentially deleterious effects of day care for infants were studying babies' reactions to separation from mother and contact with unfamiliar strangers. Because of what was known at the time about the development of infants growing up without their mothers in orphanages and other institutions, many thought that the repeated separations of infant from mother (and vice versa) that day care invariably entails would increase the risk of insecure relationships developing between child and mother (Blehar, 1974; Fraiberg, 1977). The time apart from the parent could disrupt and diminish the infant's sense of the physical and emotional availability and responsiveness of the principal caregiver and could undermine the parent's understanding of the infant. Such processes would reduce the mother's ability to be maximally responsive to the infant's idiosyncratic needs and would thereby foster an insecure relationship.

At the time that the initial day care research was undertaken, no reliable and valid measurement strategy had emerged for the assessment of attachment security. In hopes of tapping the quality of the infant-mother attachment bond, most investigators assessed how distressed infants became upon separation from mother, how positively or negatively they reacted to strange adults, and how willing they were to leave mother's side to approach unfamiliar children (Farran & Ramey, 1977; Kagan, Kearsley, & Zelazo, 1978; Ricciuti, 1974). Ainsworth and her colleagues (1978), in contrast, appraised attachment security not simply on the basis of whether the infant became upset at separation, interacted with the strange adult, or explored the laboratory setting in the Strange Situation, but rather in terms of the entire organization of the child's behavior.

In the first comprehensive analysis of what was known about the developmental effects of day care experience, the use of the Strange Situation was soundly criticized as a means of assessing differences between young children reared exclusively by their mothers at home and children spending an extended portion of their days in the care of nonparental adults, typically in group settings (Belsky & Steinberg, 1978; Bronfenbrenner, Belsky, & Steinberg, 1976). Central to Belsky and Steinberg's critique was the fact that no evidence existed to indicate that the behaviors being measured or the characterizations of infants as secure or insecure in these laboratory assessments were predictively valid—that is, informative with respect to the future functioning of the children being studied. Although an abundance of theory suggested that secure infants would develop more competently, particularly in their relationships with others, there was simply no data at the time to indicate that this was so. In addition, skepticism was expressed that a 20-minute laboratory procedure, or some variant of it, could provide a basis for useful assessment and prediction.

Despite the empirical appropriateness of the critique to the use of the Strange Situation in day care research at the time, subsequent progress in the study of attachment led Belsky, Steinberg, and Walker (1982) to rescind their negative evaluation of the Strange Situation. And over the past decade a wealth of empirical data has emerged to document the utility of 12- to 18-month evaluations of the security of infant-mother attachment relationships, using the Strange Situation procedure, to forecast individual differences in child development during the preschool and early school years (for reviews, see Bretherton, 1985; Lamb, Thompson, Gardner, Charnov, & Estes, 1984; Sroufe, 1985). More specifically, longitudinal follow-up studies conducted by a variety of investigators across the country indicate that 12- to 18-month-olds who are judged to be insecurely attached to their mothers generally look less competent as they grow older. Not only have such infants been found, as toddlers and preschoolers, to be less empathic, less compliant, and less cooperative and to exhibit more negative affect and less self-control than their securely attached agemates (see, for example, Egeland, 1983; Joffee, 1981; LaFreniere & Sroufe, 1985; Londerville & Main, 1981; Main, 1973; Main & Weston, 1981; Maslin & Bates, 1982), but they have also been found, as 5- and 6-year-olds, to be more at risk for developing behavioral problems (Erickson, Sroufe, & Egeland, 1985; Lewis, Feiring, McGuffog, & Jaskir, 1984, for boys only; Sroufe, 1983; but see Bates, Maslin, & Frankel, 1985, for failure to replicate).

The point to be made here is not that every study comparison indicates that reunion behaviors in the Strange Situation and the attachment classifications derived from them discriminate children's subsequent functioning in other settings (Lamb et al., 1984), but rather that incontestable trends are evident in the literature regarding the future functioning of children with secure versus insecure infant-attachment relationships. In fact, even though the measurement of attachment security does not in any way provide perfect or even near perfect prediction of later development—and there is no contemporary developmental theory to suggest that it should—this approach to developmental assessment has proven as powerful as any yet developed for such young children. There can be little doubt that subsequent progress in the study of early development will prove this approach to be crude, but it is certainly more useful than anything else currently available and far more than we had only a brief 10 years ago. Perhaps most impressive about the assessment of attachment security in the Strange Situation is the recent discovery of its utility in enhancing developmental prediction when used in concert with information obtained on children's experiences in the years following the measurement of attachment (Erickson et al., 1985; Lewis et al., 1984).

INFANT DAY CARE AND ATTACHMENT RECONSIDERED

Now that it has been demonstrated that variation in attachment security, as measured in the Strange Situation, predicts later development, it is only fitting that research on infant day care continue to pay special attention to the infant-mother relationship. The virtually exclusive attention that is paid to the infant-mother relationship in this chapter is not meant to imply a lack of concern for, or interest in, the child's other relationships in and out of the family; rather it is dictated by its central place in the day care literature and by the belief that a special focus on the infant-mother relationship is ecologically appropriate. Whether in day care or not, most infants in America today establish their first attachments to their mothers (Clarke-Stewart & Fein, 1983; Farran & Ramey, 1977; Kagan et al., 1978).

Having briefly summarized several basic precepts of attachment theory and considered essential features of the history of the measurement of attachment in day care research, this chapter now turns to what is known about the development of infant-parent attachment relationships of infants with extensive nonmaternal care experience in their first year of life. The first subsection provides a very brief summary and analysis of the early studies of research on attachment and day care. This lays the groundwork for more extensive consideration of research conducted since 1980. The results of this analysis lead to a reconsideration of the appropriateness of the Strange Situation as a method of assessing attachment security in the case of infants with extensive day care experience. After a consideration of three specific reasons why it is thought that the available research remains informative, general conclusions are advanced regarding the security of infant-parent attachments in infants with varying rearing experiences.

Early Studies

Despite concerns raised by many in the late 1960s and early 1970s that day-care rearing would disrupt the attachment bond between infant and mother, initial studies of infants reared in experimental, research-oriented university day care programs providing care of the highest quality failed to provide convincing evidence that extensive nonmaternal care did, in fact, affect the developing infant-mother relationship (see, for example, Kagan et al., 1978; Ricciuti, 1974; for a comprehensive and critical review see Belsky

& Steinberg, 1978). It should be noted, however, that the first set of studies was conducted prior to the refinement of a methodology for measuring individual differences in attachment predictive of future functioning. That is, rather than focusing on children's reunion behavior toward mother following separation, and rather than making formal classifications of attachment security based on such behavior in the context of the entire organization of the child's response to being separated from and reunited with the parent, the initial studies focused on discrete behavior such as degree of distress following separation and willingness to approach or interact with strangers (see, for example, Finkelstein & Wilson, 1977; Kagan et al., 1978; Ricciuti, 1974). What was never particularly clear in much of this initial research was whether it was considered developmentally beneficial or problematical for the infant to be distressed at separation or whether the inclination to move away from the parent reflected independence or detachment. The potential limitations of the early measures were recognized by Kagan et al. (1978), who, upon finding few differences between infants reared in a high quality center and those reared at home by their mothers, noted that one valid objection to conclusions drawn on the basis of their work might be that their "methods of assessment were not sufficiently sensitive" (p. 262). They noted that it would be "wise to maintain a skeptical attitude" toward their conclusion that infant day care does not seem to have hidden psychological dangers, at least when responsibly and conscientiously implemented. This sentiment is consistent with that expressed by Rutter (1981) several years later after reviewing the literature on day care and attachment. Noting that "the evidence is inconclusive," he observed that "it is possible nevertheless that more subtle ill effects occur in some children. The matter warrants further study" (p. 9).

Later Studies

The research that has emerged since 1980 and that has focused on infants growing up in day care arrangements more typically available to most families (babysitters, family day care homes, and community centers) has produced evidence that patterns of attachment differ across groups of children with varying exposure to nonparental care in their first year of life. What is most noteworthy about this second generation of investigations is (a) its focus on reunion behavior in the Strange Situation and the formal attachment classifications derived from the organization of the infant's behavior in the procedure; (b) its reliance on videotaped protocols, which permit repeated viewing of behavior sequences for appraising attachment security; and (c) its restriction to a developmental period (12 to 18 months) for which behavior in the Strange Situation has been shown to be predictively valid (when formal classifications of attachment security are employed).

These latter two considerations are particularly important, because four frequently cited studies that focus on reunion behavior and that reveal few if any differences between infants with varying day care experience are seriously flawed methodologically. Two by Hock (Brookhart & Hock, 1976; Hock & Clinger, 1980) relied on handwritten descriptions of infant behavior in the Strange Situation, a strategy of data collection that no investigator would employ today because of the well-recognized need for repeated viewings of the child's behavior in order for accurate assessment to be made. The other two investigations by Doyle (1975; Doyle & Sommers, 1978) not only included children too young (5 months) to display the very behaviors that are essential for evaluating attachment security (resistance, avoidance, and proximity seeking) and too old (30 months) to be measured accurately in the Strange Situation, but so failed to chronicle avoidance and resistance behaviors by the children studied that one is left to wonder whether the investigators were skilled in recognizing the very patterns of behavior that are central to characterizing attachment insecurity.

In other words, despite their focus on reunion behavior, the value of these four investigations for informing our understanding of the attachment security of infants in day care is seriously limited. Unfortunately, many reviews fail to acknowledge these methodological shortcomings and end up concluding that the available data are too mixed to draw definitive conclusions. We see here, however, that when studies using videotapes to study infants 12 to 18 months of age and to focus on reunion behavior are considered, a good deal of order exists in the database. As Block (1976) noted in analyzing studies of sex differences in children's behavior, bringing an informed methodological eye to bear on available research results in conclusions quite different from those of the simple strategy of summing across studies. Simply put, not all investigations are created equal.

Vaughn, Gove, and Egeland (1980), studying a sample of economically high-risk, often single-parent families, were the first to discover that infants with (often low-quality) nonmaternal care in their first year were more likely to display insecure-avoidant patterns of attachment than were infants reared exclusively by their mothers. Some 3 years later, studying a sample of infants from two-parent, middle- and upper middle-class homes being reared in family day care (involving one caregiver and one to eight other children), Schwartz (1983) reported that those infants in full-time day care displayed significantly greater avoidance of mother when studied at 18 months of age than those cared for by their mothers. Jacobsen and Wille (1984) also chronicled a relation between infant day care usage and infant-mother attachment. In contrast to infants with little or no child care (<3 hours/week) or with moderate amounts of such care (<20 hours/week), those in care on a relatively full-time basis (20–54 hours/week) were disproportionately likely to be classified as insecure when videotaped in the Strange Situation at 18 months (31.2% and 31.4% vs. 61.5%). Moreover, when Wille and Jacobsen (1984) studied a subsample of infants, each of whom had been paired with a securely attached child in order to observe peer interaction, they discovered that those classified as insecure-avoidant averaged the most hours in care per week, followed next by those classified as insecure-resistant, with those classified as secure averaging the least amount of care.

This association between extensive nonmaternal care initiated in the first year of life and insecure infant-mother attachment has recently been replicated by Barglow, Vaughn, and Molitar (1987) in their investigation of affluent families in which those using in-home babysitters for more than 20 hours per week were compared with those that relied exclusively on maternal care. Not only did the infants with extensive nonmaternal care display significantly more avoidance on reunion with mother, but they were significantly more likely to be classified as insecure-avoidant in their attachment, as well as insecure more generally. This same set of findings has also emerged from Belsky and Rovine's (1988) investigation of 149 families enrolled prenatally in two longitudinal studies of infant and family development. More specifically, infants who averaged 20 or more hours per week of nonmaternal care (in a variety of arrangements including center care, family day care, and babysitter care) evinced significantly more avoidance behavior and, as a result, were significantly more likely to be classified as insecure in their relationships with their mothers.

In considering these and other data, one set of investigators hypothesized that the timing of entry into care might account for the heightened risk of insecurity among day care infants. In accordance with arguments developed by Hoffman (1984) and Scarr (1984), Chase-Lansdale and Owen (1987) reasoned that maternal employment initiated in the first half of the infant's first year would pose less of a risk for the infant-mother relationship than would nonmaternal care initiated thereafter. Care initiated during the period in which the attachment bond was forming was presumed to be less stressful than that begun after the bond had crystallized. To test this prediction, only infants whose mothers had returned to work on a full-time basis prior to the infant's 6-month birthday were studied; when compared with infants whose mothers remained at home full-time, no differences in rate of insecurity emerged, leading the investigators to conclude that timing of entry into day care was an important determinant of the relation between maternal employment and attachment security.

Careful consideration of the design of the Chase-Lansdale and Owen investigation raised questions, however, about the conclusions they first drew from their results. More specifically, the families at first seemed to have been recruited into the research project when their infants were 1 year of age, whereas in Barglow et al.'s (1987) and Belsky and Rovine's (1988) studies, which failed to find that risk of insecurity was reduced when mothers returned to work early in the infant's first year, all families had been recruited into the research program prior to the infant's birth. This difference raised the possibility that selection bias in subject recruitment in the Chase-Lansdale and Owen study might have inadvertently influenced their results. Could it have been that their study, which was planned specifically as an investigation of maternal employment and which enrolled most families when infants were 1 year of age, systematically (although unintentionally) excluded the very families most likely to find the dual-earner situation particularly stressful and, conceivably, insecurity-promoting? That is, could it have been that by the time infants were 1 year of age those families most likely to decline the invitation to participate in a study of maternal employment were those experiencing the most difficulty with this situation, whereas those who found it to work well were most likely to accept the invitation to participate? And thus, could it have been that the study design used by Chase-Lansdale and Owen may have led to an underestimation of the heightened risk for insecure infant-mother attachment that was discerned in investigations that enrolled families in the study process prenatally, before families had a sense of how infant-parent relationships were developing (Barglow et al., 1987; Belsky & Rovine, 1988)?

As it turns out, evidence that it apparently did is found in the Chase-Lansdale and Owen investigation. For reasons that are not quite clear, 10 of the 40 families in their sample in which mothers returned to work on a full-time basis were enrolled in the research program prior to the infant's birth. When comparisons were made between the 10 infants whose families were enrolled in the research process prenatally and the 30 whose families were enrolled when the infants were 1 year of age, it was discovered that the rate of insecurity in the two subgroups was decidedly different, with risk of insecurity being more than three times greater in the prenatally recruited families than in the postnatally recruited families (60% vs. 18%). The same pattern of lessened risk for insecurity among children whose families were recruited postnatally emerged when insecurity of infant-father attachment was considered (80% vs. 28%). In fact, despite the limited size of the samples on which these comparisons were made, it is noteworthy that the differences in rates of security/insecurity as a function of timing of recruitment is highly reliable when infant-mother and infant-father attachment relationships are considered simultaneously [x^2 (1) = 15.63, $p<$ .0005]. Further evidence of the importance of timing of subject recruitment is suggested by a second, small sample study by Owen in which all families were enrolled prenatally (Owen & Cox, in press). It was found in this group that among the infants of 10 full-time working mothers, the rate of infant-mother insecurity was 60%—exactly the same as that of the prenatally recruited subjects of full-time working mothers in the Chase-Lansdale and Owen investigation—whereas in the case of infants with no nonmaternal care experience it was just 33%.

When the data are compiled across the only five studies of infant day care/maternal employment that involved nonrisk families, utilized formal classification criteria for assessing attachment security, and considered extent of nonmaternal care experienced in the first year of life, a strong and highly reliable association between extensive nonmaternal care and attachment security emerges (Barglow et al., 1987; Belsky & Rovine, 1988; Chase-Lansdale & Owen, 1987; Jacobsen & Wille, 1984; Owen & Cox, in press). Despite the inclusion of all subjects from the Chase-Lansdale and Owen investigation, in which rate of insecurity of children with extensive nonmaternal care was found to be underestimated because of the late enrollment of most subjects in the research program, it turns out that infants in nonmaternal care for more than 20 hours per week are 1.6 times more likely than their counterparts with less (or no) care to be classified as insecure in their relationships with their mothers [x^2(1) = 15.21, $p<$ .0005].

Whereas 43% of infants with extensive day care are classified as insecure in their attachments, the comparable figure for infants with less than 20 hours per week of nonmaternal care is 26% (see Table 2.1). And when the findings from the Chase-Lansdale and Owen study are adjusted for the bias evident in their data to reflect the rate of insecurity discerned in their prenatally recruited subsample, the insecurity rate of infants with more than 20 hours per week of nonmaternal care jumps to 51% across the five

TABLE 2.1
Security of Infant-Mother Attachment and Extent of Nonmaternal Care: Cross-Study Analysis*

| | | Extent of Nonmaternal Care | | |
		>20 hours/week	<20 hours/week	Total
Attachment Security	Secure	100	233	333
	Insecure	76	82	158
	Total	176	315	491
		x^2 (1) = 15.21 $p < .0005$		

*Barglow, Vaughn, & Molitar, 1987; Belsky & Rovine, 1988; Chase-Lansdale & Owen, 1987; Jacobsen & Wille, 1984; Owen & Cox, in press

studies, a figure that is virtually twice that of infants with less extensive day care experience in their first year.

Only one investigation of nonrisk families other than the five whose data are included in Table 2.1 has examined the relation between infant day care experience and security of infant-mother attachment. Although Howes and her colleagues (Howes, Rodning, Galluzzo, & Myers, in press) report in their investigation of some 115 infants that "middle-class children attending either centers or family day care homes were no more likely to be insecurely attached than children cared for primarily by their mothers" (ms. p. 24), the analyses conducted did not distinguish between infants with more than 20 hours and those with fewer than 20 hours per week of non-maternal care and so could not be included in our cross-study analysis. In view of the results just summarized, such a distinction appears critical. Recall that not only did Chase-Lansdale and Owen (1987, prenatally recruited sample) and Owen and Cox (in press) discern an association between nonmaternal care and insecure relationships in their investigations of mothers employed on a full-time basis, but in three studies that distinguished the extent of maternal employment/nonmaternal care, it was only infants who averaged more than 20 hours per week of day care initiated in the first year who were at heightened risk of insecurity. In fact, had these latter investigations not made this critical distinction regarding extent of nonmaternal care, they too would have failed to discern any association between infant day care and infant-mother attachment security. It remains quite possible, therefore, that Howes et al.'s failure to discern an association between infant day care experience and infant-mother attachment security is a direct result of their failure to consider the extent of nonmaternal care that infants experienced in their first year of life.

Consideration of extent of care also appears critical for understanding the development of the attachment bond between infant and father. Even though only two investigations have considered the infant-father relationship as a function of day care in the first year, it is noteworthy that the exact same findings emerge from both studies. Chase-Lansdale and Owen (1987) and Belsky and Rovine (1988) both report that boys who average 35 or more weeks in care are significantly more likely than other infants to be classified as insecure in their relationships with their fathers by the end of the first year. And, as a result, these sons are significantly more likely than other children to have two insecure infant-parent attachment relationships, a pattern of relationship development that has been shown consistently to be associated with less competent functioning (Belsky, Garduque, Hrncir, 1984; Main & Weston, 1981).

Interpretation

On the basis of the findings just reviewed, it is clear that when methodologically informed distinctions are made between studies, a strong and highly
reliable association exists between extensive nonmaternal care in the first
year of life and elevated risk of insecure infant-mother attachment (and insecure infant-father attachment in the case of boys). To be noted, however,
is the fact that most of the chronicled insecurity as indexed by behavior in
response to the presumed stress of the Strange Situation takes the form of
avoidant insecurity, in which infants maintain a psychological distance
from their parents by refusing to acknowledge the parents' return to the
laboratory, by averting gaze from them on re-entry into the testing room,
or by aborted approaches in which the child first makes a move toward the
parent only to veer away. This pattern of insecure-avoidant behavior is
noteworthy, because some scientists contend that this style of behaving,
when displayed by infants who routinely experience separations from their
parents, may not index insecurity but rather a familiar strategy of coping
with separation or even possibly precocious independence (Clarke-
Stewart & Fein, 1983). Basic to this line of reasoning are the assumptions
that the Strange Situation may be experienced differently by infants in day
care than by those reared in their own homes by their mothers on a full-
time basis and, consequently, that what is currently rated as avoidance
when standard coding conventions are used is not true avoidance in the in-
secure-attachment sense of the word.

     Because developmentalists continue to debate the meaning of
heightened avoidance and the use of the Strange Situation with infants with
extensive day care experience, it is useful to consider the kind of evidence
that would confirm the ideologically attractive, scientifically plausible, yet
empirically unsubstantiated contention that it is inappropriate to compare
children who vary in their routine experience with infant-parent separation by using a procedure that is designed around normatively stressful en-
counters with strangers and separations. Most compelling would be
evidence that so-called "true" avoidance can be distinguished from "true"
independence, because it is the contention of some that the latter is con-
fused with the former in the case of infants with extensive day care experience, and that such infants are actually more independent but no more
avoidant than infants with fewer than 20 hours per week of nonmaternal
care. Also significant would be evidence that the developmental sequelae
of secure and insecure attachments—especially of insecure attachments—
as measured by the Strange Situation differ in home-reared infants and infants with extensive nonmaternal care, indicating that what has been classified as insecure behavior in the latter group reflects something different

from what it reflects among infants reared exclusively at home by their mothers. Finally, evidence indicating that infants with extensive day care are less stressed, particularly at the hormonal level (e.g., cortisol), by the Strange Situation than are infants with little or no nonmaternal care would also raise serious questions about the appropriateness of this research paradigm for understanding the developmental correlates of extensive day care in the first year of life. Evidence consistent with any one of these considerations would seriously undermine the previous conclusion that extensive nonmaternal care initiated in the first year of life is associated with heightened risk of insecure infant-parent attachment; evidence consistent with all three considerations, moreover, would convincingly demonstrate that comparative studies of infants with varying day care experience using the Strange Situation are totally uninterpretable.

In view of the fact that the critical studies have yet to be conducted, even though alternative interpretations of avoidance and criticism of the use of the Strange Situation in the case of day care–reared children have been advanced since at least 1983 (Clarke-Stewart & Fein, 1983), there are three basic reasons why the concerns currently raised about the interpretation of the association between extensive infant day care and insecure infant-mother attachment remain unconvincing. And these, it should be noted, go beyond Sroufe, Fox, and Pancake's (1983) demonstration that the so-called precocious independence displayed by infants classified as insecure-avoidant forecasts later dependence during the preschool years, as a dynamic transformational theory of development would suggest, rather than independence, as advocates of the avoidance = independence position would predict. The first to be considered deals with similarities in the preschool functioning of children with extensive day care in their first year and of children with insecure-avoidant attachment histories; the second with the differential rates of insecurity discerned in the prenatally and postnatally recruited families with full-time working mothers in the Chase-Lansdale and Owen investigation; and the third with infant, maternal, and family characteristics that distinguish secure and insecure infant-mother attachment relationships in the case of infants with extensive day care experience.

Reason One. The first reason for questioning the notion that insecurity is erroneously measured in the Strange Situation in the case of infants with extensive day care experience has to do with what is known about the subsequent development of infants with such experience and of infants with insecure-avoidant infant-mother attachment histories. Not only do several investigations indicate that day care–reared infants, as toddlers and preschoolers, are more likely than children without extensive day care experience to be aggressive, noncompliant, and even socially withdrawn (e.g., Barton & Schwarz, 1981; Haskins, 1985; McCartney, Scarr, Phillips, Grajek, & Schwarz, 1982; Rabinovich, Zaslow, Berman, & Heyman, 1987; Rubenstein, Howes, & Boyle, 1981; Schwarz, Strickland, & Krolick, 1974; Vandell & Corasaniti, 1988; see Belsky, 1988, for summary), but patterns of behavior much like these have been found to be developmental sequelae of insecure-avoidant infant-mother attachments (Erickson et al., 1985; Main & Weston, 1981; Maslin & Bates, 1982; Sroufe, 1983). Although such convergence of findings from two independent lines of research does not demonstrate that the toddler and preschool functioning of infants with extensive day care experience in their first year of life is, at least in part, a function of their earlier insecure attachment relationships, the available evidence is certainly consistent with that line of reasoning. As a result, it seems more parsimonious to presume that insecurity is accurately assessed in the Strange Situation in the case of infants with multiple separation experiences than to presume otherwise.

Reason Two. The findings emerging from the internal analysis of the Chase-Lansdale and Owen study (1987) also provide grounds for questioning the notion that the Strange Situation, with its repeated separations, inaccurately measures insecurity, particularly insecure-avoidant relationships in the case of infants with extensive day care experience. If this were so, then why would the rate of insecurity observed in the subsample recruited into the research program prenatally be so high (60%) and that of the subsample recruited at the end of the first year be so low (18%)? If it was experience with repeated separations that erroneously resulted in the overestimation of insecure infant-mother relationships, then one would not expect sample recruitment differences to result in these strikingly different rates of insecurity; after all, infants from families recruited pre- and postnatally had equivalent day care experience.

Although it might be argued that the dramatic difference in rate of insecurity in the prenatally and postnatally recruited subsamples is an artifact of the small number of prenatally recruited families ($n = 10$), three points must be noted. First, the difference between the two subsamples is statistically reliable in spite of the limited sample size [$x^2(1) = 7.07, p < .01$]; second, and as already noted, another study (Owen & Cox, in press) with an identically small number of prenatally recruited families using full-time nonmaternal care generated as high a rate of insecurity (60%); and finally, the rate of insecurity discerned in these two small-sample studies is only somewhat higher, but quite in accord with, those generated by Barglow et al. (1987), Belsky and Rovine (1988), and Jacobsen and Wille (1984) for infants exposed to 20 or more hours of nonmaternal care in their first year (47%), whereas among those enrolled postnatally in the Chase-Lansdale and Owen study the insecurity rate of those whose mothers worked full-time ($n = 30$) is much lower (18%).

In sum, it remains totally unclear how the notion that insecurity is erroneously appraised in the case of infants with extensive day care experience can be used to account for the dramatic difference in the rates of insecurity in the two subsamples of infants in full-time nonmaternal care in the Chase-Lansdale and Owen (1988) investigation. Although selective postnatal enrollment of families coping well with the dual-earner arrangement would seem to account easily for the Chase-Lansdale and Owen data, the fact that infants from the prenatally and postnally recruited families had equivalent amounts of separation experience represents a serious challenge to the argument that the elevated rate of insecurity discerned in a number of studies using the Strange Situation paradigm is an artifact of day care–reared infants' repeated exposure to separation.

Reason Three. The third reason why it remains difficult to embrace the alternative hypothesis as to why infants with extensive day care experience in their first year are at heightened risk of being classified as insecure in their relationships with their mothers involves the within-group variance that is so evident in the data presented in Table 2.1. As the table shows, many infants who experience 20 or more hours of nonmaternal care in their first year do not succumb to the risk of insecure infant-mother attachment that is probabilistically associated with extensive day care experience. A pressing issue that faces the scientist as well as the policymaker, as a result, has to do with the specification of conditions associated with increased and decreased risk of insecurity. But if it indeed is the case, as some contend, that the Strange Situation is inappropriate for use with infants with extensive day care experience, then we should not expect to be able to distinguish the conditions that result in some of these children establishing secure relationships and others establishing insecure relationships. Only if attachment security and insecurity in these infants are being accurately assessed using the Strange Situation should we expect to find lawful reasons why some children experiencing more than 20 hours per week of nonmaternal care develop secure attachments to their mothers, whereas others do not. If security and insecurity are erroneously measured in the case of infants in day care, then it should not be possible to account for why some are classified one way and some the other, or the factors that do distinguish between such infants should not be in accord with basic theoretical tenets of attachment theory.

It happens to be the case, unfortunately, that this issue of within-group variation in the case of infants has not received the extensive empirical attention that has been devoted to day care during the preschool years. Although there is an abundance of evidence identifying the conditions of quality care that promote optimal development among 3- to 5-year-olds (see Belsky, 1984, for review), many fewer studies of variation in the development of infants in care during their first year of life have been undertaken (for summary, see Belsky, 1988). And among these, only a handful focus on attachment security in the attempt to account for why some infants with extensive nonmaternal care establish secure relationships with their parents, whereas others do not. In fact, with the exception of Belsky and Rovine's (1988) research linking center-based care with heightened risk of insecure infant-mother attachment and father care with decreased risk of such insecurity in the case of infants with extensive nonmaternal care experience, and also Suwalsky, Zaslow, Klein, and Rabinovich's (1986) study linking multiple care arrangements with increased risk of insecurity, no such investigations have examined aspects of the care setting or situation itself as a determinant of which infants in day care develop insecure infant-mother attachments and which do not. This is one reason why I have argued that it is inappropriate to assume that quality of care, rather than the timing and extent of infant day care, is the principal determinant of variation in the development of infants with day care experience (Belsky, 1986, 1988). However plausible and attractive this line of argument (Phillips, McCartney, Scarr, & Howes, 1987), the fact of the matter is that too few studies have been conducted to draw such a conclusion, and among those that have been conducted there is simply too much inconsistency.

The principal reason why more is not known about the characteristics of the child care arrangement that foster or undermine infant-mother attachment security is that investigations of attachment and day care/maternal employment have obtained their samples via direct contact with families rather than through contact with child care settings. When the latter strategy is adopted, extensive data are usually obtained on the quality of child care or other aspects of the day care milieu, but family factors and processes, including attachment relationships, are (relatively) neglected (e.g., Howes & Stewart, 1987); when samples are obtained by contacting families directly, the reverse tends to be true (e.g., Barglow et al., 1987; Belsky & Rovine, 1988).

Although this unfortunate state of affairs limits conclusions that can be drawn regarding child care conditions that do or do not increase risk of insecure infant-mother attachments, the available evidence does illuminate child characteristics and maternal and family factors that are related to whether or not an infant with extensive nonmaternal care does indeed develop an insecure relationship. In fact, it is the differences that have emerged between day care–reared infants with secure and those with insecure infant-mother attachments and between their families that provide perhaps the most convincing evidence that insecurity is being accurately measured among infants with extensive nonmaternal care in their first year. Not only are the differences that emerge theoretically meaningful but, as we see here, some of the very evidence that points to the validity of Strange Situation assessments of day care–reared infants raises questions about the actual contribution of infant day care to the development of insecure infant-parent relationships.

First let us look at the characteristics of the child. The characteristic that has emerged most frequently in studies seeking to determine which infants with extensive day care experience are most susceptible to developing insecure infant-mother attachment relationships is gender. Consistent with evidence suggesting that males are more vulnerable to stress in general (Rutter & Garmezy, 1983) and to maternal employment during the preschool years in particular (Bronfenbrenner & Crouter, 1983), three separate studies indicate that boys are more likely than girls to be classified as insecure in their attachments to their mothers when they experience extensive nonmaternal care in their first year (Barglow & Vaughn, 1987; Belsky & Rovine, 1988; Benn, 1985). Although the pattern of heightened risk for males does not achieve statistical significance in any of these three studies, when the data are compiled across the three studies a strong trend emerges that is of borderline statistical significance [$x^2(1) = 3.54, p< .06$]; 49% of boys are classified as insecure (39/80), whereas only 34% of girls (25/74) are similarly appraised.

These data are consistent with findings mentioned earlier indicating that sons with more than 35 hours of nonmaternal care are at heightened risk of being insecure in their relationships with their fathers (Belsky & Rovine, 1988; Chase-Lansdale & Owen, 1987). Noteworthy, too, is the discovery emanating from an analysis of a subsample of women considering or planning (prenatally) to return to work in their infants' first year that those who bore sons were significantly more likely to change their prenatal plans and remain at home with their babies (Volling & Belsky, 1987). Apparently, parents, when they have the choice, are responsive to the differential risk that the data are only just beginning to reveal.

In view of the fact that most investigations of infant day care/maternal employment and attachment have obtained samples via individual contact with families rather than via child care settings, it is not surprising that the data that have been obtained on maternal and family characteristics are more extensive and of a better quality than those that have been gathered on characteristics of the child and of the day care setting. And consistently the evidence suggests that families using more than 20 hours per week of nonmaternal care in the first year and rearing securely attached infants differ from those rearing infants who, by the end of their first year, are insecure in their attachments to their mothers. In this writer's opinion it is these data, even more than those pertaining to child gender, that highlight the sensitivity of attachment assessments of infants exposed to repeated separations in their first year. It is also these data, as we see later, that raise questions concerning the role of extensive nonmaternal care in the first year in fostering insecure infant-mother attachment relationships.

Benn's (1985, 1986) investigation is perhaps the most convincing in revealing differences between mothers of secure infants with extensive experience in nonmaternal care and those of insecure infants with such experience. Not only did the mothers of the secure infants in her study evince, in the course of 8 hours of interview, "greater competence, emotional responsivity, warmth, and acceptance of motherhood" (Benn, 1985, p. 7), which Benn labeled "maternal integration," but it was also found that the differences between employed mothers of secure infants and those of insecure infants on ratings of sensitivity to and acceptance of the infant (i.e., measures of mothering) became insignificant once a composite index of maternal integration was statistically controlled. Such results led to the conclusion "that the effects of maternal employment on mother-son attachment are mediated primarily by the mother's underlying emotional state" (Benn, 1986, p. 1230) and that maternal "acceptance and sensitivity are overt manifestations of maternal integration which become associated with related child development outcomes because [of] their connection to this more underlying property of mothers" (Benn, 1985, p. 12).

Quite consistent with this line of reasoning are the findings of three other investigations linking features of mothers' personality and emotional responsiveness to the attachment security of infants with extensive day care experience. Belsky and Rovine (1988) observed that mothers of insecure infants evinced less sensitivity to the feeling states of others on a prenatally administered personality measure of interpersonal affect than did employed mothers of secure infants; Barglow and Vaughn (1987) found (using the California Personality Inventory) that insecure infants had mothers who were overcontrolling of feeling and impulse and overly concerned with the opinions and desires of others; and Ainslie (1987) reported that in a sample of families using good quality center care since their infants' first year, mothers of secure infants experienced more distress upon placing the child in the center than did mothers of insecure infants. This latter finding is in keeping with that of Everson, Sarnat, and Ambron (1984) indicating that 2-year-olds who behaved in ways that have been found in other research (Matas, Arend, & Sroufe, 1978) to be characteristic of toddlers with insecure infant-mother attachment histories (i.e., less cooperation, compliance, persistence, and prosocial behavior) had mothers who were more "willing" and less "reluctant" to use day care soon after the infant's first birthday. Considered together, the entire set of findings, consistent with expectations derived from attachment theory, underscores the importance of mother's openness to the feelings of others, as well as to her own emotions, in fostering secure infant-mother attachment.

In addition to personal attributes of mothers, more general aspects of families have also been implicated as determinants of which infants with extensive day care establish secure relationships with their mothers. In the Ainslie (1987) research, insecurely attached children came from households in which conflict was higher and cohesion lower (on the Family Environment Scale) than did infants with comparable day care experience who were secure in their attachments to their mothers. And in the Belsky and Rovine investigation, mothers of insecure infants expressed less contentment with positive features of their marriage even before the infants were born than did mothers who also used nonmaternal care extensively but reared secure infants. Thus, both investigations highlight the fact that in households in which infants are in nonmaternal care for more than 20 hours per week and establish insecure relationships with their mothers, it is not just the relationship between infant and parent that seems to be developing poorly.

Conclusion. These three reasons lead to the conclusion that insecurity is not erroneously measured in studies of day care infants. Even though the arguments advanced may individually be insufficient to discount the notion that estimates of insecurity in the case of infants with extensive nonmaternal care in the first year are inflated as a result of confusing independence with avoidance, collectively they are as persuasive as the alternative point of view, which remains empirically unsubstantiated. Indeed, in the face of the evidence just considered, the burden of proof would appear to rest on those who argue that it is possible that the Strange Situation mismeasured insecurity in the case of infants with extensive day care experience. Although future research of the kind considered earlier may demonstrate that to be the case, for the time being it remains more parsimonious to assume that bias of measurement of avoidance or insecurity is not the serious problem in day care research that some would have us believe.

This should not be read to imply, however, that the Strange Situation is completely adequate for assessing attachment security, or even that attachment security is the only construct that studies of day care should consider. Rather, it is to argue that until alternative measures have proved to be better, the Strange Situation should not be abandoned and its findings should not be discredited simply because of the ideologically attractive possibility that it is mismeasuring insecurity in infants exposed to repeated separations from parents in the course of their day care experience.

GENERAL CONCLUSIONS

Although the foregoing analysis leaves little reason to abandon the conclusion arrived at earlier—that more than 20 hours per week of infant day care, as typically experienced in this country, is associated with increased risk of insecure infant-parent relationships—it does raise questions about the actual role that day care plays in the development of insecure infant-parent, and particularly infant-mother, relationships. The data summarized here pertaining to conditions of maternal and family functioning that appear to heighten the risk of insecurity raise the very real possibility that it is not day care experience but rather experience in the homes of some infants with extensive nonmaternal care that is responsible for the development of insecure infant-parent attachments. If this were indeed the case, then it would be expected that infants with 20 or more hours per week of day care in their first year would be no more likely to develop secure attachments to their parents if they received less nonmaternal care. Although there exist no data at present to refute this possibility, there are two important reasons why it is premature to accept such a conclusion.

The first reason has to do with the heightened risk of insecurity discerned in the case of boys with extensive nonmaternal care. Because studies that do not deal with child care have not found males to be more likely to be insecurely attached to their mothers, and because the interaction between gender and day care does not appear to be confounded with family processes associated with heightened insecurity, the evident risk for males with more than 20 hours per week in nonmaternal care cannot be accounted for by events occurring in the family. For the time being this risk must be attributed to the day care experience itself. In fact, in view of the finding that families are more likely to keep sons at home (Volling & Belsky, 1987), one is left to wonder whether the risk discerned in the case of males is actually underestimated in the available research. Evidence that it might be is provided in studies of older children indicating that negative developmental consequences associated with maternal employment among preschool children appear restricted principally to boys from lower- and working-class families (Bronfenbrenner & Crouter, 1983); it is in these households, of course, that mothers have the fewest opportunities to remain at home.

Another reason why it seems premature to draw the conclusion that family processes and not day care processes account for the association between extensive nonmaternal care in the first year and increased risk of insecure infant-parent attachment has to do with the within-group analyses conducted by Belsky and Rovine (1988). When these investigators sought to determine whether the factors that distinguished secure and insecure infant-mother attachment relationships among infants with extensive nonmaternal care also distinguished secure and insecure attachments among infants with less than 20 hours per week of nonmaternal care, they could find no evidence that the same processes were at work. What this suggests, of course, is that risk of insecurity is heightened among infants with extensive day care experience as a result of the interaction of family and day care processes. Unfortunately, the exact nature of these interactive processes is not well understood.

Phillips, McCartney, Scarr, and Howes (1987) have argued, on the basis of evidence gathered on older children, that it is the quality of maternal care that is most important in understanding which infants do well and which do poorly in day care. In view of the fact that several recent studies indicate that the quality of care that toddlers and preschoolers experience is directly related to characteristics of their families, with families under stress and with more limited economic and personal resources securing lower quality care (Howes & Olenick, 1986; Howes & Stewart, 1987; Phillips & McCartney, in press), it may be the confluence of family and day care stress that is responsible for the risk of insecure infant-parent relationships that has been discerned in a number of investigations. In any event, the now repeatedly discerned correlation between family factors and day care quality makes problematic any attempts to attribute developmental outcomes associated with day care solely to variation in the quality of care. Family processes as well as child care processes must be considered (Belsky et al., 1982; Howes & Olenick, 1986).

Obviously, this must be the thrust of future research. Howes and her colleagues (Howes et al., in press) have initiated such an inquiry using an innovative design in which the functioning of 18-month-olds in family day care homes was examined as a function of the security of infant-mother and infant-caregiver relationships. Consistent with studies of attachment relationships with mother and father (Belsky et al., 1984; Main & Weston, 1981), it was discovered that infants with two insecure relationships, one with mother and one with caregiver, functioned most poorly. Additional evidence suggested that "children who are securely attached to their mothers may be better able than children insecurely attached to their mothers to compensate for child care arrangements that promote insecure attachments to caregivers" (ms. p. 24), as the former children appeared more socially competent in child care than those insecurely attached to both mother and caregiver.

In considering future research pertaining to the actual processes responsible for the association between extensive nonmaternal care in the first year and elevated risk of insecure infant-parent relationships, it is recommended that more attention be paid to interactional processes in the family and how they may be affected by more than 20 hours per week of day care. Although the findings of several studies suggest that the infant's interactional experiences with mother and even with father vary as a function of day care experiences (Pedersen, Cain, Zaslow, & Anderson, 1983; Schwartz, 1983), further investigation is required.

One potentially fruitful avenue of inquiry may involve the parents' knowledge of the infant as an individual and the sensitivity of the care that is provided. It is conceivable that the experience of being apart from the infant for an extended period of time and then re-establishing contact after a tiring day at work may make it especially difficult for a mother to get to know her infant in the individualized way that may be a prerequisite for providing the sensitive care that is thought to promote a secure attachment bond (Ainsworth, 1973). It is also conceivable that the very reason why aggression and noncompliance during the preschool and early school-age years seem to be associated with extensive nonmaternal care initiated in the infant's first year is that parents have not developed the relationship base and acquired the parenting skill that may result from extensive daily contact with the infant; as a result, they may simply be less effective socialization agents, and the child may be less prone to adult influence. The coercive processes that Patterson (1980) has identified as operating in families of aggressive school-age children may emerge in nascent form during the preschool years simply because parents have had less opportunity to get to know their children in the individualized way that should enable them to regulate their children's behavior in a manner that fosters competent functioning and affective self-regulation.

Even though it is certainly true that such expert knowledge and parenting skill can develop in the face of extensive nonmaternal care (and does not always develop when infants are exclusively home-reared), it may still be the case that extended time away from the infant can undermine the development of such expertise and skill. This would seem particularly likely when a parent's own psychological and interpersonal resources are limited or when the family-work interface is particularly stressful. To the extent that under these or other conditions extensive time apart from their children undermines parents' skill in rearing their infants, interventions would be called for to facilitate the development of parenting expertise. Clearly there is much to learn about the conditions and processes that are responsible for the heightened risk of insecurity in the case of infants with extensive day care experience. Once such knowledge is gained, it is just as clear that the risks that are currently so evident should be preventable.

DISCUSSION

A number of objections were raised to Dr. Belsky's conclusions. Dr. Scarr cited evidence from findings in a retrospective study in Bermuda (not yet published) that showed no relationship between child care experience and later outcomes in a group of 8-year-olds. (A prospective study is currently underway following up children who were in the original day care sample and are now 8 or 9 years of age. The results of the two studies will be published together.)

Dr. Lamb pointed out that not everyone believes that the Strange Situation predicts as well as Dr. Belsky suggests. The degree to which there is prediction varies across different types of families, and researchers should be cautious about generalizing from the existing predictive literature to the sorts of families that have been studied in the day care studies. He feels that the Strange Situation is not a pure measure of quality of attachment; there are indications that other things in babies' lives affect the way they behave in the Strange Situation. He cited data from the Grossmans indicating that within the avoidant-insecure group there are actually two subgroups—so-called "avoidant but secure" and "avoidant-insecure," so that some avoidant infants may be independent or simply used to separations.

Dr. Lamb stressed that we need to know more about who is becoming insecure and who is not. The majority of babies in day care do not show insecure attachments to their mothers, so clearly day care in itself does not explain insecurity. Families do not assign themselves randomly to day care and non–day care, and it may be that other factors in the families account for the differences. He urged that researchers go beyond the day care experience to look at some of the other factors that may be better predictors of risk, and that they be careful about how they define risk and using behavior in the Strange Situation as a pure index of risk.

Dr. Phillips also felt that questions of family circumstances and quality of care are very important and that focusing on age of entry into child care oversimplifies the problem. The issue is not even which families use day care and which do not; studies within day care populations show that families with lower socioeconomic status and families with higher levels of stress use lower quality care. She pointed out that the Haskins study looked at children in two different types of day care, measuring amount of child care, and although it found higher rates of aggression in children who had spent considerable time in the Abecedarian day care centers, it found the lowest rates of aggression in another sample of children in licensed day care centers.

Dr. Belsky agreed that there are limits to the Strange Situation as an assessment and stressed that it is the attachment data in concert with data on older children that he considers noteworthy. Regarding the question of whether the Strange Situation offers the same prediction depending on whether or not the child has had extensive infant child care, he mentioned a study of the 2-year-old functioning of children with differential child care experience. Vaughn and his colleagues found that secure home-reared children looked much more competent than insecure home-reared children but that both secure and insecure children with infant day care experience looked no different from insecure home-reared children. Security appeared to be a positive correlate of children who are home-reared.

Dr. Belsky acknowledged that there clearly is no uniformity across the data concerning the effects of early child care on later functioning, although he cited several other studies whose findings are consistent with Haskins' findings in the Abecedarian project. He reiterated nevertheless that the pattern of effects of extensive day care in the first year emerges repeatedly, and he defended the validity of analyzing the data in those terms. He does not think that such care will turn out to be a main effect, the full determinant, but he believes that it is a part of the picture, interacting with other factors such as quality of care. His hope is to draw the attention of researchers to it and to encourage them to target their analyses to this question.

"We are always going to be refining our predictions," Dr. Belsky pointed out. Ten years ago, age of entry and extent of care were unknown quantities. Today they represent a refinement of our understanding, and they look simple. Ten years from now we will further specify the conditions affecting the sequelae of child care, and from that perspective they will look simple; we will want to know the mechanisms, the processes—be they physiological, psychological, or interactional—through which these conditions operate. The understanding we acquire always looks simple at the time we acquire it, but from where we used to be it's not so simple.

Dr. Belsky made clear that he does not consider his views to represent a blanket indictment of child care but that he sees a "window of vulnerability" in the two qualifications of initiation in the first year and more than 20 hours per week. Other qualifications are still unknown, and he has no doubt that the situation is more complex than the two qualifications he has cited.

ACKNOWLEDGMENTS

Work on this chapter and the research described herein were supported by grants from the National Institute of Child Health and Human Development (R01HD15496) and the Division of Maternal and Child Health of the Public Health Service (MC-R-424067), and by an NIMH Research Scientist Development Award (K02-MH00486).

3

Child Care Effects on Socioemotional and Intellectual Competence in Swedish Preschoolers

Anders Broberg
Carl-Philip Hwang
University of Göteborg
Michael E. Lamb
Robert D. Ketterlinus
*National Institute of Child Health
and Human Development*

Theoretical and practical concerns have recently stimulated a vigorous debate concerning the effects of day care on young children (see Belsky, 1986, in press; Belsky, Steinberg, & Walker, 1982; Clarke-Stewart, in press; and Lamb & Sternberg, in press, for reviews). Increasing scholarly interest in the effects of rearing and cultural contexts on children's development has reinforced a practical concern driven by the increasing numbers of dual-earner and single-parent families seeking out-of-home care for their children. Few researchers have substantiated the initial presumption that nonparental care would prove to be harmful for young children, but the conclusiveness of the available evidence is limited by the common focus on high-quality center-based care facilities providing care for socioeconomically homogeneous samples. The purpose of the research described in this chapter was to examine the effects of the quality of family and center day care on firstborn Swedish children from socioeconomically diverse back-

grounds, including in our design measures of family background characteristics and pre-enrollment measures of relevant child characteristics. The
findings discussed here were presented in greater detail by Broberg, Lamb,
Hwang, and Bookstein (1987); Ketterlinus, Bookstein, Sampson, and Lamb
(1988); Lamb et al. (1988); and Lamb, Hwang, Broberg, and Bookstein (in
press).

Although most previous research on this topic has been conducted in
the United States, our research was conducted in Sweden. One motivation
for this choice was to avoid the common confound between parental
values/ideology and type of child care. As McCartney, Scarr, Phillips,
Grajek, and Schwarz (1982) pointed out, the parents in the United States
who choose day care may well differ in important ways from parents who
choose to care for their children themselves, and these differences in ideology, rather than the type of care per se, may account for differences between
children in the different child care groups, especially when no pre-enrollment assessments are involved. We were able to overcome this problem to
some extent by limiting our study to families who had expressed a desire
to obtain center care for their children. Because the number of available
places is limited in Sweden, we selected our sample only from those
families who had formally requested center-based care. Some were successful in getting places and constituted a group of children receiving center-
based day care ($n = 53$). Others were unable to get places in centers but were
instead offered care in family day care homes; they constituted a second
group ($n = 33$). A final group of children did not enter either centers or family day care facilities; they remained at home in the care of their parents ($n
= 54$). Thus, the parents of all children had attempted to obtain center care,
and the assignment to facilities (both center- and family-based) was made
by public authorities. Because of our recruitment procedures, we hoped
that pre-existing group differences in parental values concerning out-of-
home care would be largely eliminated.

Unfortunately, subsequent analyses revealed that there were indeed
some group differences in parental values, the correlates and extent of
which have yet to be explored (Broberg & Hwang, 1987). Thus although
our groups were probably more similar with respect to parental values and
attitudes than comparable groups in the United States would be, we cannot claim homogeneity in this respect.

One additional advantage attributable to the Swedish child care system is that the confounding between quality of home care and quality of
alternative care is greatly reduced, because most facilities are operated
under public auspices and provide care of good quality. In both the United
States and Canada, researchers have reported that children from poorer,
less child-centered, and more stressed homes tend to be enrolled in altei-

native care facilities of lower quality (Howes & Olenick, 1986; Howes & Stewart, 1987; Kontos, 1987; Phillips & Howes, 1987).

Researchers have reported that children in day care become more skillful at and engage in more peer interaction than do children who have not had equivalent amounts of out-of-home care (Finkelstein, Dent, Gallagher, & Ramey, 1978; Harper & Huie, 1985). Out-of-home care appears to have little or no consistent effect—positive or negative—either on aspects of social and emotional development or on the cognitive and intellectual development of middle-class children (Belsky & Steinberg, 1978); however, education-oriented programs may have positive effects on the intellectual performance of preschoolers from socioeconomically disadvantaged family backgrounds (e.g., Darlington, Royce, Snipper, Murray, & Lazar, 1980; Golden et al., 1978; McCartney, Scarr, Phillips, & Grajek, 1985; Ramey & Campbell, 1979). In an earlier study in Sweden, Cochran (1977; Cochran & Gunnarsson, 1985; see also Gunnarsson, 1985) found few differences on measures of intellectual or social development between children in day care and children cared for in homes by their mothers or family day care providers, although adult-child interaction was more common in the home settings than in the day care centers. Nordberg and Alin-Akerman (1983) reported that children in day care centers and family day care homes performed marginally better on the Griffiths Scale C index of intellectual development. There were also positive associations between performance on Griffiths and levels of parental education, although it was not possible to determine how these associations were mediated.

Unfortunately, researchers concerned with the effects of out-of-home care on child development have seldom considered the impact of out-of-home care in the context of other significant events in the children's lives, despite widespread agreement that development is multiply determined. In addition, much of the research has been conducted in university-affiliated day care centers of unusually high quality. Consequently, although the evidence permits the conclusion that day care *can* enhance some aspects of children's socioemotional development, it precludes the inference that day care *typically* has such effects. Many reviewers (e.g., Belsky, Steinberg, & Walker, 1982; McCartney et al., 1982) have suggested that the quality of care should indeed make a difference, and using observation-based measures of quality both McCartney and her colleagues (McCartney et al., 1982; McCartney, 1984) and Goelman (1988; Goelman & Pence, 1987) showed that children receiving high-quality out-of-home care developed better language and cognitive skills and were more empathic, sociable, and emotionally adjusted than children receiving care of lower quality. Both McCartney et al. (1982) and Goelman (1988) found that family socioeconomic status (SES)—especially as represented by maternal education level—also affected aspects of cognitive and linguistic development. In British Columbia, Goelman and Pence (1987) found that children from the most socioeconomically disadvantaged families tended to receive out-of-home care of poor quality, so that the adverse effects of unstimulating home environments were probably exacerbated by the low quality of out-of-home care. In a study of 4.5-year-olds, Holloway and Reichhart-Erickson (in press) found that absolute group size was associated with social reasoning skills, such that children in larger classes gave more antisocial responses and used more antisocial categories on the Spivack and Shure (1974) social problem-solving procedure. They also found that when the child/teacher ratio was high, the children spent less time in solitary play. The National Day Care Study (Ruopp, Travers, Glantz, & Coelen, 1979) also found an association between these two "structural" measures of the quality of day care (child/teacher ratio and group size) and children's task-oriented and social behaviors. Absolute group size is apparently a particularly important variable, such that children in small groups are less aggressive, more cooperative, more responsive, and more attentive. Kontos and Fiene (1987), however, found that structural measures of day care quality did not explain variations in child outcome.

In the research reported here, indices of family social status and repeated measures of the quality of both in-home and out-of-home care were used to explore the combined impact of these factors on aspects of both intellectual and sociopersonality development. We expected that the quality of in- and out-of-home care would be influential, whereas the type of care arrangements (e.g., home versus out-of-home care) would not be predictively important. In the past, a disproportionate amount of attention has been paid by researchers to center day care, even though family day care, about which little is known, is often considered to be the facility of choice (Klein, 1985). Both center-based and family day care facilities were included in the present study.

In addition to measures of SES and the quality of home care, parent-report measures of the extent of paternal involvement in child care were included in light of the evidence that paternal involvement is often associated with cognitive competence, peer social skills, and aspects of personality development (such as locus of control, empathy, and independence) similar to those studied here (Lamb, Pleck, & Levine, 1985; Parke, MacDonald, Beitel, & Bhavnagri, in press; Radin, 1982). Perceived social support was also included in the model because of the growing evidence that parental behavior and child adjustment are often influenced by the level of perceived support or social embeddedness. Parents who have good social support systems not only are likely to introduce their children to more social partners of all ages but also can count on material assistance that enhances both the quality and extent of parental behavior (Colletta & Gregg, 1981; Crnic, Greenberg, & Ragozin, 1981; Crnic, Greenberg, & Slough, 1986; Crockenberg, 1981, 1987). Unfortunately, researchers have yet to determine whether these effects on parental behavior are translated into differences in child behavior. Such translations should occur, however, because variations in the quality of parental behavior are associated with differences in peer social skills and the aspects of personality studied here (e.g., Arend, Gove, & Sroufe, 1979; MacDonald & Parke, 1984). We expected, as a result, that children in well-supported families would appear better adjusted, more competent, and more sociable than would children from more socially isolated families.

Individual characteristics of the children—including gender, age, perceived temperamental difficulty, and sociability—were also considered in our study. Consistent with earlier findings (reviewed by Lamb, 1982), we expected that unsociable children, and perhaps children perceived to have difficult temperaments, would perform more poorly on cognitive tests because of their reduced willingness to attend to and cooperate with the examiner. We also expected that timid, cautious children, like children who had frequent negative moods, would have fewer successful interactions with peers and (as a result) would become less socially skillful with them. Such children should also be rated lower on ego resiliency, field independence, and ego control than children who were more self-assertive and tended to have positive moods. Such relations were suggested by Thomas, Chess, Birch, Hertzig, and Korn (1963).

In choosing dependent measures, we attempted to assess four broad classes of variables: those concerning the quality of peer play, the degree of sociability with strange adults, the child's emergent personality style, and intellectual competence. Sociability, peer skills, and intellectual competence have frequently been studied in research on alternative care (e.g., Clarke-Stewart & Fein, 1983), and it was thus important to include comparable measures. The aspects of personality studied here—field independence, ego resiliency, and ego-control—have not previously been examined in the day care literature but have been considered in the context of research designed to explore the effects of parental behavior, child-parent attachment, and environmental circumstances (e.g., Block & Block, 1980; Lamb, Thompson, Gardner, & Charnov, 1985). Importantly, Block and Block have also shown that these dimensions of personality are relatively stable over time. Unfortunately, however, Block and Block's questionnaire is not suitable for use with toddlers, so we were not able to employ it in the pre-enrollment assessment phase.

DATA ANALYSIS STRATEGY

The determinants of individual differences in child characteristics and competencies 1 year after some of the subjects were enrolled in out-of-home care was assessed using the technique of "soft modeling" or Partial Least Squares (PLS). This tool, developed principally by the Swedish statistician Herman Wold (1975; Joreskog & Wold, 1982), is intended as an alternative to LISREL in the exploration of complex social phenomena that have been measured indirectly. Like LISREL, PLS summarizes patterns of correlation among multiple measures of multiple putative constructs, of which some are "determinants" and some are "outcomes" of unobservable processes. An elementary description of PLS is provided by Bookstein (1986). Analytically, PLS searches for simple consistency between the various roles that constructs are expected to play in a least-squares analysis. The coefficients reported by PLS are tightly tied to actual observable correlations between linear combinations of indicators; no correction for "attenuation" occurs to accommodate vagueness in the model or measurement error. PLS computations assess the coherence of conceptually defined clusters of variables—known as latent variables—by examining their patterns of correlations with other latent variables, rather than by examining their patterns of correlations with other members of their own latent variables. One may think of it as a sort of canonical-correlation analysis in which both steps of multiple regression are replaced by a procedure somewhat akin to principal-components analysis involving the summing of simple regressions. In a model, each latent variable is computed as a weighted sum of its own indicators, using weights that are proportional to the correlations of these indicators with the other latent variables (i.e., the correlations between predictor indicators and outcome indicators). Proponents of PLS argue that it is ideally suited for longitudinal studies in which multiple measures of multiple constructs are considered (Bookstein, 1986). Because the procedure emphasizes inter- rather than intra-block correlations, it makes questions of prediction paramount. The procedure also permits researchers to determine whether coherent blocks exist and whether the distinctions between certain blocks are empirically defensible.

In Fig. 3.1, the general model examined using PLS analysis is depicted, with variables grouped conceptually in terms of their presumed interrelations. Group status was not expected to be important, but quality of home and out-of-home care, as well as the other factors discussed earlier, were expected to be influential. The measures themselves are described more fully later in the chapter.

In sum, the purpose of this research was to assess the effects of out-of-home care, in the context of other important life events and family cir-

DETERMINANTS   OUTCOMES

CHILD AGE
CHILD GENDER
INFANT DIFFICULTY

HOME BACKGROUND:
Father's Hollingshead I
Mother's Hollingshead I
Belsky & Walker Positive I, II, III   PEER PLAY—III
Belsky & Walker Negative I, II, III   Howes, Sum 3-5
                                                Positive Peer Bids
                                                Negative Peer Bids

HOME—Total, I, II, III
SUPPORT I:
Maternal Grandparents (Father)
Maternal Grandparents (Mother)   SOCIABILITY with Strange
Paternal Grandparents (Mother)   Adult, III
Paternal Grandparents (Father)
Friends/Neighbors (Mother)
Friends/Neighbors (Father)

FATHER INVOLVEMENT I, II, II
GROUP: PERSONALITY: II, III
Home/Family Daycare/Center Care   Field Independence, Mother
                                                Ego Resiliency, Mother
SOCIABILITY with Strange Adult, I, II   Ego Undercontrol, Mother
                                                Field Independence, Careproviders
PEER PLAY: I, II   Ego Resiliency, Careproviders
Howes, Sum 3-5   Ego Undercontrol, Careproviders
Pos. Peer Bids
Neg. Peer Bids

QUALITY OF ALTERNATIVE CARE I, II, III   INTELLECTUAL COMPETENCE
Belsky & Walker Positive
Belsky & Walker Negative
Hours/Week of Alternative Care
Group size
Child/caregiver ratio
Age range
Age mixture

FIG. 3.1.   The proposed model depicting the determinants and outcomes included in
the analyses.

cumstances, on several aspects of social, personality, and intellectual
development. Among the potential influences considered were the nature
and quality of in-home and out-of-home care, perceived social support,

various indices of socioeconomic status, and reports of the child's temperament.

METHODS

Subjects

One hundred forty firstborn children (70 girls) from Göteborg, Sweden participated in the study. They ranged in age from 11 to 24 months (M and median = 15.9 months; SD = 2.9 months) at the time of initial interview/assessment. Names of two-parent families on the waiting lists for child care facilities were obtained from municipal authorities in all areas of the city. Parents were then individually contacted by the research staff and invited to participate in the research; 75% of those contacted agreed to participate. Hollingshead (1975) scores showed that the children came from a range of middle-class backgrounds.

Procedure

After agreeing to participate in the study, all families were visited in their homes by a member of the research staff. During this visit, parents were interviewed about their education and occupations, their social networks, father involvement, and their child's temperament. The child's initial response to the visiting adult was also scored, and the HOME Inventory (Caldwell, 1970) was completed. A second visit was then arranged. On this occasion, the child was observed interacting at home for 30 minutes with a familiar peer (selected by the parents) of roughly the same age. Those children in the alternative care groups began out-of-home care within 2 weeks of the two home visits. Six weeks later their child care facilities were visited by a member of the research staff, who rated the quality of care, using Belsky and Walker's (1980) checklist, and obtained information about class or group composition, staffing patterns, and the like.

Both 1 year (Phase II) and 2 years (Phase III) after the first interview, the families were visited again. During one visit, stranger sociability was again assessed, parents were interviewed about child care arrangements, and the mother completed a Q-sort description (the California Child Q-set, or CCQ) of her child that measured field independence, ego resilience, and ego undercontrol (Block & Block, 1980). At this time the quality of home care was also sampled with the Belsky and Walker checklist and the HOME Inventory. During the second visit, the child was again observed interacting for 30 minutes with a familiar peer of the parents' choice. On a subsequent visit to the child-care facility (for children in the two out-of-home care groups), the quality of care was sampled and a teacher who knew the child well described the child's personality, using the CCQ (in Phase II only). Trained psychologists administered Scale C of the Griffiths (1954, 1970) Developmental Scales, typically in the child's home. More information about the measures follows. Complete details are provided in the original research reports (Lamb et al., 1988, in press; Broberg et al., 1987).

Measures

Family Background and Home Environment. Maternal and paternal Hollingshead scores—weighted sums of the education and occupation scores for each parent—were computed as instructed by Hollingshead (1975). The Hollingshead scales, although developed in the United States and now somewhat dated, have been employed successfully in previous studies conducted in Sweden (e.g., Cochran, 1977; Frodi et al., 1982).

The quality of home care was tapped using four measures in each phase: Caldwell's (1970) HOME Inventory, Belsky and Walker's (1980) checklist (both positive events and negative events scores), and a measure of father involvement. In Phases I and II, observers completed the HOME Inventory for infants as instructed by Caldwell (1970). The 45 items on this well-known inventory measure the amount of stimulation available in the home environment. In Phase III, observers completed four subscales—IV ("Pride, Affection, and Warmth"), VI ("Modeling and Encouragement of Social Maturity"), VII ("Variety of Stimulation"), and VIII ("Physical Punishment")—of the preschool version of HOME (Caldwell & Bradley, 1984), which was more appropriate for the age of the children at this time. The four subscales were chosen because pilot testing revealed little variability on the other subscales. Scores on the four subscales were combined into a single index for analytic purposes.

The Belsky and Walker checklist includes 13 positive and 7 negative events, and the observer notes whether or not each occurred at least once during a 3-minute-long "spot sample" unit. The environment was sampled three or four times per occasion, and the numbers of negative and positive items per occasion were then averaged for purposes of analysis. Further details are provided in Belsky and Walker's (1980) scoring manual.

Paternal involvement was estimated from the full-day diary recalls provided by the two parents, who were asked to recall the previous day and the previous nonworking day from midnight to midnight. From this information we extracted estimates of the number of minutes fathers spent with their children. Estimates of father involvement were computed by combining the weighted sums of the weekday (x 5) and weekend (x 2) scores.

Perceived Support. During the initial (Phase I) interview, 23 questions were asked independently of mothers and fathers about the contacts with and support received from maternal and paternal grandparents, other relatives, friends, and neighbors. Three different composite measures were then computed for each parent: perceived support from *maternal grandparents*, perceived support from *paternal grandparents*, and perceived support from *friends and neighbors*.

Quality of Alternative Care Settings. In our previously published reports (Lamb et al., 1988; Lamb et al., in press) the quality of care provided in the alternative care settings was likewise assessed with the Belsky and Walker checklist described previously. The alternative care settings were assessed three times: once 3 months after enrollment, again 9 months later, and finally 24 months after enrollment. Another measure of out-of-home care was the number of hours spent by the child in alternative care each week.

Four structural measures of the quality of alternative care were included in Study 2 only. Two traditional structural measures were added: absolute group size and the child/caregiver ratio. In addition, we included two new indicators: the age range of children in the setting and the proportion of children in the group whose ages were within 12 months of the target child's age.

Child Characteristics. Temperament was assessed using Rothbart's (1981) Infant Behavior Questionnaire (IBQ), a standardized 87-item parent report measure of infant temperament. Analyses involved only one composite measure: following Frodi et al. (1982), we computed a score for perceived difficulty of temperament by adding the IBQ score for anger/frustration to the inverse of the scores for positive emotionality and soothability, before dividing by 3. Possible scores ranged from 1 to 7, with high scores indicating that the child's temperament was perceived to be difficult.

In Phase I, sociability was assessed upon the observer/interviewer's arrival at the child's home, using a procedure developed and more fully described by Stevenson and Lamb (1979; Thompson & Lamb, 1983). The child's response in each of eight contexts was rated on a 5-point scale, with 1 indicating a fussy, unfriendly response and 5 indicating an outgoing, positive response. In addition, the observer recorded his or her overall impression of the child's sociability on a 9-point scale. The nine ratings were then added. In Phase II, the sociability assessment procedure was altered to accommodate the increased age of the children. The child's response in each of five contexts was rated on 5-point scales similar to those used in Phase I. In addition, the observer recorded an overall impression on a 9-point scale, and the six ratings were then summed. In Phase III, a single 9-point rating scale, similar to the overall impression scale employed earlier, was used to rate the overall sociability.

Child Personality. The child's score for field independence, ego resilience, and ego undercontrol were computed by correlating the ratings assigned by the mothers or care providers on the 100-item CCQ with the criterion scores for the most field independent, ego resilient, and ego undercontrolled child supplied by the Blocks. These correlation coefficients were then used as scores in all subsequent analyses. Mothers completed Q-sorts in Phases II and III; alternative care providers completed them in Phase II only.

Peer Skills. In each phase, the children were observed interacting at home with familiar peers. The 30-minute-long peer interaction sessions were divided into 15-second observation units followed by 15-second breaks for data entry. For each observation unit, the observer recorded the incidence of any of 23 discrete behaviors or states and also rated the quality of the peer play, using Howes' (1980) 6-point rating scale, on which 0 is scored when no play is observed and 5 is scored when there is complementary and reciprocal social play. Further details are provided in Howes' (1980) coding manual.

Three peer interaction scores were derived for the purposes of analysis: positive peer-related behaviors (the sum of the observed incidences of initiate play, imitate, vocalize, touch, proffer, accept, and laugh/smile),[1] negative peer-directed behaviors (the composite total for reject bid, turn away, take away toy, take toy from, have toy taken from, throw, defensive struggle, offensive struggle, strike/hit, and cry; see footnote 1), and Howes 3-5, the total number of units during which the play was rated a 3, 4, or 5 on the Howes scale.[2]

Intellectual Development. We used Scale C of the Griffiths (1954, 1970) Developmental Scales, which in Europe is the most widely used measure of early intellectual performance. At the ages studied here, Scale C calls for children to be asked to name a number of objects and colors; to explain the proper use of objects; to describe the actions and activities depicted in a picture; to explain how to address an everyday problem (e.g., "What do you do if it's raining and you want to go out?"); to tell what different things are made of; and to repeat sentences of increasing length. All items are organized by increasing level of difficulty, with a baseline determined by successful completion of six successive items and termination signalled by six successive failures. Criteria for success are fully specified, and there was near perfect agreement among the three trained examiners employed in this study. Further details are provided in the books by Griffiths (1954, 1970) and Alin-Akerman and Nordberg (1980), who conducted the Swedish standardization. All scores are converted into developmental quotients in order to adjust for variations in the children's ages.

Reliability

All observations (peer interaction, sociability, quality of care indexes) of a particular child were conducted by the same observer, one of three individuals who trained together using videotapes and pilot subjects until they achieved criterial degrees of reliability. For the peer interaction and HOME Inventory codes, criterion was set at 80% exact agreement; for sociability and the Belsky and Walker items, criterion was set at 90%. Once data collection began, 15% of the sessions were conducted by two of the observers, working simultaneously but independently. Reliability coefficients were within 5% of the criterion levels in each of the subsequent reliability assessments. It was impossible to keep observers blind with respect to the group status of the children, but they were not aware of the explanatory model guiding the research, nor of the expectations that group differences would not be significant.

RESULTS

Preliminary Analyses

Preliminary analyses of variance revealed that children in the family day care group were younger, came from families of higher social status, and were rated less ego-controlled in Phase III than were children in the other two groups. Analyses of the alternative care measures revealed that the center care settings received higher scores than the family day care settings on the Belsky and Walker positive and negative indices in both the first and second assessment phases. These differences were predictable in light of the greater number of children in the center care groups and are not important in the context of the within-group analyses emphasized here. On average, center care children received more hours of alternative care per week than children in the family day care group.

Viewed together, these results indicate that type of child care, as predicted, had little effect on the children in this study. Overall, the results suggest that the children in the three groups were more similar than different and came from similar backgrounds, although the children in the family day care group came from higher social class backgrounds.

Having demonstrated that group status was not a major determinant of individual differences among children, we next turned our attention to identifying the factors that *were* influential. For analytic purposes, we considered separately the prediction of social and intellectual competence.

Study 1

Of the 140 children who remained in the study through Phase III, 115 maintained the original care arrangement through at least Phases I and II, whereas 84 maintained the same arrangement through Phase III. Preliminary analyses revealed no significant differences between those children and families who changed arrangements and the remainder of the sample. All analyses reported here were computed twice: once on the subsample of 115 and once on the subsample of 84. On occasion, the results obtained using the PLS technique varied depending on the sample employed, and in these cases both sets of results are reported. In other cases, we report only those based on the restrictively defined subsample comprising those 84 children and families who maintained the same care arrangements throughout.

Social Competence. PLS analyses identified a fairly strong model in which several of the determinants identified in Fig. 3.1 were significantly related to the personality outcome variables as assessed in Phase III. Fig. 3.2 summarizes the predictive model describing the determinants of personality ratings in Phase III. The figure shows that the latent variables of support, quality of home care III, and quality of alternative care III all helped explain equivalent proportions of the variance in the personality ratings, with the personality II latent variable being by far the most predictive. More mature ratings on the personality Q-sort were obtained at time III when the children had received more mature ratings from their mothers at time II, when parents reported higher levels of support (especially from friends and neighbors), when the home was more stimulating and fathers were more involved, and when the quality of alternative care was poorer! When the earlier personality ratings were excluded from the model, the net R fell from .63 to .46, but the relative importance of the other latent vari-

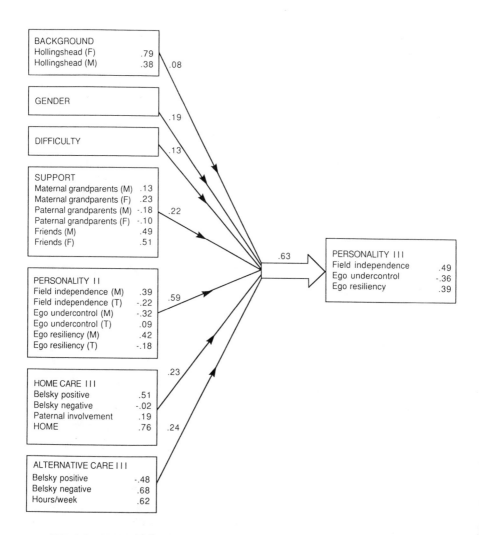

FIG. 3.2. Study 1 determinants of Phase III personality ratings. M indicates that the data pertains to mother, F to father. T indicates that the data was provided by the teacher or alternative care provider. Group status had no explanatory value and therefore is not included in the figure.

ables, and indicators thereof, was unchanged. Again, this probably reflects the fact that the earlier personality characteristics were themselves predicted by variations in family background, support, and the quality of care (see Lamb et al., 1988).

When the model was recomputed with the large sample (n = 115) of children who maintained the same care arrangements through at least Phase II, the predictive importance of the quality of alternative care and support latent variables fell to .16 and .15 respectively, whereas the coefficient for personality II rose to .67. The net R for the model rose to .68. Coefficients within the alternative care latent variable changed dramatically, such that positive Belsky scores and hours per week were positively and substantially (r = .62 and r = .77 respectively) associated with more mature personality ratings. Coefficients within the support and personality latent variables also changed, albeit in inconsistent and uninterpretable ways.

PLS analyses showed that the peer play and sociability measures tapped constructs that were quite independent of those tapped by the personality latent variables. The relevant model for the social skills outcomes is depicted in Fig. 3.3. The net R for the combined prediction was a respectable .64. Inspection of the figure indicates that the quality of home care, the quality of out-of-home care, social skills at time II, and gender all contributed to the prediction of observed social skills in Phase III, whereas background (primarily social class) and support had modest associations and perceived infant difficulty and group status were unrelated to social skills as assessed here. Children who were more sociable and playful with both peers and strange adults came from homes receiving higher scores on Caldwell's HOME and had less-involved fathers. They also spent more time in out-of-home care facilities characterized by low scores on both the positive and negative scales of the Belsky and Walker checklist. Girls were more sociable than boys. The prediction by gender, quality of home care, and quality of alternative care remained substantial (net R = .57) even when prior social skills were not included in the model. As the figure shows, this latent variable was the best predictor of individual differences in social skills at time III. This indicates that the autocorrelation between successive measures of social skills is substantial but that knowledge of prior social skills does not much enhance the degree of prediction achieved using the other predictor variables alone. Presumably this is because scores on the earlier measures of child social skills are themselves determined by variations in this group of determinants—including child gender, quality of home care, and quality of alternative care (see Lamb et al., 1988).

When the model was computed again using the large subsample (n = 115) of children who had remained in the same group through the first two phases but may have changed care arrangements between Phases II and III, the coefficients were very similar (net R = .63), although the relative importance of the hours per week variable within the quality of alternative care latent variable decreased from a coefficient of .38 to .10, the gender latent variable had a coefficient of only .16, and the coefficient for support

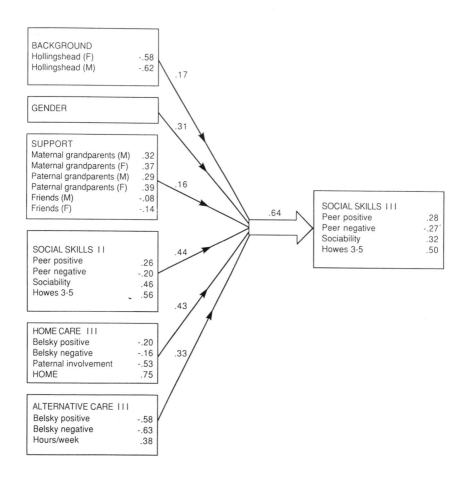

FIG. 3.3. Study 1 determinants of Phase III social skills. M indicates that mother was the respondent, F that it was father. Difficulty had no explanatory value and therefore is not included in the figure.

rose to .21. In neither model did group assignment have any impact on the social skills III latent variable.

Intellectual Competence. In Fig. 3.4 we sketch the determinants of scores on the Phase III Griffiths assessment. The best predictors of Phase III Griffiths performance were the contemporaneous (Phase III) and earlier (Phase II) measures of the quality of home care and the contemporaneous rating of the child's sociability. Although Phase I quality of home care

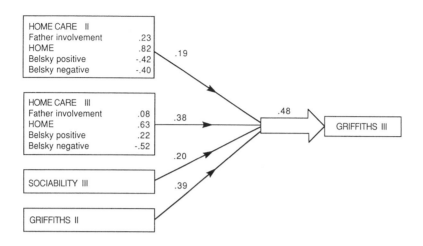

FIG. 3.4.   Best predictors of Phase III Griffiths scores.

scores were significantly correlated with scores on the Phase III Griffiths
assessment, their inclusion added little to the net R, so for clarity these
measures are not included in Fig. 3.4. Phase II Griffiths scores were correlated with Phase III scores about as highly as with the quality of home care
latent variable. Inclusion of the contemporaneous measures of out-of-
home care, family background, perceived support, and initial individual
characteristics raised the net R marginally (a maximum of .05), but none of
these latent variables contributed significantly to the prediction of Griffiths
scores and thus they are not included in the figure.

The autocorrelation between successive Griffiths scores aside, the best
predictors of developmental status at both ages (Phases II and III) were the
quality of home care and (to a lesser extent) the sociability of the child. It is
also worth noting that the latent variable tapping family socioeconomic
background did not making a significant contribution and that the correlations between the three quality of home care latent variables and the family background latent variable were modest: Phase I, $R = .41$; Phase II, $R =$
.28, Phase III, $R = .28$. This indicates that quality of home care, as assessed
here, is not simply a proxy index of socioeconomic status.

Study 2

Because these analyses are focused on the impact of the quality of alternative care, only those children who stayed in alternative care settings
through all three phases of the project were included ($n = 48$; 25 girls). Be-

cause the available sample was so small, it was not possible to distinguish between the 12 in family day care and 36 in center care facilities, even though this would have been desirable. Except for the quality of alternative care latent variables, the predictor and outcome latent variables included in the present study were the same as those examined in Study 1.

In these analyses, the latent variables of quality of alternative care were expanded to include several *structural* indices of the quality of care: absolute group size, the child/caregiver ratio, the age range of the children in the alternative care settings, and the proportion of children in an alternative care setting whose ages were within 12 months of the target child's. Associations between the quality of alternative care and indicators of intellectual competence have not yet been investigated.

Social Competence. Adding structural measures of the quality of alternative care improved prediction of both the personality and the social skills latent variables, with net R's of .70 and .77 respectively (compared with .63 and .64 in Study 1). However, the models for each outcome were somewhat different in the two sets of analyses.

In the present analyses, personality ratings by mothers in Phase III were predicted by a model that included an averaged (across the three

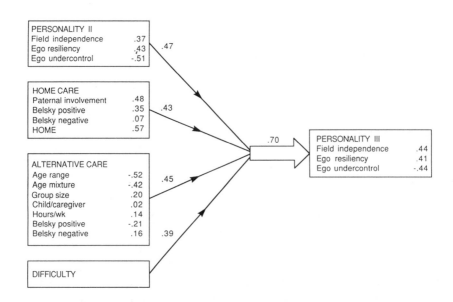

FIG. 3.5. Study 2 determinants of Phase III personality ratings. All personality ratings were provided by mothers.

phases) quality of home care latent variable, an averaged (across Phases II and III only) quality of alternative care latent variable, perceived temperamental difficulty, and earlier ratings of child personality (see Fig. 3.5). We decided to average scores on the indicators of quality on the basis of preliminary results revealing substantial intercorrelations among the relevant latent variables (within the home or alternative care situations), with no single latent variable yielding superior prediction of the respective outcomes. Difficulty and mothers' personality ratings in Phase II also predicted the averaged quality of home and alternative care latent variables.

The results of most interest involve the additional (structural) indicators of the quality of alternative care. Two (out of four) of these, the age range and age mixture of the groups, contributed most of the predictive power of the averaged quality of alternative care latent variable. Note that absolute group size and the child/caregiver ratio contributed little or nothing to the predictive power of this latent variable, perhaps because ratios were fairly homogeneous within the day care and family day care groups.

In sum, children with more involved fathers, higher HOME scores, and higher Belsky positive home scores received more mature ratings on the personality III Q-sort. (Removing personality II from the model had a negligible effect, reducing the net R to .67.) Having a mature personality was also related to being in an alternative care setting that had a narrower range of children's ages and a more homogeneous age mixture. Also, children with more mature personalities, as rated by their mothers, were earlier perceived by their parents as being more difficult. (Note, however, that the children's scores for perceived difficulty were at the low end of the 7-point scale, averaging 2.7 for children in family day care and 2.6 for children in center care.)

As in Study 1, the present PLS results show that peer play and sociability as assessed in the home were correlated with constructs independent of those correlated with the personality III latent variable (see Fig. 3.6). In the present analyses, the net R for the social skills outcome was quite high relative to the net R yielded in Study 1 (.77 vs. .64 respectively). The best predictor of the social skills III latent variable was the quality of alternative care in Phase III. The three next most important predictors (all Phase II latent variables) made approximately the same contribution to the prediction of Phase III social skills; they were quality of home care II, quality of alternative care II, and social skills II. (When the latent variable for social skills II was removed, the net R was reduced to a very respectable .71.) The measure of parental SES contributed a much smaller proportion of the predictive power of the model than the other four latent variables depicted.

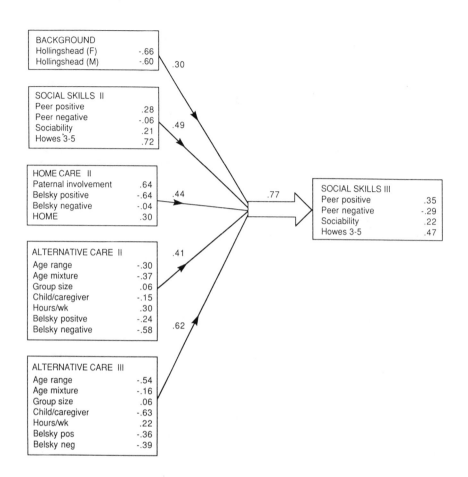

FIG. 3.6. Study 2 determinants of Phase III social skills. Difficulty had no explanatory value and therefore is not included in the figure.

Substantively, these results show that children who were, in Phase III, more sociable and playful attended high quality alternative care facilities, had more-involved fathers, and were from homes that had both high HOME scores and low scores on the Belsky positive checklist. Highly sociable children attended out-of-home care facilities in both Phases II and III that had a narrower age range and a more homogeneous age mixture and were characterized by the occurrence of fewer negative events. By Phase III the child/caregiver ratio became the most important component of the quality of alternative care latent variable. Facilities that had few children per caregiver had children who exhibited more age-appropriate social skills.

CONCLUSIONS

In Study 1, we asked whether the type of child care received by children over a 3-year period had an effect on several aspects of their development. We found that the *type* of care received by children had no demonstrable effect on their observed social skills or reported personality. This finding is largely consistent with the results of a number of studies indicating that out-of-home care beginning in the second year of life does not have reliable and consistent effects on emergent social competence (Clarke-Stewart & Fein, 1983; Lamb & Sternberg, in press; Scarr, 1985), although some researchers have reported that out-of-home care experiences positively influence the degree of involvement with peers (Finkelstein et al., 1978; Harper & Huie, 1985; Schindler, Moely, & Frank, 1987), a finding that we were unable to replicate in this sample of Swedish preschoolers.

As noted in the introduction, we expected that quality of care would be much more predictively informative than would the type of care, and this was indeed the case. In Study 1, which included children who were cared for by their parents in addition to those in family and center care arrangements, the quality of care received both at home and in alternative care settings was influential, as were measures of reported social support, prior social competence, and child gender. When we restricted our sample to those children who were in out-of-home care arrangements throughout and included additional measures of the quality of alternative care (Study 2), there was a substantial increase in the predictive power of our overall model, and the quality of alternative care latent variables gained in predictive power.

In both studies reported here, as in the analyses earlier reported involving the complete sample of 140 (Lamb et al., 1988), the quality of home care had a significant impact on both social skills and reported personality traits. In Study 1 this was the case only with regard to the quality of home care III latent variable, whereas in Study 2 the quality of home care II latent variable was a strong predictor of social skills, and a latent variable comprising the averaged measures of quality of home care over 3 years was a potent predictor of personality traits in Phase III. Except for the Study 2 results involving social skills, the most consistently informative variable was the score on Caldwell's HOME Inventory; coefficients for the Belsky and Walker checklist scores tended to be both more modest and inconsistent. In Study 2, the Belsky and Walker positive score was the most powerful predictor of social skills, but, counterintuitively, the coefficient was negative. The inconsistency of results involving the Belsky and Walker scores leads us to be cautious about any predictions involving them.

The findings concerning the association between paternal involvement and social competence varied across the two studies reported here. In Study 1, the degree of paternal involvement was negatively associated with social skills. Among the sample of children who consistently experienced out-of-home care (Study 2), the opposite relationship obtained; the degree of paternal involvement in Phases I and II was positively associated with observed social skills in Phase III. Although there was no effect of group on social skills in Study 1, our findings suggest that fathers of children in home-care situations may have become more involved in child care when their children showed poor social skills, perhaps in an effort to ameliorate the situation. It is also possible that fathers of children who were in alternative care situations throughout the study became increasingly involved with their children and that this increased involvement may have had positive effects on the children's subsequent social skills. In both studies, paternal involvement was positively associated with more mature personality ratings by the mothers.

Vandell, Henderson, and Wilson (1987) found that the quality of care experienced by twenty 4-year-olds was related to ratings of empathy, social competence, and social acceptance 4 years later. In a study of 3-, 4-, and 5-year-old American children, Kontos (1987) reported that the quality of alternative care had little impact, whereas family background characteristics had an impact on measures of intellectual and language development. Similarly, in earlier analyses involving assessments through Phase II (average age = 28 months) on data from the complete sample, Lamb et al. (1988) reported that the quality of alternative care, as assessed by nonstructural measures, had no appreciable impact on social competence. By contrast, both sets of analyses reported here, one using the same measures as in Lamb et al. (1988) and the other using an expanded model that included additional measures of the quality of alternative care, revealed noteworthy associations between quality of alternative care and both of the outcome latent variables. The second study, involving the most restrictive sample, revealed particularly strong associations between the quality of alternative care and social competence. The differences across analyses could be attributable to either sample composition or improved model specification. The less restrictive sample selection procedures employed in the earliest analyses (Lamb et al., 1988) led to the inclusion of children even when their group assignment changed before follow-up; measures of the quality of alternative care may have been rendered less sensitive as a result. It should also be noted that the internal coefficients of the alternative care latent vailables were inconsistent and somewhat counterintuitive in both sets of analyses. They indicate, for example, that sociable children spent more time in out-of-home care (as would be expected; e.g., Schindler et al., 1987) but had lower scores on the Belsky positive (unexpected) and Belsky negative (expected) checklists. In Study 1, personality maturity was facilitated by greater numbers of hours in out-of-home care, by lower scores on the Belsky positive index, and by higher scores on the Belsky negative index; in Study 2 the *direction* of these associations was the same, but the relative importance of the Belsky indices was greatly diminished. Thus, both sets of analyses again raised questions about both the validity of the Belsky and Walker (1980) checklists as measures of the quality of alternative care and their usefulness as indicators of quality relative to the structural measures of quality employed in Study 2. Although Study 1 provided limited support for the intuitive prediction that high quality alternative care would have positive effects on social competence, the results of Study 2 provide strong evidence that some structural markers of quality care have a combined impact on social competence as measured here. These structural components include those traditionally found to be associated with infant and child outcomes (group size and child/teacher ratio, e.g., Holloway & Reichart-Erickson, 1987; Ruopp et al., 1979), as well as two measures, introduced for the first time in this report, that assess peer-group composition: age range and age mixture.

Reported support had a modest association with outcome in Study 1 (especially when personality maturity was the outcome measure), and variations in internal coefficients across analyses preclude specifying the type of support that was most influential. The generally positive influence of available social support is consistent with findings demonstrating that high levels of available support enhance the quality of parental behavior (e.g., Crockenberg, 1981), and our results indicated that this may in turn have a desirable impact on children's personality maturity. However, our predictions concerning support were not confirmed in Study 2, in which available support had no impact on social competence. Perhaps the effects of alternative care quality simply "outweighed" the effects of support as measured 2 years earlier in the more restricted sample of alternative care children.

As far as intellectual development is concerned, we confirmed in Study 1 the associations between quality of home care and intellectual development (e.g., Caldwell & Bradley, 1984). Our findings thus demonstrated once again the validity of Caldwell's scales, including (in the case of our Phase III assessment) a composite score comprising 25 of the 55 items on the preschool version of the HOME Inventory. The correlations between contemporaneous measures of home care and intellectual performance obtained in Study 1 were just under .40, compared with coefficients of around .55 obtained in Caldwell's prior research with heterogeneous samples in the United States. On this account, therefore, our results are consistent with, although weaker than, results previously obtained in the United States; knowledge of the quality of home care provided the best basis for prediction of intellectual competence in children averaging 28 and 40 months of age. In the case of 40-month-olds, knowledge of earlier cognitive competence provided nearly as good information, but knowledge of both sorts of information did not significantly increase the degree to which intellectual performance could be predicted. Presumably the measurable impact of quality of home care would have been even more substantial had there been greater variability in the measure of home care, where we found less variability than, for example, in the standardization samples reported by Caldwell and Bradley (1984). Despite this, however, the HOME Inventory was the most useful source of information concerning the quality of home care.

Our results underscored the formative impact of the quality of home care and indicated that neither the type nor the quality of out-of-home care were predictively important where intellectual outcomes were concerned. These findings appear at variance with results reported by both McCartney and her colleagues (1982) and Goelman and Pence (1987), in Bermuda and Canada respectively, who found sizable associations between the quality of out-of-home care and intellectual/linguistic development in children. The divergence between their findings and ours may disappear when we re-examine the quality of alternative care in the more restricted sample and with structural measures of quality. It is also possible that threshold effects are involved, such that the quality of alternative care is influential only when it falls below a threshold level. Because alternative care facilities are generally of high quality in Sweden, it is conceivable that most could have provided at least adequate (suprathreshold) quality.

In sum, our findings confirmed that enrollment in out-of-home care during the second year of life does not have clearcut effects on diverse aspects of children's development. Whether or not such experiences are influential—either positively or negatively—depends on the quality of care received there. And regardless of the quality of alternative care, the quality of care received from parents at home remains influential. Other factors proved influential in one or more of the analyses reported here, but it was clear that the quality of care variables were the most important. It was also clear, unfortunately, that the quality of care is a slippery and multifaceted construct that requires careful measurement and interpretation to be understood properly. One goal of our ongoing research is to improve the ways in which the quality of home care and the quality of alternative care are assessed.

DISCUSSION

In addition to the Swedish study presented in the foregoing chapter, Dr. Lamb reported the recent data from a recent study in Israel concerning the effects of traditional kibbutz childrearing practices, in which babies are cared for primarily in a centralized environment by a trained professional caregiver, or *metapelet*. When the 86 infants in the study were between 11 and 14 months of age, their attachments to both parents and to the metapelet were assessed with the Strange Situation. Although the total number of insecure attachments was not significantly higher than would be found in other populations, there was an increase in the proportion of insecure-resistant attachments to metapelets and mothers, but not to fathers (Sagi et al., 1985). A follow-up study was done 4 years later, when the children were 5 years old (Oppenheim, Sagi, & Lamb, 1988). In a variety of areas of personality, social functioning, and intellectual functioning, there were consistent and strong predictors from the quality of the attachment to the metapelet, and the metapelet only; the quality of the relationship with mothers and fathers, as assessed in the Strange Situation, had no impact on the children's functioning on the variables examined.

What was remarkable about these findings, Dr. Lamb commented, was that in the kibbutz system babies are moved to another care provider at about 14 months, right after the age at which the infants in the study were assessed. Although the initial metapelet had not cared for the children in the intervening 4 years, the nature of the relationship with her, as assessed by the Strange Situation, seemed to predict the children's later outcomes. It is an open question, he noted, whether relationships would not have been found with parental attachments if indices of the children's functioning in more intimate contacts had been used.

These findings, Dr. Lamb asserted, have important implications for day care studies. We need to look at child care not only in terms of whether or not the child is out of home but in terms of what type of care the child is receiving, the quality of the care, what else is going on in the child's home, and the broader social context, which he believes is a crucial determinant of the extent to which we can predict from any measure what is likely to happen to the child later on.

Dr. Belsky asked whether the Israeli study had found any associations between relationships with parents and relationships with metapelet. He cited research by Carolee Howes (Howes, Rodning, Galluzzo, & Myers, in press) that found that toddlers who functioned best were securely attached to both parent and caregiver, whereas those who functioned most poorly were insecurely attached to both. Moreover, children securely attached to their mothers seemed buffered with respect to the liabilities associated with insecure attachment to caregivers.

Dr. Lamb replied that in the kibbutz data no such interactions were found. Infants with two insecure relationships did not develop differently from those who were insecure to the metapelet only. He also noted that there were no temperament differences related either to attachment or to later outcomes.

Dr. Lamb was asked to comment about the differences found in the infants' relationships with their mothers and with their fathers. He noted that in the kibbutz situation it is the relationship with the mother that is the most different from the traditional one. The relationship between a kibbutz father and his child is in many ways better than that between a city father and his child. Time is set aside for family interaction, when there are no other constraints and fathers can focus on their children. The mother's role is changed dramatically by the kibbutz system; many mothers do not like the system, and many kibbutzim are switching to communal living arrangements and extending the duration of maternal leave. But the fathers are in a buffered environment that makes the relationship with the child much easier than it would otherwise be.

Dr. Lamb was also asked to comment about the degree of predictive stability over time, given the lack of continuity in the metapelet. It suggests, he said, that there may be something important about the first year that has longer-term effects, at least within the context of the kibbutz system. He noted, however, that although the children change metapelet they otherwise remain in a very stable social context—the same limited community of 100 to 200 families, in a building very similar to the one they have left, with a caregiver who has been through the same training and shares the values of the first metapelet. There is another change of metapelet in a later preschool period, which the children in the study had experienced just prior to the follow-up assessment. Change is built into the system, but it is predictable change, so it may not have the kinds of effects that the instability seen in this country may have.

Dr. Scarr wondered whether the severing of the intense relationship between the initial metapelet and the child is more analogous to the death of a parent than to a change in a day care situation. Dr. Lamb felt that it is not experienced as a death, because the old metapelet accompanies the children to the new setting and stays with them for 2 weeks as they make the transition. She introduces the children and the adults to one another, makes sure that they all understand each other's needs, likes, dislikes, and styles. So the transition is not as traumatic as it might otherwise be.

Regarding the Swedish study, Dr. Lamb was asked how parental leave policies in Sweden were reflected in his studies. He noted that all the children were going into day care as toddlers; the age of entry averaged 16 months, and most of the children were between 14 and 18 months. All had been cared for at home exclusively by their parents before the beginning of the study. Almost every parent in Sweden uses parental leave, he noted. Dr. Kamerman added that the majority of married women in Sweden work part-time and therefore do not use child care in the same way as they do in the United States. They have a shorter work day and the right to make it even shorter if they choose. Dr. Lamb pointed out, however, that because there is a shortage of day care slots, parents cannot keep their children in alternative care facilities unless they work more than half-time.

ACKNOWLEDGMENTS

This research was supported by the Riksbankens Jubileumsfond of Stockholm (Sweden), whose assistance is gratefully acknowledged. We also appreciate the cooperation of the parents, children, and care providers, without whose help the study would not have been possible. Craig Abbott, Majt Frodi, Gunilla Hult, and Dr. Fred Bookstein greatly assisted in the collection and analysis of the data. Some of the research herein described was completed while Michael Lamb was at the University of Utah. This chapter is largely based on several published reports.

NOTES

[1] In Phase III, the components of these composite scores changed slightly in recognition of the children's increasing age.

[2] In one previous report, we employed as a measure the total number of occasions on which the play was rated as 2, 3, 4, or 5 (Lamb et al., 1988). The resulting Howes 2–5 measure correlates very highly with the Howes 3–5 measure, which is reported here because it appears on its face to be more appropriate for the older children.

4

Day Care and the Promotion of Emotional Development:
Lessons From a Monkey Laboratory

J.D. Higley
*National Institutes of Health and National Institute
on Alcohol Abuse and Alcoholism*
J.S. Lande
University of Virginia
S.J. Suomi
National Institutes of Health

A central goal in producing a quality day care program is to provide for infant needs. However, specifying the needs that are important to development is often difficult. One must identify children who are deprived of a hypothesized need and study them over time, a process in which maintaining experimental control is not only difficult but sometimes ethically unfeasible. Because humans take years to reach maturity, such longitudinal research is often costly, and many measurements simply cannot be performed on human children. One solution to these problems has been the use of nonhuman primates as research subjects. Nonhuman primates develop at a faster rate than humans; experimental control is less difficult to maintain; and measurements that are impossible to obtain from human children can often be readily obtained.

Psychologists have frequently used primate models of human behavior to study developmental problems. Research using nonhuman primates has often been paramount in describing variables of importance for human children's emotional and psychological well-being and their normal developmental processes. For example, Harlow's (1958) early work with rhesus monkeys reared on inanimate terrycloth surrogates was instrumental in demonstrating the importance of physical contact and security for normal development. Subsequent studies were seminal in establishing research in areas such as contingent stimulation (Anderson, Kenney, & Mason, 1977; Eastman & Mason, 1975; Mason & Berkson, 1975), fathers (for a review, see Snowdon & Suomi, 1982), and individual differences in emotional stability and coping with stress (Suomi, 1983).

Although nonhuman primates are not miniature humans with furry tails, they are our closest biological relatives and are similar to us in many respects. Some species share as much as 98% of their genetic material with humans (Lovejoy, 1981). Even rhesus monkeys share about 90% of their genetic material with humans (Sarich, 1985). As a consequence of this close genetic relatedness, monkeys and humans have similar neuroanatomy and internal physiology, such as a 28-day menstrual cycle. Like humans, nonhuman primates show complex behavioral profiles. For example, in rhesus monkey societies, each monkey must not only identify different individuals in its social unit of 20–100 members but must know the social status and rank of each of those individuals, cooperate in defense, and have the sociosexual skills to show affection and to court properly.

Like humans, monkeys are social animals from the moment of birth. During infancy and childhood they must learn the rules and skills necessary to be competent in social interactions and to control their emotions. Most primates spend a protracted period as immature, dependent infants. This prolonged period of dependency on caregivers is believed to be necessary for acquiring social skills and learning the vagaries of the environment. Because of the close similarity between developmental patterns in humans and those in nonhuman primates, monkeys have been extensively studied to understand better the various social and emotional deficits that result from different rearing experiences (e.g., Capitanio, 1986; Suomi, 1982a). What follows is a description of nonhuman primate development, with a discussion of how satisfaction of different needs leads to normative socioemotional development and how such information might be applied to the design of day care programs.

PRIMATE DEVELOPMENTAL PATTERNS

The sequence of social-emotional development is similar across most higher primates, although its rate varies according to rate of physical development. It begins with a period of close infant-caregiver contact. Over time, interactions with the caregiver decrease and interactions with peers increase. By late childhood, contact with the caregiver is less frequent, and peer interactions account for the majority of social interactions.

Infant Patterns

It is during the neonatal period that behaviors are the most uniform and unvarying across species of monkeys and apes. The predominant behaviors of this period are intimate physical contact, frequent nipple contact, and close proximity with the mother, along with caregiver restrictiveness. A likely reason why mother-infant behavior is highly stereotyped during infancy is that the physical needs of primate neonates are quite similar across species. These needs include food, thermoregulation, and transportation (Higley & Suomi, 1986). The primary caregiver, in old world primates typically the mother, provides the infant with its only food source, heat, and transportation. Without such care, the infant would die.

As infants become increasingly able to move about and to explore the environment away from their mothers, psychological needs become more important. Research has shown that curiosity is a primary factor in motivating the infant to leave its caregiver's grasp, often under the caregiver's protest. For example, when monkeys are provided a bar that when pressed will open a peephole, they will spend much time pressing the bar and looking out the peephole, even though pressing the bar provides no other reinforcers (Butler & Harlow, 1954; Harlow, 1958). The infant also expresses its curiosity through exploration. Were it not for other motivators that emerge during this period, such as fear, curiosity might lead the infant to explore too far from the caregiver's watchful eye and into danger. During infancy fears such as stranger wariness and looming fear (fear of large, tall stimuli) first emerge. When frightened or overaroused by its environment, the infant returns to the caregiver to obtain comfort and reassurance. Strong curiosity drives the infant to explore its world; fear and overarousal drive it back to its caregiver until the anxiety is reduced. This back-and-forth behavior is known as a secure-base phenomenon (Harlow & Harlow, 1965; Higley & Suomi, 1986).

If the infant has no such attachment source, exploration virtually disappears (Harlow, 1958). Studies have indicated that one of the infant's principal needs during this period is to develop emotional security. The acquisition of emotional security is based on close, intimate physical contact—what Harlow (1958) called *contact comfort*. Contact comfort serves to reduce anxiety and arousal (Candland & Mason, 1968; Harlow, 1958; McCulloch, 1939). As the caregiver repeatedly comforts the infant and reduces its arousal level, the infant gains emotional competence and spends more and more time away from the caregiver.

There is evidence that the reduction of arousal produced by contact comfort may also involve the vestibular stimulation that is provided as the caregiver carries the infant. Mason found that cloth-covered inanimate surrogate caregivers that moved or rocked were superior to stationary cloth-covered surrogates in producing emotional competence and security (Anderson et al., 1977; Eastman & Mason, 1975; Mason & Berkson, 1975). Such findings suggest that the availability of a caregiver to provide contact comfort and vestibular stimulation is important for the development of emotional stability. Similarly, the availability of a caregiver to provide such stimulation is paramount for the infant to feel secure enough to explore its environment and to gain competence in exploiting the physical and social milieu.

Caregivers also provide other important needs. Studies have demonstrated that infants deprived of opportunities to discover that certain outcomes are contingent on their behavior show higher levels of anxiety and fearfulness (Mason, 1978; Mineka, Gunnar, & Champoux, 1986). In most species, the primary caregiver provides the infant with its first contingent stimulation. Caregivers who provide adequate contingent stimulation produce infants who are less fearful and are better able to self-regulate their arousal (Mason, 1978). From these early infant-caregiver interactions, the infant learns its first important lesson concerning contingent social responsiveness—that other individuals in the troop will respond, both positively and negatively, to the infant's social signals and behavior.

When the infant experiences stimuli that do not fit into existing schema, it discovers that it can learn by observing the behaviors and reactions of others. Studies have shown that when a stimulus is potentially dangerous or to be avoided, monkeys show facial expressions that are discriminated and used to avoid negative events (Miller, 1967). When such a signal is observed, the infant quickly returns to its caregiver's grasp (Hansen, 1966). Furthermore, as the infant observes the caregiver, fears displayed by the caregiver are quickly acquired (Mineka, Davidson, Cook, & Keir, 1984). Among researchers studying human populations, this phenomenon has been called *social referencing*. Studies indicate that without an appropriate social referent, infant monkeys develop chronic anxiety and fearfulness (Bush, Steffen, Higley, & Suomi, 1987; Higley, Suomi, Hopkins, & Bush, 1986).

Childhood Patterns

As the infant strays from its caregiver to explore the environment, one of its discoveries is that there are other individuals with whom to interact. During late infancy and early childhood, one of the primary sources of social stimulation is active interactions with peers. Peer interactions consist mainly of play. Although play has historically been considered frivolous, recent studies have indicated that it is a critical component in the development of normal social roles (e.g., see Suomi, 1979; Suomi & Harlow, 1975). Play provides opportunities to develop and practice gender-appropriate social roles. Through play, infants also learn species-appropriate aggression and sociosexual skills. They learn to inhibit and express aggression appropriately as well as to express affection properly, behaviors on which future courtship and infant care are based.

In the first weeks and months of peer interactions, play behavior is brief and somewhat awkward. As the infant plays, it still uses its mother as a secure base to return to when it is frightened or overaroused. When the caregiver is not available, play behavior diminishes significantly (e.g., see Mineka & Suomi, 1978). Infants who have been deprived of a secure base during early infancy show deficits in socioemotional and play behaviors when interacting with peers (Suomi, 1982a, 1982b).

During childhood and even in infancy, there are notable sex differences in play behaviors. Males tend to engage in play more often and to show more vigorous rough and tumble play (Hansen, 1966; Harlow, 1962; Harlow & Lauersdorf, 1974; Ruppenthal, Harlow, Eisele, Harlow, & Suomi, 1974). Females are more likely to show interest in infants and to practice caregiving behaviors (Chamove, Harlow, & Mitchell, 1967).

In middle childhood, interactions with the caregiver decrease and peer interactions increase. Juveniles still return to their caregivers when frightened, but this happens less frequently, and when it is does the juvenile quickly returns to play (Hinde & Spencer-Booth, 1967). In middle childhood, play becomes central, allowing juveniles to continue practicing the gender roles they will eventually fill as adults. Gender differences become even more notable. Rhesus monkey females increase their interest in and time with infants and younger siblings (Higley & Suomi, 1986). When possible, females engage in what has been hypothesized to be practice caregiving (e.g., carrying, comforting, and grooming infants). When they are prevented by adult caregivers from interacting with an infant (juveniles are clumsy and awkward with infants and consequently infants do not relish juvenile caregiving), they often attempt subterfuge to touch or obtain access to an infant (Higley & Suomi, 1986). With an occasional exception, males seldom engage in caregiver play. Their play becomes increasingly rough and vigorous, consisting of wrestling, pouncing, tumbling, and pretend aggression. Females also engage in some rough and tumble play, but males are much more likely to do so (Harlow, 1962). Primates deprived of opportunities to play with peers show later social and emotional deficits (e.g., see Suomi, 1979). For example, males deprived of early play often show inappropriate aggression or exhibit it in inappropriate settings or toward inappropriate targets (Suomi, 1982a). Females deprived of practice caregiving are often awkward and abusive to their own infants, especially to firstborns (Hrdy, 1976).

Adolescent Patterns

By early adolescence, the juvenile exhibits relative independence from the caregiver. The caregiver is rarely used as a secure base but is still important in facilitating social interactions. The caregiver may aid the juvenile in agonistic contexts or stop aggression, and by virtue of her social rank the caregiver may determine with whom the child will interact.

As females mature and reach reproductive status, having the social support of relatives such as grandmothers is important to the birth and development of their own offspring (Berman, 1982, 1983; Drickamer, 1974; Lee, 1983a). Grandmothers may care for infants in the mothers' absence (Hiraiwa, 1981; Simonds, 1965). Having social support from relatives, friends, and/or community decreases the possibility that infants will receive inadequate treatment or maltreatment from their mothers (Plimpton & Rosenblum, 1983; Suomi & Ripp, 1983).

EVOLUTIONARY SOLUTIONS TO INFANT NEEDS

At each age, the child has needs that must be satisfied for normal development to occur. Through natural selection, primate infant developmental needs and caregiver behaviors have neatly dovetailed. In feral environments such as India, mothers, peers, and siblings each fill different developmental needs, assuring normative developmental outcomes. Mothers provide food, warmth, contact comfort, protection, vestibular stimulation, and contingent responsiveness. They provide infants their first social interactions, which Bowlby (1982) described as prototypes of subsequent social relationships. Peers are of primary import in practicing social roles. Because of the seasonal nature of births, nonhuman primate children are guaranteed age-matched peers with whom to play and practice social skills. Siblings and children from previous years provide more sophisticated interactions and support in play bouts (Berman, 1982; Lee, 1983a).

Because primates increase capacity to learn, they show a relatively high degree of flexibility in the types of environments to which they can adapt. Most nonprimate mammalian behavior is highly responsive to unlearned response patterns and internal hormonal factors. Even without previous experience, most nonprimate mammalian adults are capable of food acquisition, reproduction, and parental care. Unlike nonmammalian species, primates who develop in isolation fail to acquire the necessary skills to exploit their environment (Suomi, 1982a). Primates must learn sophisticated skills in order to live and interact in their social group and to take advantage of their physical environment. As a result of the time needed to learn these skills, primates go through protracted periods of infancy and childhood during which they learn these necessary skills. The ability to learn new behaviors is an evolutionary adaptation that allows primates to change their behaviors and to adapt to a wide range of different environmental niches throughout the world.

Macaque species are one of the most successful primate groups. They are widely distributed across the Asian and African continents from the cold, snowy mountains of Japan to the arid deserts of Morocco (Roonwal & Mohnot, 1977). These species show different behaviors depending on the environment to which they have adapted. For example, some rhesus monkeys can be found in rural forestial environments with an altitude as high as 6,000 feet above sea level. Other rhesus monkeys live in urban environments, where they can be seen sitting atop homes in populated cities and sleeping in the gardens and yards of the temples (Southwick, Beg, & Siddiqi, 1965). Still other groups of rhesus monkeys have successfully exploited vastly different ecologies such as the tropical island of Cayo Santiago (e.g., see Rawlins & Kessler, 1986). In all the cases discussed here, the rhesus populations have increased over time, and the infants have developed high levels of psychological sophistication. Thus, infants are able to develop physically and psychologically in diverse physical environments.

Mothers are not the only individuals capable of caring for infants. Although mothers are usually the primary caregivers, other individuals such as males and grandparents are also capable of providing for infants' needs and often share in the infants' socialization (Higley & Suomi, 1986). With the exception of nursing, every form of caregiving behavior typically provided by mothers has been seen in other individuals in the troop, including the typically uninterested adult males. Among other closely related primates such as colobinaes, unrelated females may even suckle infants (e.g., see Higley & Suomi, 1986). Siblings, subadult females, and related childless adult females are more likely than anyone else except the mother to display caregiving behaviors (Higley & Suomi, 1986), but the absence of caregiving behavior does not indicate an inability to show care for infants. For example, although adult male rhesus monkeys are one of the least likely groups to show caregiving to an infant—in one study, after approximately 1,000 hours of observation of a troop only two incidents in which males cared for infants were observed (Lindburg, 1971)—another study indicated that when female caregivers are not present adult males display as much interest in infants as do adult females (Lande, Higley, Snowdon, Goy, & Suomi, 1985). In the latter study, prior experience with infants, rather than gender, was the major determinant of an individual's interest in infants. Other studies have shown that in the absence of adult females, males will exhibit all caregiving behaviors with infants, except, of course, nursing (Gibber, 1981; Redican & Mitchell, 1973). Furthermore, infants reared by these males develop in a normative fashion (Redican & Mitchell, 1973). When given the chance, then, males can successfully care for infants. Thus, there is no reason to suppose that for normal development to occur the infant's caregiver must be its mother. Biology has simply placed the infant's mother in that role because of the infant's need for nourishment, something that in feral environments only the mother can provide.

LESSONS FROM NONHUMAN PRIMATES FOR DAY CARE PROGRAMS

The success of others in providing adequate care is dependent on the caregiver's ability to fill the child's needs. For each of the developmental phases described earlier, children have different needs. In designing the curriculum and facilities of day care programs, therefore, consideration should be given to the age and developmental requirements of the children.

Considerations for Infancy Programs

Nonhuman primate studies suggest that relative to programs for other age periods, infant day care programs should give greater importance to physical needs. Among both human and nonhuman primates, infancy is a period of frequent disease and mortality (Drickamer, 1974). Because infants and toddlers are at highest risk for injury and disease, infant day care programs and regulations should give special consideration to prevention of disease and injury.

Important psychological needs during infancy include the development of security and emotional stability, in which infants need to learn to regulate their fears and anxieties. Calming and comforting infants should be paramount caregiver tasks during this period. Studies with nonhuman primates demonstrate the importance of training caregivers to use contact comfort and vestibular stimulation to alleviate infants' fears and anxieties. Other studies indicate that infants seek to maintain an optimum level of arousal (Mason, 1970). By using contact comfort and vestibular stimulation, caregivers can maintain infants' arousal within an optimum range. As we have seen, exposure to contingent responsiveness is important to infants in developing the ability to self-regulate arousal. Inappropriate responses to infant cues increase arousal and anxiety. Caregivers should therefore be trained to recognize infant cues and to respond sensitively and contingently to such cues in order to allow infants to develop the capacity to maintain their arousal within an optimum range.

In learning emotional and social competence, there is a clear need for infants to experience social interaction. Nonhuman primate research indicates that the best physical environments are no substitute for quality social interaction (Davenport & Menzel, 1963; Pratt, 1969). However, different classes of individuals fill different needs. During infancy and toddlerhood, peers lack the sophistication to respond sensitively and contingently to the child's needs (Bush et al., 1987; Chamove, Rosenblum, & Harlow, 1973; Higley et al., 1986). Early in life, therefore, other children cannot replace adults, and in the design of infant child care programs special consideration should be given to the adult caregiver/child ratio. The ratio should allow infants sufficient access to adult caregivers so that the caregivers can be used as a secure base from which to explore the environment. The staff should be large enough so that infants' fears and anxieties are responded to promptly. Studies with nonhuman primates indicate that even when caregivers are present, if they cannot sensitively respond to infants' needs, the infants may develop anxiety or affective problems (Rosenblum & Paully, 1984). Similarly, consideration should be given to crowding, for studies with monkeys have shown that overcrowded environments inhibit emotional growth and play (Elton & Anderson, 1977).

As the infant develops, other factors become increasingly important. Although late infancy is devoted to building social bonds with the primary caregiver, studies with nonhuman primates indicate that infants can build bonds with caregivers other than their mothers (Hrdy, 1976; Redican & Mitchell, 1973). In the development of these bonds, however, caregiver stability is important. Studies with monkeys indicate that infants who experience frequent turnover of caregivers develop aberrant social bonds (Sackett, Griffin, Pratt, Joslyn, & Ruppenthal, 1967). Clearly, although individuals other than the primary caregiver can comfort and care for an infant, time must be given for such relationships to develop. These findings suggest that in addition to maintaining a low ratio of children to caregivers, quality child care programs should work to minimize staff turnover to allow sufficient time for caregiver attachment bonds to form.

Considerations for Preschool Programs

As the infant becomes more sophisticated in responding socially, peer interactions increase in importance. Day care programs for preschoolers should therefore provide and encourage peer interaction. Role-playing games and toys that facilitate social play are good tools for promoting such interaction. Programs with limited resources can be designed to capitalize on children's proclivities to play with peers by structuring activities around peer play. In designing programs with more structured activities, planners should not forget to provide time for social play.

An often-overlooked variable in child care is familiarity of peers. Studies with nonhuman primates indicate that by late infancy or early childhood children form preferences for familiar peers (Higley, Hopkins, Suomi, Hirsch, & Orman, 1985). Although comparable studies have not been done with humans, such research suggests that the turnover of children in a program may be important because novel peers may cause anxiety and wariness (Higley et al., 1985; Thompson, Higley, Byrne, Scanlan, & Suomi, 1986). On the other hand, familiar peers and siblings are capable of alleviating infants' fears (Higley et al., 1985), suggesting that they might be used to facilitate a child's adaptation to day care by accompanying the child on entry into the program.

Ameliorating Distress During Social Separations

One of the most difficult problems to deal with in a day care program is the effect of separation from the primary caregiver. Nevertheless, nonhuman primate studies indicate that brief social separations are probably the norm for infant and juvenile monkeys. Nonhuman primate mothers forage while infants play; infants may stray to play with peers; forced separations may be imposed on infants following the birth of siblings or as mothers seek consort relations with males (Agar & Mitchell, 1975; Lee, 1983b). From the infant's perspective, however, social separations pose a crisis event, because loss of a caregiver for more than a brief period can be potentially life threatening.

Studies with monkeys indicate that taking into consideration a child's age and circumstances can help to ameliorate separation trauma. During early infancy, caregivers are largely interchangeable; separation distress can therefore be alleviated readily by other caregivers who provide for the needs characteristic of this age. Almost any adult can usually comfort the infant quickly by providing contact, vestibular stimulation, warmth, and food. When infants reach an age where they have become attached to the primary caregiver, however, caregivers are no longer interchangeable. Stranger fear and fear of novel environments preclude the infant's being easily comforted by an unfamiliar caregiver. Studies with nonhuman primates indicate that distress can be minimized during social separation if it occurs in familiar surroundings, during familiar activities (Mineka & Suomi, 1978), and after becoming familiar with the new caregiver (Dolhinow, 1980; Mineka & Suomi, 1978).

With regard to in-home day care, having the new caregiver visit prior to the separation may alleviate some of these problems. However, because of its high cost, home care is not a practical alternative for most families. Most care occurs outside the child's own home. One solution is for the primary caregiver to accompany the child at the day care facility, thus allowing the child to become familiar with the surroundings and with the new caregivers while the primary caregiver is present. Day care workers might unobtrusively play alongside the child to facilitate familiarity. As we have noted, siblings can also accompany the child to the program and help the child adjust to the setting. Day care staff can facilitate the child's adjustment by learning to read cues and to respond appropriately—for example, not attempting to engage an overaroused child in physical play. For the first week or so, special patience should be used with the child's increased clinginess, which in most cases passes. Studies of monkeys indicate that children are more likely to prefer and bond more readily to caregivers who respond quickly and positively to the infant than to caregivers who are present but fail to show consistent interest in the infant (Champoux et al., 1982). Nor should parents be forgotten. Parental distress may be alleviated in part by reassuring parents that for centuries children have undergone repeated separations without long-term negative outcomes. Parents should also be assured that when they leave, infant distress almost always disappears after a brief period.

Training Caregivers

Contrary to popular belief, studies with monkeys indicate that quality caregiving does not develop naturally. Experience with infants makes for better caregivers. The rhesus males in the Redican and Mitchell (1973) and Gibber (1981) studies described earlier had no previous experience in caring for infants. When they were given an infant, they were initially clumsy and awkward, at times carrying the infant upside down; with practice, however, they improved. Another example comes from females who are giving birth for the first time. Firstborns are at higher risk for maltreatment by their mothers than later-borns (Drickamer, 1974; Ruppenthal, Arling, Harlow, Sackett, & Suomi, 1976). Maltreatment is more likely if the mother's early experiences with infants were limited (Harlow, Harlow, Dodsworth, & Arling, 1966; Ruppenthal et al., 1976; Suomi, 1978) and even more likely for females who were raised in isolation or without early physical contact with adult caregivers (Suomi, 1978; Suomi & Ripp, 1983). Some suggestion has been made that infants learn to be caregivers by having care given to them (Suomi, 1978). This may provide the basis for the finding that rhesus monkey infants reared with unresponsive surrogates are at higher risk for later neglect or abuse of their own infants (Suomi & Ripp, 1983). Again, however, with experience these mothers improve, and in most cases later-borns receive more or less normal maternal care.

Caregivers should be taught that the needs of children are age-related. Those working with infants should be taught to comfort the infant using contact comfort, vestibular stimulation, and contingent responsiveness. Infants provided with contingent stimulation show increased emotional stability (Anderson et al., 1977; Eastman & Mason, 1975; Mason, 1978; Mason & Berkson, 1975; Mineka et al., 1986). Indeed, studies with human children have confirmed that contingent stimulation is an important part of developing secure attachments and predict that knowledge and use of contingent stimulation would facilitate the development of secure attachment bonds between the caregivers and chidren in day care programs (see Ainsworth, Blehar, Waters, & Wall, 1978, for a review).

Respecting Individual Differences

Even when children are reared outside optimum limits, some individuals thrive; conversely, not all children reared under the best of circumstances fare well. In considering the effects of day care and designing quality day care programs, it should always be remembered that different individuals have different needs, weaknesses, and qualities. Programs should be sensitive to the existence of individual differences and should build in enough flexibility so that caregivers can tailor the curriculum to the needs of different individuals. For example, timid monkeys who usually withdraw and avoid social challenge or interactions will become more socially competent with consistent support from caregivers (Suomi, in press). Thus, although preschoolers generally seek peer interaction, timid preschoolers may seek adult support and through such support thrive and develop normally. As children get older, aggression becomes a problem, but not for all individuals. Again, the program must have a plan for dealing with these individual differences.

IMPORTANCE OF SOCIAL SUPPORT
FOR CAREGIVER COMPETENCE

Finally, studies indicate that day care can offer a valuable resource for high-risk parents. A small but persistent proportion of our monkey-breeding colony population neglect or abuse their offspring. This pattern shows continuity across time and births. Abuse increases in frequency during times of stress, especially if females are isolated from social support; however, studies have shown that when these females are provided social support, abuse and neglect often stop (Plimpton & Rosenblum, 1983; Suomi & Ripp, 1983). Social support may be even more crucial for some individuals, such as female monkeys who are prone to depression (Suomi & Ripp, 1983). Such studies provide an empirical basis for the argument that federally supported day care programs in economically deprived areas, although costly, may not only provide an economic resource so that mothers can remain employed but also prevent or ameliorate abuse and other negative treatment of children.

DISCUSSION

Dr. Suomi was asked to spell out the research paradigms used in his separation studies. In some studies, he explained, animals are reared in a laboratory nursery for the first days of life and at about 1 month of age assembled into peer groups, with which they continue for the duration of their childhood years. In other studies, animals are reared in cages with their mothers but no physical interaction with other animals, and in still other studies the animals are reared in more complex social groups. In each case, separation studies begin at about 6 months of age. The animal is removed from the familiar environment and kept by itself for up to 4 days. In studies in other laboratories, he noted, separation has involved other paradigms such as being moved into a strange group, with or without a familiar individual.

All such separations yield measurable results, although they may differ in intensity. They can also produce profound responses among animals more than 1 year in age. In fact, some of the most severe separation reactions ever observed in Dr. Suomi's laboratory were with adult animals who had lived together for over a decade. Typically, the animal becomes withdrawn and exhibits signs of depression. There are striking patterns of individual differences, however. About 20% of the experimental population appear to be at risk for a severe reaction to prolonged or profound stress, regardless of the type of separation or manipulation. This characteristic appears to be highly heritable, or at least to have a highly heritable component.

Dr. Suomi noted that in the wild separations are normal events. The severity of the infant's reaction depends on the support system available and the temperamental characteristic of the infant. Although such reactions as withdrawal and anxiety may appear to be negative, in a dangerous environment they might serve to keep the infant animal out of trouble and enhance its chances of survival. In other circumstances, they might be a real disadvantage if there are resources to be exploited and the animal lets others get in its way. It is also conceivable that an individual can overcome its characteristic response to stress by learning to channel it into an effective coping strategy. Thus the variability of this characteristic among rhesus monkeys can be seen as nature's way of covering all bases, making it possible for these monkeys to live in many different places and in many different circumstances; no matter what the environment, some individuals will survive.

Studies in cross fostering "high-reactive" infants—infants who have been bred to be at risk for developing problems in response to stress—are now under way. When such infants are cross fostered with females who show unusually high nurturant and protective behaviors and low levels of rejection, especially around weaning, the infants actually leave these mothers earlier and explore more during development than do nonreactive individuals, even nonreactive individuals cross fostered to a nurturant mother. And although they show extreme behavioral reactions to a brief separation in the absence of social support, they quickly revert to the normative phase when social support is provided.

These high-reactive animals have now been placed in peer groups, in some cases with an old male/female pair who serve as "foster grandparents." Those with a history of a nurturant mother seek out the foster grandmother and, using her as a basis of social support, become the dominant members of the group, maintaining their dominance up to puberty. Under these circumstances the high-reactive individuals do better than high-reactive animals cross fostered to other types of mothers and better than more normative individuals whatever their background. In response to questions about sex differences among the high-reactive animals, Dr. Suomi replied that no clear differences had yet emerged but that the data to date is mostly on animals who have not yet reached puberty; if differences do exist, they would be expected to appear at that time.

Dr. Suomi was also asked whether there were age differences between competently nurturing and incompetently nurturing females and whether a learning process appeared to take place in the social support system. He noted that it is difficult to tell what might actually be transmitted in a support system, but that it is clear that when there is a challenge or threat from the outside the family mobilizes around itself, so that those with newborn infants do not have to worry so much about defense and can pay attention to the infants. Family members also serve to prevent others from handling the infants. Studies of animals reared without such support systems demonstrate that younger mothers are the highest risk group, especially with their firstborn offspring. Once these mothers have had some positive contact experience with their firstborns, however, even if they do not take very good care of them, that experience appears to trigger relatively normal behavior toward their subsequent offspring. Most of these data come from laboratory experiments, Dr. Suomi noted. In the normal case of a female growing up with a troop, she is surrounded by family members having infants to which she would be permitted access, so she would probably have some experience handling infants before she actually has her own. Support and experience can come in a variety of forms, and it does not take very much experience to ensure relatively normal caretaking thereafter.

ACKNOWLEDGMENTS

Our appreciation is extended to Lisa Tillema and Brad Dowd, who assisted in the preparation of this chapter.

5

Child Care, Women, Work, and the Family:
An International Overview of Child Care Services and Related Policies

Sheila B. Kamerman
Columbia University School of Social Work

The child care debate in the industrialized world cuts across national lines, even though the specifics vary from country to country. For some people concerned with the well-being of children, the central child care issue is what it does for children. Does the program enhance children's cognitive and social development? Does it compensate for early deprivation? Does it assure good physical care and protect children from inadequate parenting? For others, child care is viewed largely as a service for parents, especially mothers, in order to facilitate work while children are young. Still others stress the rewards for society. They raise questions about the role of child care in increasing or decreasing female labor force participation rates, in socializing children into the society's values, and in raising a more productive citizenry. All these issues appear in international as well as U.S. discussion, as does interest in the effects of care on such diverse domains as child development, school performance, fertility, marriage, and public expenditures.

Given all these concerns, the motivation for child care policies at a specific time and place is complex. Short-run labor market demands are only one aspect of national child care policies; long-term human capital investment can be as significant. Nonetheless, the changing roles of women at home and in the work force and the substantial growth in female labor force participation rates have clearly had an impact on the supply of child care services in the European countries. Several countries with lower proportions of women in the work force, however, have comparable policies and equally high or even higher rates of coverage (see Table 5.1); they have other concerns.

This chapter focuses not on the debate nor on the rationale for policy but rather on program and policy outcomes. I discuss the different policy "models" and packages and briefly illustrate alternative policy strategies and approaches to delivering child care services. I conclude with some comments on current trends and issues and the contrasts with U.S. policies and programs. Although the focus here is on child care, it should be noted that these policies in turn can be fully understood only in the context of the array of family policies in place in these countries, including the cash benefits that support parenting and health insurance coverage. Given the limitations of space, however, such policies are not addressed here. Finally, although the focus is on western Europe, occasional illustrations are drawn from other countries.

SOME TERMS DEFINED

Child care policy includes the whole range of government actions designed to influence the supply of and/or demand for child care and the quality of

TABLE 5.1
Labor Force Participation Rates of Married and Single Women with Children Under 18, and Child Care Coverage Rates for Children of Different Ages, Selected Countries

Country	Year(s)	*Percent of Mothers in Labor Force*		*Percent of Children in Child Care*	
		Married	*Single*	*Aged 0–3*	*Aged 3–5*
Belgium	1981	33		16	95
Britain	1982–84	49	39	2	43[a]
Denmark	1980	80	85	44	85
F.R. Germany	1985	42	60	2	76
France	1981	50	78	24	95
Italy				5	90
Sweden	1986	83	85	73[b]	
U.S.	1987	64	67	20[c]	70[d]

[a]These data are for children aged 3–4, because compulsory school begins at age 5. [b]These data are for all children aged 1 to 6, from the time parental leave ends until compulsory school begins at age 7. [c]Est., 1984–85. [d]Est., 1984–85, largely part-day.

care provided. These activities may include direct delivery of child care services; direct and indirect financial subsidies to private providers of care through grants, contracts, and tax incentives; direct and indirect financial subsidies to parents/consumers, through grants and tax benefits to permit or facilitate access to services or to permit parents to remain at home (and stop working) without loss of income; and the establishment and enforcement of regulations pertaining to the quality of care.

Child care services include family day care (care in the home of a nonrelative); all types of group facilities for the care of children under compulsory school age (day care centers, public and private nursery schools, prekindergartens and kindergartens, Head Start programs); and before- and after-school programs. These services include part-day and full-day programs. Relative care is not included, nor occasional babysitting, nor (although one could argue otherwise) care provided within a child's own home. Nor am I discussing here care for children with special needs.

The best-developed child care policies in Europe are those having to do with parenting leaves to care for infants and with child care services for children aged 3 to compulsory school entry. Therefore, I begin by discussing these policies and later discuss the less well-defined and less well-established policies involving child care services for the children under 3 and for after-school programs.

INFANTS: CARE FOR CHILDREN 0–1

The first component of a child care policy package addresses the needs of infants and their employed parents at the time the child is born and immediately thereafter. Maternity and/or parenting policies for working parents include paid, job-protected leaves, often supplemented by additional unpaid, job-protected leaves. In addition to such job-protected leaves, with their cash benefits, assurance of the same or a comparable job on return, and protection of seniority, this policy package includes full health insurance and/or medical care coverage. It is designed to assure babies a good start in life and to protect maternal health while maintaining income. More than 100 countries around the world have such leave policies, including all of Europe, Canada, Israel, and many developing countries (Kamerman, 1988; Kamerman & Kahn, 1988). An infant is assured at least 2 to 3 months of maternal/parental care, and usually about 5 to 6 months in the European countries.

The availability of maternity and parenting policies is not just a function of high labor force participation rates. Although among those countries with high rates only the United States is without statutory policies, many

countries with far lower rates have enacted such laws, and the most extensive and generous policies are in the European countries. Countries at the
cutting edge are moving to extend these benefits further for all mothers, or
for all mothers with modest incomes, until children are aged 1.5 , 2, or even
3, not because of evidence of negative effects on children of out-of-home
care but because of a melange of other factors, including economic considerations and parental preference, described later in this chapter.

One result of these leave policies, of course, is that out-of-home infant
care (care for children under age 1) is not an issue in many European
countries. Even in countries with very high labor force participation rates
among women with children under 3, rates far higher than those in the
United States (75% or higher in Denmark, Finland, and Sweden), very few
children under age 1 are in care. Because virtually all working women who
give birth are covered by such policies, the child is cared for at home by at
least one parent for a good part of the first year. Just *when* a maternity or
parenting leave ends determines when child care services are needed, and
for those countries with shorter leave policies infant care services are essential.

In most countries, the benefit that is provided to protect the family
against loss of income following childbirth is equal to either 100% of the
mother's or parent's insured wage (the maximum wage covered under social insurance) or 90% (that wage less social insurance contributions), or a
portion of the insured wage (60 or 75%). And in most countries (but not
Sweden or Canada) the benefit is tax free.

Although the specific programs vary from country to country, the job-
protected leave is always part of employment policy, whereas the cash
benefits provided to offset lost wages are always considered part of the social insurance or social security system. All the benefits are financed
through social insurance funding as either a contributory or noncon-
tributory benefit. In several countries, the employer and the government
jointly bear the bulk of the burden or the total cost, whereas in others such
as Canada the employee also contributes. A country's health insurance system (including the paid sick leave program) is the system most likely to
carry administrative responsibility for maternity benefits. Israel, however,
views this as an independent social insurance benefit; Britain mandates
payments by the employer but provides reimbursement; and Canada and
Austria deliver the benefit through the unemployment insurance system.
The particular system employed is as much an artifact of the governmental structure of a country as it is of earlier history and ideology.

The traditional maternity policy stems from a history of legislation
designed primarily to protect the health of pregnant working women, new
mothers, and their infants. Only since the 1960s has the link with employ-

ment become stronger and more important. The policy as currently implemented in several countries involves a paid maternity leave for working mothers that begins from 2 to 6 weeks before expected childbirth and lasts from 8 to 20 or even 24 weeks after birth (see Table 5.2). During that period, women who qualify on the basis of prior work history are permitted to take time off from their jobs without loss of fringe benefits or seniority, receive a cash benefit provided much like unemployment or disability insurance, and have the same or a comparable job saved for them when they return to work at the end of their leave. For example, employed women in France are guaranteed the right to a 16-week, job-protected maternity leave, paid for under sickness benefits and replacing about 90% of wages up to a specified maximum. They may take up to 6 weeks before anticipated birth and 10 weeks after. More time off is permitted and paid for if the child is a third or subsequent child, or if the birth is complicated, or in the case of multiple births. In Canada, working new mothers have the right to a 17-week leave, paid for through the unemployment insurance system for 15 weeks at the rate of 60% of wages.

A second model is premised on the importance of parenting and involves fathers as well as mothers in caring for new babies. A parent insurance benefit provides protection to the new mother before birth and for 6 to 12 weeks after birth but then permits fathers to share equally or partially in the remainder of the entitlement to the post-childbirth leave. Like the maternity leave, parenting leave includes job, seniority, and benefit protection. The prototypical illustration for this parent insurance model is Sweden, where for the first 12 months following childbirth employed parents have the right to a job-protected leave from work. They receive a cash benefit equal to 90% of the wage of the parent who is on leave, up to the maximum wage covered under social security, for 9 months, and a fixed minimum benefit is available for the remaining 3 months. (A nonworking mother would also be entitled to a minimum cash benefit during the year, but there are very few such women.) Parent insurance can be used to cover a complete leave from work or can be prorated to permit part-time work by either parent, for full pay, until the 9 months of pay is used up. Thus, a working mother might take off a full 3 months, after which she and her husband might share child care between them, each working half-time for 6 months or three-quarters time for 9 months, without significant pay loss. Current government proposals include expanding the 1-year leave to 18 months by 1991.

In addition, Swedish parents have the right to take an unpaid but fully job-protected leave until their child is 18 months old and to work a 6-hour day (without additional financial compensation) from the end of the parental leave until their child is 8 years old.

TABLE 5.2
Paid Maternity/Parenting Leave Provisions in Selected Western Countries

Country	Date	Duration of Paid Leave	Available to Fathers Y = Yes	Supplementary Unpaid or Paid Parental Leave
Benefit Level at 100% Earnings[a]				
Norway	1984	4 months	Y	Y
Austria	1987	16 weeks		10 more months, at lower level[b]
F.R. Germany	1987	14 weeks[c]	Y	1 year at flat rate[d]
Portugal	1984	3 months		Y
Netherlands	1984	12 weeks[c]		
Benefit Level at 90% of Earnings				
Sweden	1987	9 months plus 3 months at flat rate	Y	up to 18 months; 6 hour work day, up to 8 years
Denmark	1987	24 weeks	Y	Y
France	1987	16 weeks[c]		up to 2 years
United Kingdom	1987	6 weeks + 12 weeks at flat rate		Y maternity leave
Benefit Level at 80% of Earnings				
Finland	1987	11 months	Y	Y
Italy	1984	5 months[e]		Y
Belgium	1984	14 weeks		
Ireland	1982	14 weeks		
Benefit Level at 75% of Earnings				
Spain	1982	14 weeks		
Israel	1984	12 weeks		
Canada	1984	17 weeks, 15 paid		
Benefit Level at 50% of Earnings				
Greece	1982	12 weeks		

[a]Up to maximum covered under Social Security.
[b]Plus 2 years for low-income single mothers if they cannot find child care.
[c]6 weeks must be taken before expected birth; in other countries this time is voluntary.
[d]Last 6 months available only on an income-tested basis.
[e]100% paid for first 4 weeks; 2 months' leave before birth mandated.

All Swedish working mothers take advantage of the parent insurance benefit, and about 85% return to work by the end of the leave, or by the time their child is 1 year old. In 1981, 22% of eligible fathers took at least some part of the leave, in addition to the 2 weeks' paid leave all fathers are entitled to at the time of childbirth. On average, fathers took 47 days of parental leave, as compared with 265 days for women. Clearly, women still play the dominant role in child care and assume primary responsibility, but fathers have increased their use of the parental leave substantially since it was first established in 1974 and continue to do so. Current estimates are that more than one quarter of the eligible fathers now take a partial leave.

The European Economic Community (EEC) has proposed (but not yet adopted) a directive that would require all member countries to mandate a minimum parental leave of 3 months per worker per child, although individual countries may fix a longer period. This would mean that in a family where both parents work there would be a total entitlement of at least 6 months' full-time leave, to be divided equally between mother and father. Both parents could not be on leave at the same time, nor could the right to a leave be transferred from one parent to another. The leave would be longer for single parents or for parents of a handicapped child. A cash benefit is recommended, but the details are left to the individual member states; any payment, however, would come from general revenue, not from employers. An estimate of the costs to employers of introducing a 3-month leave, including disruption, recruitment of substitutes, and other costs, is that it would increase the total wages and salaries bill by less than 0.01% (Equal Opportunities Commission, 1986).

The years of greatest expansion for maternity and parenting policies were the decades of the 1960s and 1970s, decades that experienced an extraordinary growth in the number and proportion of women, especially young married women, entering the labor force. If maternal and child health concerns underlay the initial development of these policies, the expansion in these two decades was more a reflection of labor market needs, concerns about declining fertility, and issues having to do with the equality of men and women. Developments in the 1980s have slowed, along with the decline in the growth in social benefits generally. Nonetheless, these policies have been protected and in some countries even expanded. Maternity and parenting benefits are modest social policies, but if the goal is to assure children a good start in life, they are an essential part of any country's child care policy.

PRESCHOOL PROGRAMS: CARE
FOR CHILDREN AGED 3 TO 6 OR 7

A second component of child care policy, involving the care of children between age 3 and compulsory school entry (usually age 6), is also firmly established throughout Europe. In contrast to the United States, countries in Europe are increasing the coverage of children in this age group in some form of group care program, whether or not the child has a working mother.

These programs are all heavily subsidized and operate largely within the public sector.

The pattern that dominates the continental European countries, both eastern and western, is preschool education (preschool, kindergarten, prekindergarten, nursery school), operated under educational auspices as part of the public education system (or publicly subsidized in the private systems). The programs cover the normal school day and year, with more or less enriched and developmentally appropriate curricula depending on the country. They are free and voluntary, and children participate to the extent places are available.

There are two other models, of far less significance: (a) a freestanding, autonomous, special child care program (not a part of the educational system) in Sweden and Finland, for all children under age 7 (when compulsory primary school begins), designed to serve the children of working parents; and (b) a dual system in Britain (and other Anglo-American countries) of social welfare day care for neglected and/or abused and/or deprived children and part-day, educational nursery school for middle- and upper-class children. By and large, in this model women with children under compulsory school age (age 5 in Britain) do not work, and if they do it is part-time.

The coverage or enrollment pattern in most countries with a preschool program is fairly similar: full coverage for 4- and 5-year-olds and nearly that for 2.5- and 3-year-olds. Thus, the French *ecole maternelle* serves almost all the 3-, 4-, and 5-year- olds and close to half the 2-year-olds, primarily those aged 2.5 and older. The Belgian pattern is similar. Denmark, Italy, and Germany have somewhat lower rates, as do the eastern European countries, but participation by 75%–85% of the cohort is found in all these countries. Coverage rates in Sweden and Finland are slightly lower, but for a full work day rather than a school day. Coverage in Britain is inconsistently counted, at best modest, and generally described as very inadequate.

The French *ecole maternelle* exemplifies the preschool model. France and Belgium are among the countries with the most extensive preschool programs in the world. In France, the *ecole maternelle* dates back to the 19th century, although its major growth has been since the 1950s. It is a publicly financed program operated as an integral part of the French educational system. The local facilities may be situated next to or in a primary school, but they are often freestanding, completely separate structures.

All children aged 2 years and 3 months or older are eligible to participate, although there are usually not enough places for all the 2-year-olds whose parents want them enrolled. The program clearly provides child care to the children of working parents, but participation is by no means limited to these children. Only where there is a shortage of places for 2-year-olds do the children of working mothers get preference.

The program is conceived as an educational program, with the emphasis on cognitive development placed in the framework of a developmentally appropriate curriculum. The hours follow the pattern of the normal school day, generally 8:30 a.m. to 4:30 p.m. Lunch is available at school, and many preschools (and primary schools) also have after-school programs as well. The basic preschool program is free; parents pay income-related fees only for lunch and for the after-school program. On Wednesday, when French schools are closed (they are open for a half day on Saturday), there are other special programs available, but also on a fee-paying basis.

Although the French regard these programs highly, group size and staff/child ratios would not satisfy American child development experts. Groups are large, as many as 25–30 or more 4-year-olds with one teacher (and sometimes an assistant). Nonetheless, the programs are enormously popular and are viewed as an essential socialization experience, whether to prepare children for school or to expose them to a valuable opportunity for peer play, growth, and development. French research has found that children who do not participate in these programs are likely to be disadvantaged when they begin school (Kamerman & Kahn, 1981).

Coverage rates are extraordinarily high. Despite the fact that only about half the mothers of children aged 3 to 5 are in the labor force, more than 95% of the children of this age participate in these programs (Ergas, 1987; Kamerman & Kahn, 1984; Moss, 1988). Moreover, because the programs are available to 2-year-olds as well, even if not to all whose parents wish them to participate, almost half the 2-year-olds are enrolled, and the waiting list is long. Although parents may choose to have their younger children participate only part of the day, most children are enrolled for the full day. Even among the 2-year-olds, about half attend the full school day.

The Belgian pattern is very similar, with comparable coverage rates for the 3- to 5-year-olds and children entering at age 2.5. The school day is slightly shorter, from 9:30 a.m. to 3:30 p.m., but after-school programs are increasingly available as well. Although parents may opt for a part-day program, most children participate a full day.

The Italian *asilo nilo* is also similar but is operated under more diversified auspices (Saraceno, 1984). It is interesting to note that although less than half of all women with children aged 3 to 5 are in the work force, close to 90% of the children in this age group are in preschools. Almost two thirds of these programs, in particular those in the north, are open for a full school day (8:30 a.m. to 3:30 p.m. or 4:30 p.m.), and most children participate for the full program.

In Denmark, coverage is a little lower despite far higher labor force participation rates of mothers. More than 75% of women with children of this age work. Coverage rates for the Danish preschool program are about 85%, with 60% in programs that cover the full work day and the remainder in either school-day or part-school-day programs. More importantly, the quality of these programs far surpasses that in many of the countries described earlier. Staff/child ratios are far higher, the groups are much smaller, and quality is far more regulated as well.

Despite relatively low labor force participation rates of women with preschool-aged children, German policy mandates coverage for at least 75% of all 3- to 5-year-olds in preschool programs. These are largely part-day, like the German primary school, and operate from 8:00 a.m. to 1:00 p.m. About one-fifth of these cover a longer school day. Like primary schools, these programs are under the aegis of state and local governments rather than the national government. Ninety percent of the costs are subsidized equally by the state, regional, and local governments; the remaining 10% is covered by parents' fees.

Unlike the pattern of preschool programs under educational auspices, which dominates most of Europe, in Sweden and Finland child care is a separate, freestanding, autonomous institution under social welfare auspices. These programs serve all eligible children under age 7, when compulsory school begins. Given the parenting leave policies of these countries, this means that the programs cover children from about age 1 or a little younger.

Using the Swedish program to illustrate this model, we can note that the child care services in Sweden offer the highest quality of out-of-home care available anywhere. Quality is stressed far more extensively than in most other countries. Standards of group size, staff/child ratios, and caregiver qualifications are based on extensive research and are rigorously set and enforced. These programs are all heavily subsidized, but parents do pay income-related fees, usually equal to about 10% of average female wages (Kamerman & Kahn, 1981).

Swedish programming stresses sibling (age-integrated) groups, in contrast to the age-segregated groups that exist in the preschool programs in most other countries. Children aged 2 or 2.5 to 6 may be placed in the same group, although special age-appropriate activities are incorporated into the curriculum.

Although these are universal programs and all children are eligible, priority is given to the children of working parents, especially single mothers, and the children of immigrants. Because about 80% of the mothers of children under 7 are in the work force, the demand for these services is still well beyond the supply. In 1986, about 60% of children between the ages of 1 and 7 were in municipal (public) child care programs, and another 13% were in private care. Child care services expanded enormously in the 1960s and 1970s with the growth in female labor force participation and the concern with protecting the well-being of children under circumstances of rapid social change. Economic constraints precluded the full realization of the child care service goals envisioned in the 1970s, but the programs grew nonetheless. Recently there has been renewed attention to child care in Sweden, and a new commitment to increasing the supply has been announced. Beginning in 1991, all children aged 1.5 and older are to be guaranteed a place in a child care center. With the parallel commitment to extending the parental leave to 18 months, all children of working parents will be assured of parental care (if the parents wish) until they are 1.5 years old and then a place in a high-quality child care program.

Child care services for children aged 3–6 increased dramatically throughout Europe beginning in the 1960s, largely because of two factors. The dramatic growth in female labor force participation rates contributed substantially by increasing the political pressure for more services; women's groups stressed the importance of these programs, and labor unions in Europe, far more than those in the United States, have made increased government support for child care a priority item on their agendas. At the same time, there has been growing emphasis on the contribution that programs for young children can make to improved socialization and better preparation for primary school. Thus the combined pressure from the educational and child development side and the needs of working parents have made these programs an integral part of good social policy generally and have provided a broad-based political constituency in support of them.

Preschool programs are largely public, or at the very least publicly funded if delivered through private, nonprofit auspices. Throughout much of Europe, these programs are thought of as an essential component of child and family policy generally and of child care policy in particular, and the goal is universal coverage for all. As Peter Moss (1988) found in his study of the 12 member countries of the European community, there is an almost universal demand among parents for preschool for children aged 3 and older, and wherever these programs are available children attend them for a full school day whether or not they have working mothers. This is the child care policy goal of the European countries; many have achieved it, and others are rapidly approaching it.

CARE FOR THE UNDER-3-YEAR-OLDS

A critical issue in much of Europe is child care for children from about age 1 to age 2.5 (Commission of the European Communities, 1984; Ergas, 1987; Kamerman & Kahn, 1981; Moss, 1988). Here the picture looks more like that in the United States, in that in contrast to the public programs just described, the delivery system is highly diversified. Family day care homes and group day care centers (*creches*) both exist, but there is not enough of either. About one third of the women in Britain and Germany who were surveyed earlier in the 1980s indicated that they had not returned to work following post-childbirth leave because of the unavailability of child care. In Denmark and Sweden, public subsidies are provided to permit three or four families to share the costs of a caregiver and to provide care in the home of one of the families (or rotate). In France and Finland, a subsidy is also available to help pay for in-home care.

In the countries in which preschool programs are part of the education system, programs serving the under-3s are often under health ministry auspices. As already indicated, in Sweden and Finland the programs serving children of this age are combined with those serving the older children described earlier and thus constitute an autonomous child care program administered under social welfare auspices.

Extensive public subsidies are provided to these services, but unlike the preschool programs these services are neither free nor universal. Parents pay income-related fees that account for between 10% and 50% of program costs, depending on the country. Only in France do payroll contributions by employers help to finance these programs. Fees for group programs are often not very different from those for publicly sponsored family day care.

Regardless of the program type, these services for very young children are designed primarily to provide care for the children of working parents. Eligibility is limited to these children and to children with special social or psychological needs for care. Priority for acceptance goes to children of working parents, in particular those in single-parent families; children in low-income families; children in need of protective or compensatory programs; immigrant children; and in some countries, such as Sweden and Italy, physically handicapped children.

The infant/toddler group programs do not have consistent or uniform curricula, and the family day care programs have even less (Moss, 1988). Programs usually operate 10–12 hours per day and are often open from 6:30 a.m. to 6:30 p.m. Children usually attend a full day. In some countries, such as Denmark and Sweden, where mothers are likely to work part-time, children may be in care only part of the day. In southern Europe these programs usually close for about 1 month during the summer, but else-where they are open all year. Although age of entry is often closely linked to the length of the maternity/parenting leave, new places are often avail-able only in September, when the older children leave the program to enter the preschool program. Shortages exist everywhere; no country describes an adequate supply of services for this age group (Moss, 1988).

The dominant program mode for this age group is family day care, often because the supply of places in group facilities is so limited, not be-cause parents prefer this type of care (Moss, 1988). In contrast to the United States, much of the family day care in countries such as Denmark, Finland, France, Germany, and Sweden is under public sponsorship, with providers often recruited, trained, supervised, and supported by municipal child care administrators or local social agency administrators and staff. In many countries a significant group of private providers also exists.

In contrast to the maternity/parenting benefits (where coverage is al-ready universal in Europe) and the preschool programs (where coverage is universal in some countries and approaching that goal in others), coverage for the 1–2 age group is limited at best and varies widely from one country to another (see Table 5.1). Moss (1988) reported that about 10% of the under-2s are currently in care in those countries that are the child care service "leaders." A larger proportion of the 2-year-olds is served in countries like Belgium, France, and Italy, where the preschool program accepts 2- or 2.5-year-olds. At present, among these countries, Denmark has by far the most extensive coverage; about 44% of the under-3s are in some type of out-of-home care, largely full-day. In France, about 25% of the under-3s are in care. This includes about 10% of the under-2s, most in family day care, and about 45% of the 2-year-olds, in preschool, usually from 8:30 a.m. to 4:30 p.m. The pattern is similar in Belgium, but the coverage is only for about 16% of the cohort, and the preschool day for the 2-year-olds is shorter (6 hours instead of 8), and about half attend for only a half-day session. In Britain, there is practically no care for the under-2s, and what there is is for protective pur-poses only, not for the children of working parents. Coverage rates in Ger-many are about 2%, despite the fact that 30% of children of this age have working mothers; in Italy the rate is 5%.

Finland is the only country that has made expanded coverage for the under-3s the primary goal of its child care policy. The government expects that by 1990 there will be sufficient places in family day care or group care facilities to care for all the children whose parents want them in out-of-home care. Current estimates are that this means adequate coverage for about 45% of children under 3, with another 10% cared for in their own homes by caregivers whose salaries are partially subsidized by the govern-ment. This estimate is premised on the extension of parental leave, to cover care for the remainder of the cohort (45%), who would be at home with a parent. Finland is also planning to institute a shorter work day for parents of infants/toddlers, following the Swedish policy.

Until recently, expanding the supply of services for children of this age has been the most important child care policy for this age group. Now, however, some countries are beginning to rethink this policy, or to modify it. In its place is a growing trend to extend parenting leaves in some form, to make it possible for one parent to remain at home until a child is 1.5, 2, or 3 (Kamerman & Kahn, 1987). Indications of such a policy, which began in Hungary, have emerged in such western European countries as France, Finland, Germany, and Austria, and it is being discussed in several other countries as well. The rationales offered include the extraordinarily high costs of satisfactory out-of-home infant care, a belief that young children are better off if the mother stays home for a while, and a desire to encourage low-skilled women to stay out of the labor force in a period of high unemployment.

SCHOOL-AGE CHILD CARE

Although there is general recognition of the need for supplementary programs for preschool and primary school children when school hours do not coincide with working hours, or when school is closed but jobs continue, there is no systematic coverage anywhere (Moss, 1988). Moreover, there is very little data on what is available or on the quality of what does exist, and there is a general conviction that the supply is inadequate. There seems to be a growing pattern of expanded provision of after-school programs, but there are no consistent policies or systematic data.

Where the school day lasts 6 to 8 hours, part-time work is possible, and in many countries women with young children work part-time. In some countries, such as Sweden and Finland, the current trend is to move toward a 6-hour day for working parents with children under age 8. Where the school day is a short day, as in Germany (4 hours, between 8:00 a.m. and 1:00 p.m.) or in Norway until children are aged 10, clearly there is need for supplementary programs. Fortunately for working parents in many of these countries, legislation mandates that they have far longer vacations than parents in the United States, and the school year is longer than in the United States. A month or longer of vacation makes it easier to cope with the 6 to 9 weeks of school summer vacation, but there still can be problems.

CONCLUSIONS

Almost all the industrialized countries other than the United States have recognized the necessity of establishing maternity/parenting policies that permit working parents some time off after childbirth to recover physically and to adapt to parenting and to a new baby. Their policies are designed to permit parents to do this without losing employment or income. Most countries now include adoptive as well as natural parents in their policies. The only differences among the countries have to do with the length of the leave, the level of the benefit, and the inclusion of fathers as well as mothers.

Almost all the European countries have acknowledged the importance and value of preschool programs for 3- to 5-year-olds whether or not their mothers are working, for socialization and educational reasons as well as for the role these services play in caring for children while their parents work. These programs are increasingly universal and free, and even if voluntary they are used by all children whose parents can obtain a place. Even those countries that have established an autonomous child care program separate from the education system are aiming toward universal coverage, and all stress age-appropriate and developmentally appropriate programming. These are publicly funded programs and often publicly operated as well. Variations in quality are the most dramatic difference across countries, as more and more countries strive to expand supply to cover the whole cohort.

There is a growing recognition of the importance of expanding the supply of child care services for the under-3s as well. There is parallel concern, however, with the quality of these programs and even more with their cost. Coverage is nowhere near adequate in any country, and only Sweden and Finland have announced any significant commitment to expanding these services. Other countries are looking to the extension of parental leave as an alternative approach to expanding out-of-home care.

Finally, in contrast to the United States, there are no proprietary child care programs anywhere in Europe except for a few in Britain, the country with the least adequate provision of any of the major European countries. Nor is employer sponsorship viewed as of major significance or the way to achieve needed coverage, despite an earlier history of such sponsorship, especially in Italy.

In Europe, child care is viewed as a public responsibility. Although some think in terms of facilitating women's employment, others emphasize the child development consequences of these policies and programs. Either way, the countries are prepared to invest heavily in these policies and to continue to do so. The ultimate question is why, despite the far greater investment in child development research in the United States and our knowledge of what is good for children, we continue to dither about who should do what and who should pay. Clearly, we know what to do, but we have lacked the commitment to act.

DISCUSSION

In discussing Dr. Kamerman's presentation, participants sought explanations for the differences in European and American policies regarding parental leave and child care. High percentages of government spending for defense proved not to offer a satisfactory explanation; Dr. Kamerman pointed out that Sweden spends a relatively high percentage of its budget on defense. Attitudes toward taxation have a bearing, however. There are some European countries that tax more than we do and yet have higher per capita gross national product. It is a combination of such variables as per capita wealth, female labor force participation rates, and birth rates, along with a long history of social insurance benefits, that makes the costs of the European programs acceptable.

Dr. Kamerman noted that the history of maternity leave for working women, as a social insurance benefit, goes back to 1883 in Bismarck's Germany. By World War I many of the European countries had such policies in place, and within a short time after World War II all of them did. It began as a health policy for women and children, and although pro-natalism certainly played a role in certain countries at certain times, particularly during the Depression and right after World War II, policies having to do with children did not decline during the baby boom, which occurred in Europe as well as in the United States. Interestingly, the history of child or family allowances (cash benefits based on the presence and number of children in a family) does not provide any clearcut evidence of positive consequences on fertility rates; at most, parents may have their first child somewhat sooner and the second closer to the first, but in general birth rates in Europe are no higher and in some cases are lower than they are here, despite the policies that are supportive of children.

In the United States, Dr. Kamerman commented, policies that could be construed as pro-natalist have in the past been rejected because of racial and religious issues. During the 1960s in particular, when child allowances were being debated, the fear was that such policies would benefit minority children and support the position of the Roman Catholic Church, at a time when there was much racist and anti-Catholic feeling. These attitudes have acted as obstacles to doing more for children (Kamerman & Kahn, 1988).

Differences in the women's movement in Europe and the United States are also reflected in the role it has played in policies for children. The feminist movement in Europe has been based on a belief in the importance of women's roles as mothers and wives, and policies designed for women have had to consider this aspect of women's lives. Moreover, the organized feminist movement in many of the European countries took as its primary target low-income women and their families, whereas in the United States much of the concern has been for individual rights for women, job equity, affirmative action, and other economic and employment issues for better-educated professional women. The debate is now converging, Dr. Kamerman feels; there is recognition in this country that the feminist movement must consider women in their family roles, and a number of the European countries are seeing the need to pay more attention to women in their work roles.

Dr. Kamerman rejected the explanation that European countries are more caring societies. Studies comparing the economic situation of the elderly and of children in various countries suggest that where the elderly are concerned, the United States does about as well as many of the other advanced industrialized countries. The situation of children is very different; the economic situation of children is far worse in the United States than in any one of about eight other major industrialized nations (Kamerman & Kahn, 1988).

One important difference that Dr. Kamerman noted lies in the structure of government and the allocation of responsibilities for certain domains, in particular for education. In our federal structure, the states have primary responsibility for education and for family law issues. In many of the European countries, by contrast, the national government has primary responsibility for education. One of the factors that prevented the early development of a firm base for a national policy on child care was the debate about whose responsibility it was. When you have an administration that would prefer not to take the financial responsibility, it is very easy to say that that is not an appropriate federal role but a state and local government role. This is not an insurmountable barrier, however, she noted; both Canada and West Germany have federal governments and are moving ahead in this area.

Another major difference lies in the different motivations behind the development of child care initiatives. The preschool programs in the European countries were established largely because they were considered to be good for children's educational and social development. They happened to fit with the growth in labor force participation by mothers of young children that began, as it did here, in the 1960s; thus, there was a convergence of constituencies. The beginnings of this kind of convergence of constituencies in this country can be seen in the school-reform movement, reaching down to preschool, and in the recognition of the social benefits of preschool programs.

Dr. Kamerman was asked how American firms operating in Europe and Canada reacted to the parental leave policies that are so different from policies in this country. She replied that they find it acceptable and are fulfilling mandatory requirements.

ACKNOWLEDGMENT

The main source for this chapter is earlier research and ongoing monitoring of these developments. The most recent updating of the European community is much facilitated by the completion of the very valuable report by Moss (1988).

6

Child Care and Federal Policy

Susanne Martinez
Legislative Assistant to Senator Alan Cranston

The percentage of children—particularly children under 1 year of age—whose mothers are in the work force has increased dramatically in the past two decades. Yet the United States has no national policy regarding child care nor anything that even remotely resembles a coordinated approach to dealing with the escalating demand for child care. Federal child care policy can be characterized as fragmented, inconsistent, and virtually nonexistent.

DEMOGRAPHIC CHANGES

Whether the statistics are discussed in terms of mothers in the work force or children whose mothers are in the work force, the numbers are staggering. For the vast majority of children and families, labor force participation of mothers is today's reality.

The most recent data available from the U.S. Department of Labor (1987) indicate that as of March 1987 52% of the mothers of children 1 year old or younger were in the labor force. Five years earlier, the proportion was 43%, and in 1977 it was only 32%. In terms of the children affected, in 1987 50% of those under age 1 had mothers in the labor force, whereas in 1977 only 31% of the children under age 1 fell into that group.

For older children, the statistics are even more dramatic. In 1987, about three fifths of the mothers whose youngest child was between the ages of 2 and 5 were in the work force. About the same proportion of all children under 18—three fifths—had mothers in the work force. In 1985, this translated to 20 million mothers, including 8.2 million mothers with children under the age of 6, and 33.5 million children under 18, with more than 9 million under age 6 and 14.7 million between the ages of 6 and 13 (U.S. Bureau of Census, 1986).

This phenomenon crosses all family structures and all economic levels. Although divorced mothers were the most likely to be in the labor force, with a participation rate of 80%, in 56% of the married-couple families both husband and wife were earners at some time during the past year (U.S. Department of Labor, 1987).

As significant as these figures are in terms of today's families, there is every indication that in the next decade the number of children whose mothers are in the paid work force will continue to grow. The Children's Defense Fund (1987c) projects that if current trends continue, by 1995 34.4 million children over 6 will have a mother in the work force, as will 14.6 million children under 6.

Both in the case of mothers who are heads of households and those who are married, economic necessity is a driving force behind their work force participation. Two thirds of the women in the work force either are sole providers or have husbands who earn less than $15,000. One out of five families with children is now headed by a woman. This translates into 6.3 million women with 11.2 million children under 18. Sixty-eight percent of these women heading a household are in the work force (U.S. Bureau of Census, 1986).

The economic pressures upon women in two-parent families have also been strong. In 1985 the Joint Economic Committee issued a report on family income indicating that the real income of most American families declined significantly in the past decade, with the most severe decline between 1979 and 1985. Only the addition of a second wage earner kept many of these families in the middle-income brackets.

The vast majority of women in the labor force are working full-time. Seventy-one percent of the mothers in the paid work force work full-time. This is true for mothers of very young children as well. Sixty-five percent of the mothers of children under the age of 3 who work outside the home work full-time (U.S. Department of Labor, 1985).

For most of these full-time workers, adjustment of schedules to allow for child care responsibilities is not a real option. Flextime, for example, is available to only about 6% of the full- time workers, and only about 10% of the dual-career couples are able to work different shifts so that one parent can always be at home with the children (Population Resource Center, 1984). Alternative child care becomes a necessity for these families while parents are at work.

WHERE ARE THE CHILDREN?

The most recent data indicate that the majority of children under the age of 5 with an employed mother are cared for outside of their own homes. Forty-six percent are cared for in the home of another, with 25.4% in the home of a nonrelative. Almost 20% of the children under 5 with an employed mother are cared for in child care centers (Select Committee, 1987b).

National information on the availability of adequate child care, sketchy at best before 1980, is virtually nonexistent for the years since the Reagan administration took office. The last national data, released by the federal government in 1980 and 1981, indicated that there were some 900,000 slots available in child care centers and 5.2 million in family day care homes (Children's Defense Fund, 1982). That represented less than one place in three for the children—then 22 million—under the age of 13 with employed mothers. Despite the absence of data collection by the federal government, reports from individual states and local communities indicate that the lack of available choices for parents in need of child care assistance has gotten worse in the intervening years. For example, in 1987 the Children's Defense Fund reported nearly 30,000 children on waiting lists for state-subsidized child care in the state of Florida. A 1985 report from the California Assembly Office on Research estimated that 1.6 million children in that state needed care outside the home while their parents worked, yet there were only 6,600 licensed child care centers in California, with a capacity for 330,000 children, and 33,400 licensed family day care homes, with a capacity of 198,000 children.

The Select Committee on Children, Youth, and Families, after a year-long series of hearings and investigations into the area of child care, said of the problem in a 1984 report:

> Waiting lists for family day care homes and centers for infants and after-school programs for school-aged children are commonplace. Child care for children who are ill or disabled is extremely limited, as is care for abused and neglected children, and for children of teen parents. Even preschool care, the most widely available of all child care, is inadequate in many communities. (p. ix)

The lack of adequate child care has a variety of implications. A 1987 survey by the American Federation of State, County, and Municipal Employees found that almost one third of the respondents with a child under 18 had been forced to give up either a job or a promotion because of lack of adequate child care. The Census Bureau has estimated that more than 2 million school-age children regularly spend some period of time without adult supervision after their school day ends and before a parent returns home (U.S. Bureau of Census, 1987b). Other sources suggest that the number of latchkey children is much higher. For example, the Children's Defense Fund (1982) has estimated that between 6 and 7 million children under the age of 13 are probably left to fend for themselves for a significant part of their day.

Moreover, even where child care is available, the cost is often beyond the means of many families. The average cost of full-time child care is $3,000 a year for one child. For a typical family, child care is often the largest family expense following shelter and food. For a low-income family, the costs can be virtually impossible to meet. A minimum-wage earner working full-time, year-round, earns only $6,700 per year; the average child care cost would absorb almost 50% of that income (Alliance for Better Child Care, 1987a).

By virtually every account and every measure, the demand for child care services throughout the nation vastly exceeds the supply. Parents and families experience enormous problems in finding and paying for satisfactory child care. Availability, affordability, and quality are constant issues in the field of child care.

THE FEDERAL ROLE IN CHILD CARE

The child care crisis has resulted in an enormous increase in the amount of interest and concern at the federal level in dealing with this problem faced by millions of American families. The increased national attention on child care has led to the introduction of a number of new proposals in Congress.

Historically, the federal government has been involved in a substantial way in addressing child care needs in this country (Martinez, 1986; Norgren, 1981). For example, during the Depression, a day care program was established under the Federal Emergency Relief Administration (subsequently the Works Progress Administration, the WPA). By 1937, some 1,700 centers were operated under this program. The purpose of the WPA child care program, however, was to create jobs for unemployed adults. The needs of children and their parents were secondary. Funding for these centers was decreased as the economy improved and adults were able to locate jobs in the private sector.

Similarly, a federally funded day care program was established during World War II under the Lanham Act to enable women to work in war-related industries. Most of the programs established under this program closed immediately at the end of the war, when women were no longer perceived as necessary in the work force.

In the early and mid-1960s, federal financial support for child care programs was authorized under the Social Security Act for welfare mothers participating in work programs. Again, the impetus—discouraging welfare dependency—was in response to adult needs, rather than as part of a long-term commitment to supporting the needs of children and their families.

In the early 1970s, driven in large part by the war on poverty, Congress did pass a far-reaching, comprehensive child care bill, authorizing $2 billion to fund construction and operation of child care centers. The 1971 legislation, supported by a broad coalition of organizations, including labor unions, church groups, social welfare advocates, women's groups, and citizens' organizations, had been declared by the *Washington Post* to be "as important a breakthrough for the young as Medicare was for the old" and "a vehicle for a new national effort to make childhood liveable" (cited in Edelman, 1976). That legislation, which was in the form of an amendment to the Economic Opportunity Act of 1965, was vetoed by Richard Nixon with an inflammatory veto message that stated: "For the Federal Government to plunge headlong financially into supporting child development would commit the vast moral authority of the National Government to the side of communal approaches to child rearing over the family center approach" (Nixon, 1972, p. 1178).

Again, however, the 1971 legislation was part of a larger effort aimed at enhancing the economic status of low-income families and impoverished communities. Child care had not yet become a mainstream need for all families. Indeed, in 1971, it wasn't. Only about 30% of the mothers of preschool children were in the work force at that time, and the vast majority of these children were cared for in their own homes.

In subsequent years, as the number of working mothers of young children increased, renewed efforts to develop a comprehensive strategy for addressing child care needs began. In 1975, child care legislation proposed by then-Senator Walter Mondale was crushed under a right-wing mail campaign that used the theme of the Nixon veto—that federal support for child care would lead to sovietization and communal child rearing (Subcommittee on Children and Youth, 1976). In 1976, presidential candidate Jimmy Carter pledged to work for the development of a comprehensive child care bill that would help states and localities meet child care needs. However, when the Carter administration was asked to take a position on legislation introduced in the Senate by the chairman of the Senate Subcommittee on Child and Human Development, Senator Alan Cranston, the Carter administration delivered conflicting messages. Although President Carter's chief advisor on women's issues, Sarah Weddington, chair of the Carter administration's Interdepartmental Task Force on Women, had told the Senate Labor and Human Resources Committee that "employed women with young children must be assured of high quality child care, if we as a nation are to take full advantage of the potential for improving the lives of all Americans in the future" (Labor and Human Resources Committee, 1979, p.42), a month later the Carter administration took a different position when confronted with actual legislation to achieve that goal. Testifying on behalf of the Department of Health, Education, and Welfare (HEW), the administration's witness contended that the federal government was already making a substantial commitment to child care, through programs like Head Start, AFDC, and the IRS child care tax credit. "Given the size and nature of this commitment," the HEW witness testified, the Carter administration did not "believe that another categorical program for child care is warranted" (Subcommittee on Child and Human Development, 1979, p. 223). The opposition of the Carter administration helped bring efforts to pass a comprehensive child care bill to a halt.

As the 1970s came to an end, federal policy on child care was in disarray. Efforts to develop a coherent, coordinated program had, for various reasons, failed dismally. What existed was a series of fragmented programs providing fiscal assistance to help meet the costs of child care for some families. Some direct support for child care was available to low-income families through the social services program authorized under Title XX of the Social Security Act. These Title XX funds were available to the states to meet the social services needs of a variety of groups ranging from foster children to elderly and disabled persons. Child care for welfare recipients was one of the services for which Title XX funds were utilized. Prior to 1981, an estimated 21% of Title XX funds nationally was expended on child care services (Committee on Ways and Means, 1985). States were required to give priority for Title XX services to families on welfare. Although low-income families not receiving welfare assistance were technically eligible for Title XX–supported child care programs, rarely was any funding actually available for these families, given the limited number of spaces available in such programs.

In addition, some federal funding was available to help subsidize child care programs directly. For example, the salaries of some child care workers were subsidized through the public employment program authorized by the Comprehensive Employment and Training Act (CETA). Funds for food in child care programs serving low-income families were made available through the child care food program of the National School Lunch Act.

Head Start, although not a child care program, provided federally funded child development services in communities throughout the nation. In 1980, some 362,000 children were served in Head Start programs. Only a handful of programs, however—less than 15% in 1984—provided full-day services.

Indirect support for child care costs existed in two other programs: the AFDC income disregard and the child care tax credit. Under the AFDC income disregard, employed welfare recipients are allowed to deduct the costs of child care from their earnings when computing the amount of welfare benefits they are eligible to receive. Since 1976, families with income tax liabilities have been eligible to use a child care tax credit to offset their tax liability. The tax credit, which today constitutes the largest single federal expenditure in the child care area, primarily benefits higher-income families. In 1979, almost 80% of the credit was claimed by families with incomes over $15,000 (General Accounting Office, 1982). In 1981, the credit was expanded and targeted toward more low-income families. Nevertheless, the bulk of the benefits continue to go to higher- income families. In 1985, 64% of the credit was claimed by families with incomes over $20,000 and 6% by families with incomes below $10,000. Twelve percent went to families with incomes over $50,000. The total cost of the credit in 1985 exceeded $3 billion (Stephan, 1987).

Although the 1970s had begun with great expectations for addressing child care policy at the federal level, they ended with little accomplished. Then the situation rapidly got worse.

First, in 1980 Congress voted to suspend the Federal Interagency Day Care Regulations (FIDCR), marking the first time since federal standards for federally funded child care had first been established in 1968 that the federal government had totally abdicated any responsibility for ensuring that child care programs supported by federal funds meet any basic minimal health and safety standards (Congressional Record, 1980).

Second, the 1981 Reagan administration budget cuts slashed deeply into the already inadequate child care funding sources. Title XX was cut from $3.1 billion to $2.4 billion, and provisions earmarking a portion of Title XX funds for child care were eliminated (Public Law 97-35). Other programs that had provided support to child care programs were either wiped out entirely, like the CETA program, or cut back drastically. Funding for the child care food program, for example, was cut in 1981 by 30%.

The immediate impact of the 1981 federal funding reductions on state child care programs was devastating. A state-by-state survey done by the Children's Defense Fund in 1983 found that 32 states were providing Title XX child care to fewer children than in 1981, despite the increased numbers needing such care. The total combined federal and state funding for Title XX child care dropped by 14% between 1981 and 1983, and numerous states imposed or increased fees for child care services, making it harder and harder for low-income families to afford Title XX child care programs. Thirty-three states lowered their child care standards and 32 cut back on child care staff (Blank, 1983).

The AFDC child care income disregard for employed welfare recipients was also cut back. A ceiling of $160 per month—roughly $40 per child per week regardless of age—was placed on the amount an AFDC mother could deduct as a work-related expense (Public Law 97-35).

At the same time that massive cutbacks were being imposed upon programs that provided direct support to low-income families in need of child care services, the child care tax credit was significantly increased in the 1981 tax reform legislation. However, a provision that would have made the credit refundable—thereby helping the lowest-income families—was approved by the Senate but rejected in conference by the House of Representatives (Public Law 97-36). Although more families were able to benefit from the child care tax credit as a result of the 1981 legislation, most of the benefits continued to go to higher-income families. As a result of the 1986 tax reform legislation, it is estimated that even fewer low-income families will receive any assistance in meeting child care costs from the child care tax credits, because most will have no tax liability to apply the credit against.

RENEWAL OF SUPPORT FOR CHILD CARE

In the mid-1980s, the pendulum began to swing back for social programs generally, and for child care programs in particular. As the consequences for families of the dismal economy of the early years of the Reagan administration became more and more apparent, a series of events occurred.

First, Congress began to restore some of the funds that had been cut from programs like Title XX. In 1984, Title XX funds were increased to $2.75 billion. Although the Reagan administration's budget proposals continued to seek further reductions in social welfare programs, a bipartisan majority in both houses of Congress emerged to reject any further cutbacks.

Second, a bipartisan coalition began to form, not simply to oppose further funding reductions but to support new initiatives aimed at helping the millions of families hit hard by the Reagan recession of the early 1980s. For example, in the 98th Congress, bipartisan legislation (S. 951) was introduced to provide health care coverage for newly unemployed workers and their families. An emergency program was created in 1983 to help provide food and shelter to needy families (Public Law 98-8). And a series of measures was enacted to expand Medicaid services for low-income women and children (Public Law 99-272; Public Law 98-369).

Concern about the problems arising because of inadequate child care provided the impetus for the creation of several new child care programs. An amendment was added to the 1984 Human Services Reauthorization Act (Public Law 96-558) to authorize $20 million for grants to states to support the establishment of school-age child care programs and child care resource and referral programs, which help families find child care in their communities. Another amendment was passed that added $25 million in funding for training programs for child care workers (Public Law 98-473).

The Senate passed an amendment to the 1986 Continuing Appropriations bill requiring each state utilizing Title XX child care funds to review the adequacy of its child care licensing and regulatory system and submit a report to the Secretary of Health and Human Services identifying those areas where improvements could be made. Although this provision was deleted in the House-Senate conference, strong support for this initiative was expressed in the House debate by the ranking Republican member of the House conference committee (Congressional Record, 1985).

The House of Representatives approved legislation (not acted upon in the Senate, however) authorizing the Department of Housing and Urban Development to establish demonstration programs for child care in public housing projects. Legislation was enacted as part of the 1986 Higher Education Act (Public Law 99-498) authorizing child care services to be provided to low-income college students.

A $1.5 million program was enacted as part of the 1986 Head Start authorization (Public Law 99-425) to provide scholarships for low-income child care providers seeking to earn child development associate credentials. A demonstration program was also established (Public Law 99-425) authorizing the development of programs to provide respite child care for families in crisis and child care for disabled children.

In the 100th Congress, a number of other child care initiatives were introduced in both the House and the Senate by Republican and Democratic members alike. The proposals range from legislation to help family day care providers obtain home mortgage financing (S. 1300) to legislation to promote the establishment of model federal child care standards (S. 934). There was also bipartisan support for legislation that would substantially increase funding for Title XX–funded child care (S. 1309/H.R. 2577/S. 1070/H.R. 1365). Other measures providing new federal funds to support child care services were also introduced (e.g., S. 4, S. 1678, H.R. 1001).

Finally, the need for adequate child care services played a major role in the debate over welfare reform. The welfare reform legislation introduced in both the House and the Senate in the first session of the 100th Congress contains substantial provisions relating to child care services for welfare recipients. This legislation, for the first time, mandates that mothers of very young children work as a condition for receiving welfare assistance and requires that child care services be made available to these families.

Although the number of child care initiatives that have been approved in the past several years and the growing list of new proposals represent an encouraging trend, the progress being made is somewhat illusory. The legislation thus far enacted has generally authorized very limited amounts of funding, often as demonstration projects, not ongoing service programs, and the actual release of federal funds to implement these new programs has been extremely slow. For example, the Reagan administration persistently refused to issue the regulations necessary to implement the 1984 Dependent Care Block Grant program. These regulations were not finally issued until April 1986, months after Congress had appropriated the necessary funds to establish the programs.

In some instances, the legislation itself has had severe shortcomings. For example, Congress has provided funds to help set up child care resource and referral programs but prohibited any of the funds authorized from being utilized to operate such programs.

Another striking example of an incoherent policy is in the area of child care provider training. Although one new law authorizes assistance to help child care workers secure the training needed to upgrade their skills, a bill has been introduced recently that would require states to exempt family day care providers from state licensing requirements as a condition for a state to receive any federal financial assistance under the new program (H.R. 1572). At the same time, the Reagan administration continues to push for legislation to eliminate substantial numbers of family day care providers from the child care food program—a program that has proved a tremendous success in getting unlicensed and unregulated child care providers to seek licensure and to participate in child care training and support programs.

Half of the $25 million authorized in 1984 for child care training was returned by the states to the federal government after virtually every state determined that one of the requirements for acceptance of the new money—establishment of a system of criminal-record checks for all child care workers—was prohibitively expensive and of limited value in protecting children from potential abuse in child care settings.

In short, the hodgepodge of responses at the federal level to the child care crisis has produced a long list of new initiatives in a patchwork, crazy-quilt pattern, which sometimes makes little sense and in other instances is in conflict with itself.

REBUILDING THE 1971 COALITION:
A COMPREHENSIVE APPROACH

It has become increasingly clear to a number of child care advocates and policymakers that continuing this pattern of fragmented child care initiatives makes little sense. Although the tremendous need for adequate child care services for working families has driven child care to a new visibility and priority at the federal level, the lack of a coordinated approach to addressing this program has serious drawbacks.

From the standpoint of child care advocates at the state and local level, federal initiatives establishing small demonstration programs focused on narrow, targeted categories of families and children can be exceedingly frustrating. A great deal of effort sometimes produces very little substantial return. For example, while the California legislature was considering legislation to provide $100 million to establish and operate child care programs for school-age children, California child care advocates were called upon to lobby for enactment of the federal dependent care block grant, which authorized less than $20 million for start-up costs for such programs throughout the entire nation.

From the standpoint of policymakers as well, the fragmented system made little sense. In the summer of 1986, the Senate Assistant Democratic Leader, Senator Alan Cranston, wrote to a number of organizations concerned with the well-being of children and families to urge them to put together a new coalition that would focus the attention of Congress on the child care crisis in America and compel action on a major child care initiative (*Congressional Record*, 1987). This suggestion received an enthusiastic response from virtually every organization contacted. After many months of discussion, planning, and consensus building, in the spring of 1987 these groups announced the formation of a new entity called the Alliance for Better Child Care (ABC). Representing a broad spectrum of groups ranging from child advocacy groups like the Children's Defense Fund to professional groups like the American Academy of Pediatrics, the Alliance has helped develop a far-reaching child care bill, the proposed "Act for Better Child Care Services," which would authorize $2.5 billion to help states expand child care resources and subsidize the costs of providing child care services for lower-income working families.

This effort marks the first time since 1971 that a broad-based coalition has come together to work for a comprehensive approach to meeting child care needs. The ABC bill introduced on November 19, 1987 (S. 1885/H.R. 3660) by a bipartisan group of senators and representatives, including the chairs of the subcommittees with jurisdiction over child care legislation in both houses, is aimed at making the federal government a full partner in a federal-state-private partnership effort to increase child care options and make affordable, high-quality child care more readily available to working parents.

POLITICAL REALITIES AND THE FUTURE
OF FEDERAL CHILD CARE POLICY

At first glance the goals of the Alliance for Better Child Care may seem unrealistic in light of the enormous obstacles facing any new spending programs at the federal level. With the national debt and the federal deficit continuing to mount, prospects for enacting any new federal spending programs may seem dim.

In the past several years, however, a series of new programs has been approved by Congress and signed into law because the issues involved demanded both public attention and a federal response. For example, in the fall of 1986, Congress passed legislation authorizing $1.7 billion in new spending aimed at combating drug abuse (Public Law 99-570). At the same time, it authorized approximately $1.5 billion in new federal spending to implement an immigration reform bill (Public Law 99-603). More recently, Congress approved new spending of almost half a billion to address the needs of homeless Americans (Public Law 100-77). And in January 1987 President Reagan requested Congress to approve a new worker-retraining program as part of the trade legislation that would authorize almost $1 billion in new spending to help workers displaced because of adverse trade conditions.

As the need to address the child care crisis in America moves to the top of our national agenda, there is ample evidence to suggest that the federal government can find the resources to help meet this national need. Obviously, the federal government acting alone cannot provide the solution to the child care crisis. But the federal government can and should play a constructive role in helping to assure that the millions of working families in need of adequate child care services have access to the programs and services they want and need. The real question is not whether the federal government is going to play a more important role in addressing the child care problem, but what kind of role it is going to play. Elected officials, responding to the real needs and demands of their constituencies, are already moving forward with a diverse array of initiatives.

Researchers in the field of child development can make important contributions to the debate on how child care programs can best be developed to enhance the welfare and well-being of children. But one point needs to be clearly understood. As Marian Wright Edelman of the Children's

Defense Fund told a Senate subcommittee looking at child care issues in 1978, "Public policy. . . should proceed from reality" (Subcommittee on Child and Human Development, 1978). The reality for an ever-increasing number of children and families is that child care is a necessary service for family economic self-sufficiency and stability. The growing national consensus on this issue is demonstrated by the virtually unanimous agreement in the current drive toward welfare reform that mothers—even of very young children—are expected to be part of the work force.

A majority of children in this country are going to spend significant parts of their early years in child care settings. The challenge is to make sure that adequate and affordable services are available for these children and their families.

DISCUSSION

The nature of the political process and its relationship to the child care issue were elaborated during the discussion period. A concern was expressed regarding the way in which research in child care is used politically. Rather than leading public policy, it becomes ammunition for one side or the other in a battle for legislation. Ms. Martinez replied that research, particularly research focused on practical applications, has a role in the development of responses to problems, but that it does not play a part in the political decision about whether there will be a response in the first place. Political responses occur only when politicians detect a need in their constituencies. She gave as an example the introduction of a new child care bill by Senator Orrin Hatch of Utah, a conservative Republican, who presented his bill by profiling a number of his constituents and commenting, "I will admit that I believe it is far preferable for parents to care for their own children; but I have been persuaded by the facts that our policy choice must be to enable citizens to work without fear for the safety and well-being of their children."

Dr. Kamerman noted that the research is most influential on public policy when the findings are consonant with the values and political position of those reviewing the research. She pointed to the example of Head Start; the politics surrounding this program were such that it was consistently supported despite negative findings with regard to its effects, until positive consequences were eventually demonstrated. In another example, when researchers demonstrated the negative consequences of the 1981 cutbacks on Medicaid eligibility for low-income children, a move was begun to reinstate some of the provisions that had been cut.

Both Ms. Martinez and Ms. Blank stressed the importance of having a legislative package ready when the "window of opportunity" opens and legislators are ready to consider an issue. Such opportunities happen suddenly; an event may occur that inspires members of Congress to take an initiative that has been sitting on the shelf and push it through. The drug abuse bill, which authorized almost $2 billion of new spending, was passed in just such a way in response to the death of a well-known athlete. Even when a comprehensive bill is not passed as a package, bits and pieces of it may be adopted over the years. This was the case with a far-reaching child health bill that was filibustered and blocked in 1980; over the next 6 years sections of it were enacted until virtually the entire bill had been made law.

Child care can also be related to other concerns of Congress. Looking at welfare reform, legislators can see the relationship between child care and self-sufficiency. They are concerned about the shrinking youth work force, and they can be shown that child care is the place to begin to lay the foundations of basic skills. They are aware of the studies that show that lack of child care makes women less productive at work, and they are worried about the economic consequences. As such issues come up, child care advocates have to be ready with a legislative package.

Ms. Martinez sees some hope for child care initiatives as a result of a "startling coalition" in which fiscal conservatives who want to reduce the national debt will be willing to work with liberals to curb defense spending. She feels that child care has steadily moved upward on the national agenda. The outcome of the 1988 election will be important in determining what happens in the next few years, and even the extent to which child care is an issue in the presidential campaign will be a factor in enhancing its prospects. She is encouraged by the fact that Republicans as well as Democrats are moving ahead with initiatives. It is not going to be easy, she cautioned, and the prospects for any new spending this year are not great, but as politicians learn the importance of child care to their constituents, they will respond.

7
The Federal Role in Child Care

Senator Orrin G. Hatch
(R-Utah)

Defining a federal role in child care has always been a thorny public policy issue, and the extreme ends of the philosophical continuum concerning such a policy are well established. At the one end is the view that the federal government can be effective in providing for children only if it is able to govern the program directly. At the other end is the view that any governmental role will result in the bureaucratization of childrearing. Although Congress has approved program-specific child care assistance for welfare recipients and low-income families through programs such as Title XX, the Job Training Partnership Act, the Carl Perkins Vocational Education Act, and Head Start, advocates of the latter view have prevailed thus far and have prevented passage of any comprehensive child care legislation. Most notably, in 1971, President Richard Nixon vetoed legislation calling for federal child care centers on the grounds that government should not be in the position of affecting children's psychological or emotional development.

There are three basic reasons for this aversion to a broad federal child care policy. First, American society in recent decades has clung to the ideal of a two-parent family, one parent working and one in the home. Although the statistics clearly show that this family structure is no longer the norm, support for any child care legislation is an admission that this ideal is no longer achievable for the majority of American households. To the extent that Congress reflects its constituency, many members are hesitant to take action that acknowledges this fundamental change in American life.

Second, Congress has been, and should continue to be, budget conscious. A federal child care program costs money. Regardless of one's views on the efficacy of legislation in this area, its price tag cannot be disregarded. Public funds spent for child care have the same short-run impact on the deficit as funds spent for any other purpose. Cost was certainly one of several factors contributing to President Nixon's veto of the 1971 bill.

Third, the issue of who cares for children, and under what circumstances, is a highly sensitive one. It has often been said that government cannot play God; neither can it play parent. The very word "federal" implies a substantial degree of standardization, to which a sizable number of citizens are opposed. Perhaps an obvious example of such homogeneity is the suggestion of some that federal funds should not be used to assist child care programs sponsored by religious institutions unless the church or synagogue agrees to remove all religious elements from both the program and the facility. This, of course, would automatically limit parents, despite their preferences, to secular surroundings for their children.

Given, however, that circumstances have changed since the early 1970s, today's question is not so much *if* the government has a role in child care but rather one of *what* that role should be. It should be acknowledged at the outset that government cannot by itself solve the triad of problems that make up the child care issue: availability, access, and quality. The need is simply too great. For example, Congressional testimony has pointed out that the average cost of child care is $3,000 per year per child (Children's Defense Fund, 1987). In 1985, there were 11.2 million children living in families headed by women. More than half these children (53.6%) were living in poverty (U.S. Department of Labor, Women's Bureau, 1986; Children's Defense Fund, 1987). It would, therefore, cost $18 billion annually to provide adequate child care for these children. Clearly, this level of federal expenditure is not possible.

Further, the tactic of subsidizing direct services (i.e., the direct payment of funds to eligible individuals or to child care providers who enroll children from eligible families) while attempting to address the problem of access to child care for low-income individuals, fails to address the problem of availability. Unless a child care initiative also promotes the creation of new child care opportunities, a program of direct subsidies will succeed only in bidding up the price of existing child care spaces and reducing the benefit of the subsidy to low-income families.

Subsidizing direct services for low-income families also has the effect of bifurcating the child care market. If federal funds are used to provide subsidies to low-income families, through vouchers, direct payments, or contracts with child care providers to enroll eligible children, low-income families are necessarily limited in their choices of child care settings and providers. If a family receives a subsidy that is less than the amount of the going rate for child care in that community, that family must seek out a provider who charges less than the market rate in order to stretch the value of the subsidy and lower its out-of-pocket costs. Child care offered at less than the market rate may be of questionable quality. If a public agency contracts with licensed child care providers to provide a certain number of slots for children from low-income families, parents of those children are restricted to those providers and will most likely have to spend considerable time with their names on a waiting list. In short, this approach creates one system of choice for upper- and middle-income parents and another system, of uncertain quality and limited choice, for low-income families.

The government may, of course, stipulate that families receiving subsidies utilize only the services of qualified providers. This requirement would provide some quality assurance, but, as previously discussed, it would also increase the competition for licensed child care slots, raise the price of child care, and reduce the value of the subsidy.

Rather than finance direct services exclusively, a federal initiative should emphasize the expansion of quality child care programs. This could be accomplished in several ways. First, funds could be used to capitalize various locally developed and operated child care projects in the public, private, and nonprofit sectors. This "bottom-up seeding" approach is desirable because it permits flexibility and welcomes innovation. It relieves the stigma of "federal control" of child care and encourages a community's long-term commitment to maintaining the project. A sliding fee scale imposed for each project would permit low-income parents the same choices as middle- and upper-income families at a reduced cost.

Second, any legislative effort to address the child care issue must look seriously at how the liability crisis has exacerbated the shortage of child care. The fear of defending lawsuits brought for nonintentional torts has discouraged otherwise willing private companies and nonprofit organizations from opening child care facilities. Family-based providers often do not carry any liability insurance. Legal reforms, which protect the right to sue and obtain redress while also providing reasonable protection for the child care provider, coupled with lower-cost liability insurance more readily available through a liability insurance pool, would be significant incentives for thousands of would-be child care providers.

Finally, tax law could be amended to provide additional incentives for the private sector to become involved in child care. Businesses, for example, would be more willing to establish on-site child care programs for the benefit of their employees if they were given a tax credit to help offset costs. Additionally, current tax regulations could be streamlined to assist family-based providers who, under current law, are treated as small businesses and are therefore subject to the same quarterly filings of estimated tax and withholding, FICA taxes, and other requirements as any business. Such burdensome regulations have discouraged many family-based providers from seeking licensure and from registering their availability with resource and referral networks.

In sum, child care is a federal problem only in the aggregate. The government's role should be one of facilitating solutions to the child care crisis, not of trying to solve it itself. Previous legislation failed in part because it did not recognize the financial limitations as well as the policy pitfalls inherent in proposals emphasizing direct subsidies and federal standards. Successful federal legislation must take into account the cultural and economic diversity among regions, states, and families. Programs should be locally devised and controlled and should be governed by quality standards set for that state based on the recommendations of an advisory council of experts, including parents and providers. The private and nonprofit sectors should be encouraged to get involved through the lightening of such governmentally controllable burdens as liability and taxes.

It will take the participation of every sector in our society to address the child care shortage, not just a few public agencies. Legislation will be successful if we do not repeat the mistakes of the past and, instead, develop a program having enough flexibility to meet the needs of every neighborhood in America.

8

Crafting the Future of Child Care

Congressman George Miller
Chairman, Select Committee on Children,
Youth, and Families

Child care is as essential a service for American families in the 1980s as housing, food, health care, and education. Ample research demonstrates that the demographics of work and family life have changed in the past two decades as more mothers have entered the work force. This fundamental change has tremendous significance for the debate about child and family policy as we begin to plan for the 21st century.

CHILD CARE TODAY

This historic shift in family needs has been documented extensively in hearings conducted by the Select Committee on Children, Youth, and Families since 1983. In more than 75 hearings spanning a broad range of issues, child care emerged time and again as one of the most critical needs of families, regardless of geographical location, ethnic group, or income level. (See, for example, the following hearings before the Select Committee: "Children and Families in Poverty: The Struggle to Survive," February 25, 1988; "America's Families in Tomorrow's Economy," July 1, 1987; "Children and Families in Poverty: Beyond the Statistics," November 6, 1985; "Families with Disabled Children: Issues for the 80s," April 19, 1985; and "Teen Parents and Their Children: Issues and Programs," July 20, 1983.)

In a specific investigation of child care in 1984, the Select Committee held field hearings to collect information directly from employers, state and county officials, the clergy, and health-care providers in communities across the nation. Virtually every witness identified child care as a key element of any effort to achieve a productive work force and stable community. (See the list of Selected Hearings Addressing Child Care in the Appendix.) Following this investigation, the Select Committee reached a bipartisan consensus determining that mothers were working out of economic necessity and that the federal government has a major role to fill in developing child care services.

The Need for a Universal System

It is increasingly clear that the United States has a need for a universal system of child care—a need long recognized and met in many other Western industrialized countries. This does not mean that the United States should develop a uniform system of child care run solely by the federal government. It does mean that any child care system must recognize and respond to the diversity of families at all income levels as well as the changing demands of their lives. Child care must be universally available to all families who need it, when they need it. As children grow from infants to toddlers and preschoolers, to school-age children, and then to preteenagers, families find that their child care and after-school care needs change dramatically. At the same time, parental preferences regarding the type, location, and philosophy of child care may change. Their decisions can be influenced by a new job or by a divorce or remarriage. Given this range of factors, any system must allow enough flexibility to accommodate the diversity of family needs and situations. And last, but certainly not least, a community-based care system must allow for the broadest possible range of providers—schools, family day care homes, centers, businesses, and religious institutions.

Some people argue that making child care universally available is tantamount to an abdication of parental responsibilities. Far from it. Public policies must facilitate parents' ability to fulfill their dual responsibilities of rearing children and supporting them economically. If parents are to do so, they must be able to choose from many child care options. But there will be no opportunity to choose unless the supply of child care is made adequate to meet demand. The current fragmented and haphazard system of care services forces too many families to patch together whatever mix of child care they can find. As a result of the lack of services, children left unsupervised have suffered tragic injuries and even death.

Inequities in Current Federal Programs

The new national child care system is not being designed on a tabula rasa. Local communities, the private sector, and the federal government have long been involved in providing direct and indirect support for child care services. The Select Committee has documented the success of a wide variety of private and public sector child care initiatives. (See, for example, the hearings listed in the Appendix for May 21 and June 18, 1984; March 10, 1987; and June 22, 1987.)

The federal government's support for child care has a long history, beginning with the short-lived Lanham Act, which established child care services for children of women working during World War II. In the early 1970s, Congress enacted Title XX of the Social Security Act to consolidate federally supported social services programs with a protected set-aside to enable states to fund child care for low-income children and children in the care of state protective services. With the institution of the block grant concept in 1981, states now determine how much of their Title XX funds to allocate to child care services, and in what form. The 21% cut in Title XX funds in fiscal year 1982, however, and the meager increases in federal support for Title XX since then have not allowed the program to keep pace with inflation, let alone the demand for services. As a result, many states have markedly reduced the level of child care services they provide through this program (Blank, this volume).

Another major source of direct federal support for child care is the Child Care Food Program, which provides meals for low-income children in child care centers and family day care homes. This program, the principal source of technical assistance and training for family day care providers, also suffered severe budget cuts during the early 1980s.

The single largest source of federal assistance for child care is the child and dependent care tax credit, which allows a working family a nonrefundable income tax credit for child care expenses. In 1987, revenue lost as a result of this credit reached $2.7 billion, according to the Joint Committee on Taxation (Select Committee, 1987a). The beneficiaries of this indirect support are largely middle- and upper middle-income families, because they are able to spend the most for child care and have enough tax liability to benefit from a nonrefundable credit. By contrast, federal Title XX and Child Care Food Program expenditures, which target low-income families, totaled less than an estimated $1 billion in 1987.

Many other, smaller federal child care programs (e.g., WIN, Job Training Partnership Act, AFDC and Food Stamp disregards, Dependent Care State Planning Grants, employer tax incentives, Child Development Associate Scholarship Assistance) have helped raise awareness about the child

care dilemma and have helped compensate for the child care policy
vacuum. Because of their piecemeal nature, however, they have also contributed to a fragmented and inequitable system of federal child care assistance.

As a result of this underfunded, disjointed, and constantly shifting
scenario, millions of children and families lack access to child care or cannot afford the programs in their communities. The large gap between supply and demand raises significant issues concerning future federal support.
Current federal support is not equitable, because most of the funding
benefits higher income families, and it neither expands the supply of care
nor addresses its quality.

Even the maximum relief available under the tax credit—$1,440 for a
family earning up to $10,000 with two or more children and $960 for a family earning $28,000 with two or more children—does not nearly compensate
for the cost of child care. According to the most recent data from the National Longitudinal Survey of Youth, families with a child under age 5
spend about 10% of their income for child care (Hofferth, 1987). The Census Bureau estimates that those families who pay for child care spend on
average about $2,000 annually (U.S. Bureau of Census, 1987b). Low-income
working parents who owe no taxes receive no benefit from the credit at all,
yet they carry a much greater burden, spending 20%–26% of their income
on child care.

THE TASKS AHEAD

It is generally acknowledged that child care is best based in the community,
in order to be tailored to the specific needs of families and of the community. States and localities, although they have the desire and the
creativity, do not have enough resources to meet the current need for
universal child care. The federal government can help create community-
based child care by ensuring equitable access, quality of care, developmentally appropriate education, training of caregivers, and sufficient funding.
The federal government can also facilitate partnerships among businesses,
schools, churches, and public agencies to forge the new child care system
in the most efficient and creative manner possible.

Ensuring Equity

Although median family income rose between 1970 and 1986, the rise
resulted primarily from a second adult wage earner's entering the work

force, not from increased earnings by the typical worker (Congressional Budget Office [CBO], 1988). Child care, by enabling the second earner to work, has played a key role in facilitating the rise in family income. Many families, however, are still unable to afford the entire cost of child care themselves.

There is almost universal agreement among conservative and liberal policymakers that a significant responsibility of the federal government is to aid those whose ability to purchase care is most limited. At present we are not fulfilling that responsibility. The result is that a minority of the neediest are served and that everyone, rich and poor and middle-class alike, has insufficient care to choose from.

The recent public and congressional debate on reforming the welfare system has addressed questions of child care policy for low-income mothers receiving public assistance who are attempting to achieve economic independence. The legislation enacted by the 100th Congress in 1988 guarantees low-income mothers enrolled in educational, training, or employment programs regulated child care during their period of participation and for 1 year after they leave the program and enter the work force. This is a significant advance over current policy, because it recognizes the need for a child care entitlement if women on welfare are required to participate in programs of education and training and because it provides for care during the period from dependency to self-sustaining employment. Child care assistance during this period is essential, because initial earnings are rarely sufficient to meet the family's total child care costs.

An enormous number of low-income families still need assistance paying for child care, however, including working parents at risk of slipping into poverty. One third of families living below the poverty line do not receive AFDC. In addition, in 1986 families that are especially vulnerable, including young families, low-income families with children, and single-parent families, lost significant income relative to their counterparts in 1970. Child care is essential if these families are to have any chance to move out of, or stay out of, poverty (CBO, 1988).

Policymakers must therefore determine whom the federal government will assist in paying for child care. The answer ultimately depends on political compromises. We can begin by helping those who are most financially needy and protecting others from falling into poverty as a result of child care burdens.

Ensuring Quality

Although not all families with children need financial help from the federal government, we cannot deny that there is a federal obligation to ensure the health and safety of all children, regardless of their parents' income levels. All children deserve a safe, healthy environment in which to live, grow, play, and learn. Today, with at least 2 million and possibly as many as 7 million children left without adult supervision and millions more in substandard and even hazardous child care arrangements, we have not yet fulfilled that basic obligation to the youngest, weakest members of our society (Select Committee, 1984; U.S. Bureau of Census, 1987a).

Despite the federal government's financial investment in child care, there is currently no federal oversight of child care providers. Ambiguous and unenforced federal child care regulations first established in 1968 led to a heated debate in the 1970s over the content and feasibility of federal standards. A consensus on improved minimum health and safety regulations was finally reached and delineated in the Federal Interagency Day Care Regulations (FIDCR), and by the beginning of 1980 revised regulations were promulgated. However, political concerns about the cost of implementing the final version in an election year led Congress, for the first time, to withdraw completely from federal responsibility by suspending all federal regulations.

States have been left to determine their own standards, with insufficient resources or guidance. As a result, child care standards vary enormously from state to state, as does the consistency of their enforcement. The federal government established occupational safety and health standards to guarantee American workers a basic level of safety in the workplace; it is equally appropriate for the federal government to require basic health and safety protections for our youngsters. Yet in 1988, exactly 20 years after the first child care regulations were established, the controversy over federal standards is still alive and remains one of the most important and difficult issues defining the extent of federal responsibility for child care.

Fostering the Development of Young Minds

The nation has long recognized that fostering academic and intellectual achievement is a responsibility of society as well as of the family, as illustrated by compulsory school attendance laws. Early childhood education is increasingly being recognized as a key factor in success in school and in later life, and a number of states, including Texas and South Carolina, have made preschool a part of the state school system. Head Start, the comprehensive preschool program for low-income children, has proved to be an excellent investment of federal dollars, delivering substantial paybacks in social and educational achievement and substantial savings in costs of remedial education and crime later on (Select Committee, 1988). In 1987 the Committee for Economic Development, a group of influential business executives, endorsed a massive public and private investment in early childhood education, citing it as essential to creating a technologically skilled work force for the 21st century. The group called for substantial spending for child care, creating a system of universally available child care at the highest educational standards (Committee for Economic Development, 1987).

Experts have amply documented that age-appropriate education in the first 3 years of life is vitally important to the emotional and cognitive development of children (National Center for Clinical Infant Programs, 1986; Phillips, 1987a). The federal government should lead the way in establishing high standards of early childhood education and in training caregivers to deliver the best possible care.

Training Caregivers

The Select Committee (1984) has documented that the skill and competence of child care workers are among the most significant components of a quality child care system. However, opportunities for training are limited at best. The federal government must encourage the establishment of standards of education and experience for caregivers and stimulate the development of in-service training programs for existing workers.

Until now, caregivers have subsidized the cost of child care by working for incredibly low wages, often with few or no benefits such as health insurance, vacation days, and sick leave. As a result, job turnover is high, affecting the consistency and quality of available child care. In recognizing the importance of child care workers as early childhood educators, we must also recognize that they must be paid as trained professionals. Until they are, stability and continuity of care will continue to be elusive goals. Benefits and improved, less stressful working conditions for child care professionals must be addressed as well (Pemberton, 1987; Phillips, this volume; Whitebook, 1984).

Paying for Quality

The last and most basic issue facing child care policymakers is the need for more resources. The misguided federal priorities of the past 8 years have brought the nation to the point where any new social spending must be debated in the context of a massive federal deficit produced by excessive military spending and substantial tax cuts. Congress acted in complicity with the Reagan administration in bringing about this shameful state of affairs and must face up to the social and economic requirements of creating a child care system able to meet the need.

Child care does not come cheaply, but it is a shortsighted society that is unwilling to invest as much as it can in the future of its children. We would be deluding ourselves to pretend that we can create an acceptable child care system without a substantial federal investment. The presidential candidates of 1988 are increasingly acknowledging that child care must be a component of any national policy platform, supported by public opinion that overwhelmingly cites child care as a priority. Many of the candidates are actively supporting new federal child care policies of one form or another. Congress, and the next president, must make financial support for an equitable, universally available system of child care a top budget priority.

Since 1983 we have traveled farther and faster on the child care issue than on any other public policy debate in memory. We have recognized the problem, quantified the need, tested innovative solutions, and reached a remarkable unanimity of purpose that spans the entire spectrum of American politics. Now we must put our knowledge to work, using federal policy to turn theory into practice for the good of our families, our children, and our collective future.

APPENDIX:
SELECTED HEARINGS ADDRESSING CHILD CARE
BEFORE THE SELECT COMMITTEE ON CHILDREN, YOUTH,
AND FAMILIES, U.S. HOUSE OF REPRESENTATIVES

Child Care: Beginning a National Initiative, Washington, DC, April 4, 1984.

Child Care: Exploring Private and Public Sector Approaches, Irving, TX, May 21, 1984.

Child Care: Exploring Public and Private Sector Approaches, San Francisco, CA, June 18, 1984.

Improving Child Care Services: What Can Be Done? Washington, DC, September 5–6, 1984.

Child Abuse and Day Care, Washington, DC, September 17, 1984.
Child Care: The Emerging Insurance Crisis, Parts 1 and 2, Washington, DC, July 17 and 30, 1985.
Child Care: Key to Employment in a Changing Economy, Washington, DC, March 10, 1987.
Florida's Economic Future and the Child Care Crisis for Families, Miami, FL, June 22, 1987.
American Families in Tomorrow's Economy, Washington, DC, July 1, 1987.

9

Child Care:
Issues at the State Level

Helen Blank
Children's Defense Fund

Child care is now viewed as a vital component of any public policy agenda. It is necessary to help families become and remain self-sufficient and to ensure that young children receive the support they need in key early years to grow up to be productive citizens.

Many families struggle to find and pay for decent child care. Families with incomes below or just above the poverty line, however, have fewer options, because they cannot afford good child care without assistance. Resources to help low- and moderate-income families meet the growing costs of child care or to help build a quality child care system for all families are not expanding to meet the demand.

Overall, federal and state assistance to help such families meet their child care needs has declined sharply over the past decade when the effect of inflation is factored in. At the same time, the number of families needing such assistance has grown, because more women with young children are working and because the failure of wages to keep up with inflation has meant that more working families have earnings so low they need help with child care. This is especially true for young parents, whose median family income has been declining since the mid-1970s.

The past few years have demonstrated that states alone will not be able or willing to help the large number of low-income families needing child care assistance. Nor will the states alone build a child care system that ensures that all families have access to quality child care.

TITLE XX SERVICES

In 1981 the president and Congress enacted a 20% reduction in federal funding for 1982 in the Title XX Social Services Block Grant (SSBG), the largest direct source of federal support for child care.[1] Since 1982, Congress has approved only two modest increases in Title XX funds. It failed to restore the program to its 1981 levels, much less keep pace with inflation since 1981. The federal appropriation for fiscal year (FY) 1987, after adjusting for inflation, is approximately 50% of the FY 1977 level and approximately 75% of the 1981 level.[2]

Some states, especially since 1984, have made valiant efforts to increase state funds targeted for child care through Title XX. Despite the many new programs enacted by governors and state legislators who have recognized that investing in child care is essential to their states' economic vitality, the states' overall funding for child care, when adjusted for inflation, is basically at 1981 spending levels. Twenty-eight states are spending less in 1987 for child care funded through Title XX than their 1981 levels adjusted for inflation. Only 18 states are serving more children than they did in 1981, whereas 22 states are actually serving fewer children than they did in 1981.

Millions of children remain to be helped. Even before the federal cuts in Title XX, the program served only 472,000 of the 3.4 million children younger than 6 who were living in poverty in 1981. By 1986 there were 4.9 million poor children in that age group, nearly a 50% increase, and despite increased state efforts, virtually the same number of (inflation-adjusted) federal and state dollars were available as in 1981 to serve families needing day care assistance (see note 2).

STATE CHILD CARE INITIATIVES

With federal Title XX funds losing ground to cuts, freezes, and inflation, and with almost no federal child care support through other programs, some states have moved ahead to create new child care programs funded entirely through state, or state and local, dollars. These initiatives typically have been designed to help special populations, such as families headed by teenage parents or with school-age children, to improve the availability, quality, and supply of child care. Two states experimented with new initiatives in 1987 for raising funds for child care services. New Mexico increased the fee placed on all vital records to $6, to generate $700,000 to support child care services for low-income working parents. Indiana approved a new funding source for school-age child care by passing a 5¢ per pack increase in the state cigarette tax and earmarking a percentage of this increase for public health and child care programs. Since 1985 the number of state programs has increased, most of them funded modestly.

Whether or not a state sets out to create such programs typically depends, in large part, on the health of its economy, although some states with limited resources have taken new steps that at least showed an understanding of the importance of child care, if not adding significant new resources. But even the most progressive state efforts, with only a few exceptions, have been very limited in their scope or funding. Few states have taken bold steps to address the wide spectrum of needs that must be met to help families afford child care and to create a quality child care system. As a consequence, the unmet need for child care escalates:

- Nearly half the counties in Kentucky provide no child care assistance to low-income working families.
- A recent survey of 230 public housing projects around the country with on-site child care centers found waiting lists with 96,000 children. Furthermore, the surveyors estimated that households with approximately 170,000 children might be interested in the centers' services if care were available for a wider range of children for more hours.
- In Florida, there are waiting lists for child care for nearly 30,000 children.
- In one recent 90-day period, in just three Florida counties (Orange, Osceola, and Seminole), the following were refused help because of lack of funds: 9 abused children; 176 children whose mothers applied for an employment training program but remained on welfare because they lacked child care help; 200 children whose AFDC mothers had found jobs but could not work because of child care problems; 6 children of migrant farm workers who had to accompany their parents to dangerous work sites; and 2,073 children whose families were eligible for child care assistance under the state's own criteria to help parents continue working and stay off public welfare, but for whom there were inadequate appropriated funds.
- California provides child care assistance to 7% of the over 1 million children eligible for help.
- Seattle serves 2,200 of 10,000 eligible children.
- In New York City, 144,000 children under 6 are eligible for child care, but publicly funded day care slots are available for only 1 out of every 5 children.

CHILD CARE FOR AFDC RECIPIENTS

Child care is essential to the ability of many families to become self-sufficient and move off dependence on Aid to Families With Dependent Children (AFDC). Without help in meeting child care costs, it is unlikely that a mother receiving AFDC can participate in a training program or go to work.

Good child care initiatives have been given a major boost by a welfare reform bill—the Family Support Act—passed in October 1988. While the new act has both bad and good provisions, most of the new child care provisions are good. They create new challenges and opportunities for advocates.

The Family Support Act makes five key changes in AFDC-related child care:

It expands the child care entitlement to AFDC parents in training or in school, as well as to those who are in paying jobs. Currently, states can receive federal reimbursement under the AFDC program (Title IV-A of the Social Security Act) only for child care for parents who are working and whose child care is reimbursed through the AFDC earned income disregard and, in a few states, for parents enrolled in education or training programs whose child care needs are reimbursed as a special need.

It increases the amount that can be paid for child care through the AFDC program, which means that parents on welfare may finally be able to obtain quality care.

It increases the number of ways states can pay for care. Previously, states could receive federal matching funds only for child care provided through the AFDC child care disregard. Under the disregard, parents have to pay for child care themselves and then be reimbursed for the cost of care in their welfare checks. Because of this delayed reimbursement, parents have rarely been able to purchase quality care.

It creates an entitlement to 12 months of child care for families that leave AFDC because of earned income.

It helps ensure quality care by requiring that care meet applicable state and local standards and by making the state responsible for offering assistance in locating child care and providing that assistance upon request.

The Family Support Act requires all states to establish and operate a Job Opportunities and Basic Skills (JOBS) Training Program for AFDC recipients and to include in the program a range of education, training, and employment activities. To the extent that state resources permit, parents of children age 3 and older must be mandated to participate in the JOBS Program. Parents of 1- and 2-year-olds may be required to participate. No parent of a child under age 6 may be required to participate for more than

20 hours a week, with one exception: Parents in the mandatory group who are younger than age 20 and who do not have a high school diploma must be required to participate in an educational activity and may be required to participate on a full-time basis regardless of the age of their children.

The act includes a strong child care guarantee for parents in any of the JOBS Program activities, as well as for other parents who are working or in other education or training programs. A parent has a good cause for not participating in the JOBS Program if the state fails to provide the care. The act also raises the child care disregard amount for parents working and receiving AFDC, from $160 a month per child to $175 a month per child ($200 a month for infants and toddlers). And the act for the the first time also provides federal funds for child care for parents who lose AFDC because of earnings; such parents will be eligible for continued child care on a sliding-fee basis for 12 months.

When a state implements the JOBS Program, which can be no later than October 1, 1990 (but can be as early as July 1989), it can begin to receive federal reimbursement for child care expenses for AFDC parents on an open-ended basis at the Medicaid matching rate. That rate ranges from 50% in more well-to-do states to higher levels in the poorer states and reaches 80% in Mississippi. The program of transitional child care assistance for families leaving AFDC because of earnings will be effective April 1, 1990.

States must make concerted efforts to evaluate the child care needs of AFDC recipients, to inform them of their rights to child care services, and to help link them with appropriate providers. A state must provide orientation to AFDC applicants and recipients about employment and training opportunities, including information on child care services.

For each JOBS participant, the state must do a formal assessment that includes an evaluation of child care needs. On the basis of this assessment, the state must prepare an employability plan for the participant, taking into account the need for supportive services, including child care. This plan must, to the maximum extent possible, reflect the preferences of the recipient and must explain services to be provided (including child care). The state must let participants know that they can get help in selecting appropriate child care and must (directly or through arrangements with others) provide information on the types and locations of reasonably accessible child care services.

CHILD CARE FOR LOW-INCOME WORKING FAMILIES

Most states use their Title XX child care funding to help low-income working parents in general, including those leaving AFDC. A number of recent state welfare reform initiatives have recognized that child care help must be provided after a parent is no longer eligible for AFDC but still earning such modest wages that assistance with child care is essential to continued employment. They have provided new state funds to help these parents with their child care costs. Three states—Minnesota, New York, and Virginia—recognizing the difficulty that struggling low-income working families have with child care costs, fund separate state programs targeted to parents who are poor but may not receive AFDC. Minnesota spends $13.75 million a year, New York $18.6 million, and Virginia approximately $1.5 million. In New York, families earning up to 75% of the federal poverty level are eligible for help with child care costs. However, a local social service district can obtain waivers to serve families earning up to 200% of the poverty level, or slightly above $22,000 a year for a family of four.

CHILD CARE FOR CHILDREN OF COLLEGE STUDENTS

Child care responsibilities combined with the lack of adequate child care services and assistance are major barriers to higher education for low- and moderate-income women. In 1979, the California Post-Secondary Education Commission cited the lack of adequate low-cost child development programs as a primary factor in the underrepresentation in higher education of ethnic and minority low-income female students. In that same year, during hearings conducted by the California Community and Junior College Asociation and Commission on Women, child care was "the most frequently mentioned, most critical, and most unmet need" cited during the testimony.

Child care is rarely available on campus. When it is, the cost often makes it inaccessible to lower-income students. States often refuse to give Title XX assistance in paying for child care to college students; limited dollars are targeted on working families.

State higher education funds as well as Title XX funds should be used to provide child care assistance to low-income mothers enrolled in institutions of higher learning. One approach is to subsidize child care for students' children in facilities on campus. Many colleges do not have on-campus care programs, however, and those programs that exist often have long waiting lists. Mothers should be offered help in purchasing space in community child care centers or family day care homes as well as assistance through campus-based centers. Only three states— California, Minnesota, and New York—target funds to help students enrolled in institutions of higher learning with child care expenses, at a cost to the state ranging from over $10 million in California to slightly over $4 million in New York.

CHILD CARE FOR ADOLESCENT PARENTS

Each year nearly 500,000 teenagers give birth to children. Approximately 50% of the teens who give birth before the age of 18 never complete high school. Staying in school is extraordinarily difficult for a parenting teenager, one who has all the usual problems of a girl of that age plus the special problems of being a mother and having the responsibility of raising a young child. Good child care is important not only because it allows these young women the opportunity to attend school but also because it helps them gain parenting skills by leading them to participate in child development classes and by offering them the opportunity to provide care under supervision to infants and toddlers other than their own.

Child care for teenage parents should not be limited to a few months, as is the case with some recently developed programs. The dearth of resources to help low-income families pay for child care makes it extremely difficult for a teenage mother to find new support after a few months and increases the likelihood of her dropping out of school or a training program. Assistance should be continued until a mother finishes her degree. This is important not only for the parent but for the child; young children should not be bounced in and out of child care programs.

Easy accessibility of the child care is also essential. States and cities must support programs located in or near schools where teenage parents are. They must also provide transportation for mothers and their children from home to school and to child care facilities and back. Off-campus child care must also be available to mothers seeking a GED or enrolled in non-school-based training or education programs.

A comprehensive approach is necessary to work effectively with children as well as teenage parents. The range of services incorporated into the most successful models of care for children of teenage parents includes: prenatal care and birth training; health care (for the baby and the mother) and nutrition information; child care; tutoring of the parents in academic skills; individual and family counseling; separate support groups for mothers, fathers, mothers and fathers together, grandparents, and siblings (especially sisters of teenage mothers); family planning services and counseling; help in coping with daily life experiences; and employment training.

In 1987, Maine, Minnesota, and Rhode Island joined California, Connecticut, the District of Columbia, Florida, Massachusetts, Michigan, New

York, Pennsylvania, Texas, and Wisconsin in providing some earmarked state funds targeted to mothers in high school or working toward their GEDs. The programs vary in approach. For example, Michigan assures that any parent still enrolled in high school and younger than 21 is eligible for state-subsidized child care, whereas California takes a more programmatic approach, providing over $6.5 million for child care on or near high school and junior high school campuses and requiring programs to provide an array of services, including parent education and counseling.

State programs targeted to children of adolescents, although growing in number, remain small in size. For example, Connecticut spends $214,000 of state funds to help 104 high school students with the cost of child care services. In FY 1987 Wisconsin provided help to only 72 children in child care programs in high schools.

CHILD CARE FOR SCHOOL-AGE CHILDREN

Nearly three quarters of the mothers of school-age children work outside the home. They share the dilemma of finding safe, supportive, and affordable child care for their school-age children. The consequences of the lack of school-age programs are far-reaching. A new national poll by Louis Harris and Associates found that 51% of the 1,000 teachers interviewed said that lack of after-school supervision was the primary cause of poor school performance, and 41% of the 2,000 parents surveyed said their children were often unsupervised after school.

Although the number of school-age child care programs is growing, there are still too few to meet the expanding need. California provides child care assistance to only 8,000 of the state's estimated 500,000 to 550,000 eligible children who need school-age care.

The majority of state school-age child care initiatives that do exist earmark the funds solely for programs' start-up costs. Thus they fail to provide the ongoing help that low- and moderate-income families need to use the programs, which can cost from $15 to $40 a week for each child. In 1987, however, New Jersey and Indiana did approve school-age child care appropriations that include funds to help low-income families pay for the cost of such care. School-age child care is especially important for low-income children, because these programs can help keep them "on track"—that is, help them to succeed academically and to avoid various social pitfalls.

Massachusetts will fund some extended-day programs for school-age children with part of the $10.2 million it has allocated for early childhood development and will allow $1.5 million appropriated for Head Start to be used for extending the hours of Head Start programs to make them more convenient for working parents. California is the only other state that actually allocates funds for ongoing subsidies.

Connecticut has a program to fund salaries of day care providers in before- and after-school programs, which should help lower the cost to parents. Florida, Iowa, Maine, Minnesota, New York, Pennsylvania, and Rhode Island limit their efforts to start-up costs. A Children's Defense Fund study (1986) of state school-age child care initiatives identified major roadblocks to services for poor children that also affected the overall success of school-age initiatives, including:

- Lack of continuous funding stream to help low-income parents pay the weekly fees;
- Lack of funds for transportation;
- Restrictive licensing and regulatory policies that pose difficulties for providers in receiving start-up grants or even in using Title XX child care subsidies to help families pay for care;
- Inadequate time allowed for start-up of new programs;
- Lack of special outreach to low-income families;
- Lack of space exacerbated by an unwillingness of some school boards to become involved in any way in school-age child care.

PRESCHOOL EDUCATION

Preschool education has risen higher on the agenda of a number of states since 1984. It is recognized as an important investment by key business leaders. The Committee for Economic Development recommends that the federal Head Start program be expanded to serve every eligible child and that states make the necessary investment to provide preschool services to every eligible child.

Preschool education and preschool child care are vital topics for low-income families and children. Too often each of these programs is discussed in a vacuum. Child care is considered in a custodial framework as part of an initiative to help mothers work, whereas preschool is examined as a means of furthering the optimum development of young children. This dichotomy fails to recognize the interrelationship of the two objectives, leading to contradictory or uncoordinated child care policies. For example, legislators sometimes support a quality preschool program, such as Head Start, while failing to apply any of the principles of child development learned from the Head Start experience when designing child care policies for preschool children and parents on welfare.

Low-income families benefit from child care when it helps parents reach economic independence. But child care must also help children establish a foundation of intellectual, physical, social, nutritional, and emotional well-being critical to their later success as adults.

In 1987, six states—Connecticut, Michigan, New Jersey, Oregon, Rhode Island, and Vermont—joined the 20 states that have been providing some level of state funding for preschool programs, including in some cases state funding for Head Start. Programs created from 1983 to 1987 range from $189,000 for three pilot programs in Delaware to more than $37.5 million in Texas.

Almost every state that funds preschool takes a different approach, ranging from simply passing permissive legislation under the state's school code (allowing local schools or school districts to operate preschool programs), to substantial special appropriations for preschool, to state funds to supplement Head Start.

PARENTAL LEAVE POLICIES
AND TEMPORARY DISABILITY INSURANCE

Over 50% of mothers with children younger than 1 year old are working, largely because their paychecks are crucial to supporting their families and maintaining their standards of living. Infant care, however, is not only in short supply but often prohibitively expensive. Child care costs in general are often very high in relation to women's typical wages, but newborns need especially intensive (and expensive) attention.

Paid disability leave immediately following birth is part of the social insurance systems of five states—California, Hawaii, New Jersey, New York, and Rhode Island. It allows a mother time to recover from her pregnancy and childbirth during the period in which she is considered medically disabled—generally 6 to 8 weeks—and to spend these important weeks with her infant. By not forcing the family to deplete small savings, the insurance payments also can make more of the family's resources available for child care when the mother does return to work. Temporary disability insurance paid for by the employer not only addresses the concerns of new parents but also meets the needs of other employees by guaranteeing partial salary replacement to workers who find themselves suddenly unable to work because of a serious health condition.

Temporary Disability Insurance (TDI) alone does not guarantee job security to a disabled worker, however. New parents can find themselves receiving partial salaries for several weeks but then learn that they are out of a job when they seek to return to work. TDI also provides financial assistance only during a period when a mother is medically disabled as the result of pregnancy and childbirth.

In 1987, Minnesota, Oregon, Rhode Island, and Tennessee passed parental leave legislation that does not provide wage replacement but does guarantee job security during a minimum amount of time off after childbirth. Usually both the mother and the father are protected. Although Minnesota and Rhode Island cover all employees, Oregon limits the mandate to employers of 25 or more employees, and Tennessee's law applies only to employers of more than 100 full-time employees.

ESSENTIAL ELEMENTS OF A CHILD CARE AGENDA

Whether functioning at the federal, state, or local level, and whether using Title XX funds, state funds, or other monies, public policymakers must consider a number of overarching principles in the development of each child care policy or program:

- The supply of quality child care programs must be expanded. The shortage is particularly acute in the areas of infant and school-age care. State-sponsored loan and grant programs and family day care recruitment programs, as well as business assistance initiatives, are key to stimulating the creation of necessary renovations and expansions.
- Child care must be affordable for all families. Particular attention must be paid to how a program will meet the child care needs of low-income working families or families in which low-income parents are attending school (including 4-year colleges) or participating in employment training programs.
- Child care assistance must be continued not only as parents complete training programs and search for jobs but after they are employed.
- Parents must receive the help of a sliding fee eligibility scale, with the family's contribution based on income.
- The quality of child care programs must be strengthened through standards that address staffing and training, education, parent involvement, health, nutrition, and safety issues. Adequate funding must be made available for the implementation of these policies.

IMPROVING THE QUALITY
AND AVAILABILITY OF CHILD CARE

In 1987 several states took steps to improve one or more of the components of a stable child care system. For example, the low salaries of child care providers make it exceedingly difficult to recruit and retain qualified staff. With an eye for relieving the staffing problem, Connecticut raised its extremely low child care reimbursement rates by 150% for family day care providers and by 66% for child care centers. Massachusetts pioneered in this area, allocating funds in 1986 to allow a 30% increase in child care providers' salaries.

In 1987, Minnesota, New York, Oregon, and Rhode Island began programs to start new or to renovate existing child care programs. New York's program is the largest, with the state appropriating $3 million for services and expenses of new nonprofit child care programs. Oregon established a 50% employer tax credit for reimbursing parents' child care costs or for building child care facilities. California, Connecticut, Illinois, Iowa, Maryland, Massachusetts, and Ohio already sponsor loan or grant programs or some type of business assistance to new child care providers. California makes the largest investment in this area, funding a capital outlay program that makes $7.25 million available for loans to preschool and infant care programs. Although technically an interest-free loan, the state may waive any payback, making the loan a grant, if the provider is receiving state child care funds and complies with certain contractual terms. The capital outlay program also provides $36.5 million for start-up grants to school-age programs. Finally, the California Child Care Initiatives Project, together with a match of four-to-one raised from private sources, enables six resource and referral agencies to recruit and train family day care providers.

Resource and referral programs, in addition to helping families find child care, can provide valuable services such as sponsoring family day care recruitment campaigns to expand the supply of child care or offering training and technical assistance to their communities' child care providers. It is important for states to provide operating as well as start-up costs to ensure that services to families will continue. California and Massachusetts fund the most extensive state networks of resource and referral programs. Fourteen other states and the District of Columbia provide state funds to start or operate resource and referral programs. In 1987, Iowa, Maine, Minnesota, Oregon, and Pennsylvania began new state programs to support these programs, and Michigan and New Mexico expanded their existing efforts.

Although a number of states have moved ahead in efforts to structure and fund a responsive child care system, it is clear from the efforts discussed that they cannot by themselves address the significant child care issues: affordability, quality, supply, and caregivers' wages. We will not have a cohesive child care policy in this country until the federal government joins state governments, the private sector, and parents in a new partnership expanding the resources available to address the issues of affordability, accessibility, and quality.

DISCUSSION

Ms. Blank was asked whether the effort to expand child care might be tied to the currently important issue of minority recruitment in the schools. She replied that the problem of recruitment for child care had actually been exacerbated in the states that have preschool initiatives. The latter programs, which are paying higher salaries and giving more benefits, are siphoning off the teachers in the child care programs. The education connection is thus a double-edged sword, she commented, providing some of the care for a part of the day, but still leaving an enormous need for child care, and for child care teachers. Recruitment campaigns in child care have not been adequate to meet the demand. Minnesota recruited 750 new family day care providers, but because of the large turnover in family day care this was just enough to maintain the supply and did not expand it.

One participant commented that despite the problem of availability of day care, some moderately priced programs have 10% to 15% of their slots empty. The problem is that even though these are not the most expensive programs, low-income parents cannot afford them. Ms. Blank agreed, especially with respect to some age groups. Finding care for infants is more difficult; more care is available for preschoolers, although there is a question of the quality of care that is provided in these programs.

Ms. Blank was then asked what specific role the federal government should play in child care. Should the funds go to the states, many of which do not have adequate regulations or quality control to guarantee that child care is what it should be? Or should it be a national program, more complex than just appropriation of funds?

Ms. Blank replied that the federal solution cannot be a simple block grant but that neither can it be a completely uniform system everywhere. The ABC bill has taken an approach that finds a balance between prescriptiveness on the one hand and recognition of what the states have done on the other. It sets out what the states have to do to build a decent child care system, but because some states have some of the elements of the system already in place it does not prescribe how much is to be spent in each area. There has to be accountability and the bill does set up national child care standards, but a reasonable approach will be taken to meeting those standards. The focus for centers will be on five key licensing standards: caregiver/child ratios, group size, health and safety, training and caregiver qualifications, and parent involvement. For day care homes, the issues will be maximum number of children, age of caregiver, maximum number of infants, and health and safety. When licensing standards are met and improvements in enforcement of standards are made, the state's match of federal funds goes from 20% to 15%. States have 5 years to meet the licensing standards and requirements for enforcement procedures. In defining the federal role, Ms. Blank concluded, you have to set minimum standards and lay out a structure, because although some states have a good structure in place, others have none.

NOTES

[1] Although the Title XX/SSBG is the major source of federal funds available to states to help them provide child care subsidies to low-income families, states also use the Title XX funds for a variety of other critical social services, such as emergency services, short-term foster care, and day care for the elderly. States decide how much of the federal block grant (and how much of their own funds) will be used for each of the services. This chapter uses "Title XX" to describe the funding stream, including state and federal dollars, that is used to provide the bulk of direct child care subsidy funds to low-income families. Forty-four states use Title XX funds plus some of their own revenues to provide child care assistance. Alaska, California, Montana, and Oregon use no federal funds for their child care assistance programs for working parents. North Dakota and South Dakota use no Title XX funds or state funds for child care for low-income working families.

[2] This calculation includes California, Alaska, Montana, and Oregon state spending figures for child care. Minnesota's sliding fee scale program and Virginia's separate program for working parents are not included in the FY 1987 calculation. In addition, New York's total for FY 1987 includes money for separate state programs. The state could not provide data about Title XX only. Pennsylvania as well includes state-funded programs.

10

Licensing and Accreditation of Child Care Facilities

Barbara Willer
National Association for the Education of Young Children

One of the most profound social changes in recent years has been the increased labor force participation of mothers of young children. As more and more mothers have entered the labor force, the need for supplemental child care arrangements has also increased. Although some parents can make such arrangements with family members, a growing number of families seek child care in their communities and rely on organized group facilities (child care centers) or family day care (providers who care for a small number of children in the provider's home). As the use of comunity-based services has grown, so too has the public responsibility to assure that the services parents choose offer safe environments that enhance their children's development.

A brief look at the numbers clearly documents the extent to which supplemental child care arrangements have moved from private arrangements between relatives to community-based arrangements. In 1958, care in the child's home (by relative or nonrelative) or care in a relative's home constituted 71.1% of the child care arrangements made by mothers employed full-time whose youngest child was under 5 (Select Committee on Children, Youth, and Families, 1987b). By the winter of 1984–1985, this percentage had dropped to 34.1% (U.S. Bureau of Census, 1987b). During the same period, child care in the home of a nonrelative (family day care) or organized group facility (child care center or nursery school) rose from 17.2% to 45.4%. Much of the growth in community-based services can be directly attributed to increased use of organized group facilities. Child care centers and other organized facilities, which were used by less than 5% of full-time employed mothers in 1958 (Select Committee on Children, Youth, and Families, 1987b), constituted nearly 30% of the child care arrangements of full-time employed mothers in 1984–1985 (U.S. Bureau of Census, 1987b). This trend has occurred for all ages of young children. Although organized group programs are more widely utilized for 3- through 5-year-olds (because many such programs do not accept infants and toddlers), the use of organized group programs for infants rose from 5% to 14% in less than 3 years between June 1982 and winter 1984–1985 (U.S. Bureau of Census, 1987b).

As supplemental child care arrangements have moved outside the family network, so too has the responsibility to assure that the settings parents choose provide safe, developmentally appropriate experiences for young children. There are a number of regulatory mechanisms by which the quality of child care settings can be safeguarded. Such mechanisms are both public and private, formal and informal. Licensing is central to all other forms of regulation because it establishes the requirements for legal operation, but it is only one form of regulation. This chapter outlines some of the various forms that regulation can take and in particular highlights accreditation as one method of voluntary regulation.

FORMS OF REGULATION OF CHILD CARE

Regulation of child care arrangements provides systems for maintaining good conditions for young children by setting standards, determining whether or not they are met, and applying sanctions when there is noncompliance. Standards may be set publicly for all programs or by individual parents, staff, professional organizations, or public or private funding sources. When programs do not comply with the standards, they face closing, withdrawal or nonenrollment of individual children, or loss of staff, status, or funding. In all its forms, regulation offers a powerful tool for assuring and improving the quality of services provided to young children. No one form of regulation can be considered in isolation. For example, although parents' personal standards are extremely important to assure the well-being of their particular child, public regulation is also needed to assure a safe context within which personal standards may operate for all children.

Figure 10.1 diagrams the various types of regulatory mechanisms that affect early childhood programs. Basic to all others is the licensing system, the process used by states to grant permission for programs to operate. Such permission is granted in exchange for demonstrated compliance with preset standards, which typically involve adult/child ratios, staff qualifica-

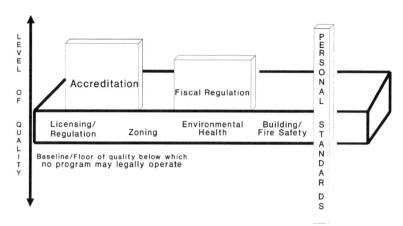

FIG. 10.1   Regulatory systems operating with regard to early childhood programs.

tions, and requirements for parental involvement, the physical environment, and health and safety.

In addition to licensing, early childhood programs—like any other community service or business—must conform with zoning regulations and sanitation, building, and fire safety codes. Together with licensing standards, these stipulations determine a baseline or floor of quality below which no service may legally operate (Morgan, 1979).

Regulatory systems that define the legal basis for operation are not the only forms of regulation applied to child care programs. Other systems include accreditation and fiscal regulation. Although licensing codes pertain to all programs except those legally exempt, these additional forms of regulation are often selectively applied. Like licensing, they set forth qualifications that must be met. In exchange, programs receive recognition, status, or funding. Generally these systems require licensure as a necessary condition for consideration.

One other regulatory system is diagrammed in Fig. 10.1—the system of personal standards. Personal standards are depicted as spanning both sides of the baseline, because they can vary greatly, depending on one's values, degree of understanding of the needs of young children, and possession of resources to act on that knowledge. These standards may be imposed by parents or practitioners, and they play an important role in determining the quality of programs actually provided. Personal standards also combine to form the basis for all other standards, as when widely shared definitions are translated into licensing codes, stipulations for funding, or accreditation criteria.

Personal standards often far exceed the public baseline of acceptability. For example, some of the states with the largest number of centers accredited by the National Academy of Early Childhood Programs, of the National Association for the Education of Young Children (NAEYC), are states with a history of less stringent state standards. We believe that this occurs because program directors whose personal standards greatly exceed the public baseline have been eager to demonstrate their compliance with higher standards.

Similarly, parents' personal standards play an important role in assuring quality. Think what would happen if every parent refused to put an infant in a group with more than six babies and fewer than two adults, the numbers recommended by NAEYC (1984). If this were to occur, 49 of the 50 states could improve their licensing standards on these aspects. Only Maryland currently limits groups of infants to no more than six and requires a staff/child ratio of 1:3. Kansas and Massachusetts come close; Kansas sets its group size at 9 with a staff/child ratio of 1:3, and Massachusetts limits group size to 7 infants and requires 2 staff members with the group. In many cases the improvements would be significant. Less than half (24) of the states currently regulate group size for infants, despite its documented importance to program quality (Howes, 1983; Howes & Rubenstein, 1985; Ruopp, Travers, Glantz, & Coelen, 1979). Of those regulating group size, 6 states permit groups of 12 or more infants (Morgan, 1987).

Because personal standards depend both on knowledge and on the resources to act on that knowledge, efforts must be geared to improving both these areas. These efforts must include large-scale public education efforts to help parents and others understand the components of high-quality programs as well as legislation and other activities to increase accessibility to good programs. For early childhood teachers, there must be increased opportunities to improve professional practice as well as policies that facilitate good practice in programs.

To summarize Fig. 10.1, public regulation establishes three levels of quality for early childhood programs: programs below the legal floor, which are operating illegally and are subject to legal sanction; programs at the baseline, which provide legally acceptable care; and programs above the baseline, which exceed the state's definition of acceptability. Personal standards may be operating at all three levels, while additional requirements may be applied to acceptable programs through accreditation or fiscal regulation. Let us now look in more detail at some of these forms of regulation that are so critical in determining the conditions under which many of today's young children spend a considerable portion of their time.

Licensing

What the three levels of quality look like varies tremendously from state to state because of variation in state licensing codes. For example, 7 states have no educational requirements for early childhood teachers, whereas 10 stipulate that teachers not only must have substantial amounts of preservice training but must complete regular inservice training requirements as well (Morgan, 1987).

The floor of quality is also affected by exemptions. In some states the floor has some fairly large holes. For example, about half the states exempt part-day programs from licensure, often because too few regulatory staff are available for enforcement. Another fairly common exemption is church-based programs (12 states), although most states impose some standards; the legality of this exemption is under court challenge. Many exempt programs voluntarily meet or exceed baseline standards, but there is no guarantee that all do.

It is important that states set some level of necessary conditions that will assure all children's well-being in any out-of-home setting. An effective licensing process, which has this as its goal, provides official recognition that the state has a responsibility to assure that families who seek child care in the community can choose among settings that provide safe, developmentally appropriate experiences for their young children. As more and more young children spend large portions of their days in such settings, this public responsibility has taken on greater significance. Licensing provides necessary consumer protection for parents and their young children; it is not an intrusion into private family matters (NAEYC, 1987).

Licensure also acknowledges the valuable public service that early childhood programs provide. Good programs nurture, protect, and educate young children while allowing parents to work or to participate in educational or job-training programs. They provide an essential service to business and industry, because parents who know that their children are safe and well cared for are more productive workers and are less likely to be absent or tardy (Fernandez, 1986; Galinsky & Friedman, 1986). Communities that have taken the lead in the provision of early childhood programs find they have a powerful incentive for economic development. And in addition to all the benefits they achieve right now, good early childhood programs are also a worthwhile investment in the future, reaping their cost many times over in savings of costly remedial programs that too often are needed when young children's needs are ignored. Because of their importance to society, states have a powerful incentive to assure that good programs are provided to all children.

A number of features are essential to a well-designed and effectively implemented licensing system (NAEYC, 1987). First, compliance must be made mandatory. The best-written regulations are meaningless unless they are enforced. Sanctions are needed so that licensing requirements have binding force. NAEYC's position on licensing suggests that enforcement provisions give the state the ability to impose fines, revoke or suspend licenses, and take emergency action to close programs in the rare cases that are dangerous to children (NAEYC, 1987).

Second, licensing systems designed to provide basic protection of children should apply to all programs, without limiting definitions, exemptions, or exceptions. Standards should be applied to all programs, regardless of sponsorship, length of program day, and age or number of children served (NAEYC, 1987). Licensing is the legal system that defines the parameters of legal operation, and equal opportunity to demonstrate compliance with licensing standards is therefore essential to assuring a fair system.

Finally, standards should reflect the nature of the setting and the number of children served. There are generally different standards for family day care and for centers, reflecting the significant differences in size and the nature of the two kinds of operation. Standards should not, however, differ in the extent to which they protect children. Current research findings related to program quality—group size, adult/child ratio, staff knowledge and training in early childhood development, parental involvement and access, positive discipline, developmental appropriateness of the program, and health and safety—should be reflected in the licensing code.

Effective licensing systems are highly visible and accessible to parents as well as to providers. Such accessibility is important to assure the effectiveness of the role of licensing in consumer protection. Moreover, a highly visible system, with standards that are commonly understood, can help to increase public understanding of the components of good quality care and can act to raise the personal standards of parents seeking care.

A highly visible system is particularly important when states use registration systems to regulate family day care. Registration does not include an inspection prior to registration. Some registration systems are completely voluntary; others rely on random inspection of homes on a rotating basis. In such systems, parents must play a particularly active role in inspecting and monitoring the quality of the program. In fact, voluntary registration systems can easily provide a false sense of security to parents. Having obtained the provider's name from a publicly maintained list, parents are often shocked to learn that no quality-control mechanisms apply.

All the stipulations mentioned here require funding for the implementation and monitoring of compliance with licensing standards. In some states, enforcement staff are ridiculously overstretched. A more than 200% increase in the number of licensed early childhood programs (NAEYC, 1985) during the budget-cutting 1980s has seriously compromised many states' ability to assure quality programs. In some states, this has led to the consideration of deregulation or voluntary regulation, especially for family day care, a solution like that of the ostrich who hides its head in the sand.

Other Legal Requirements

In addition to licensing requirements, early childhood programs are subject to building and fire safety requirements and sanitation codes. Each set of requirements is locally applied and enforced by a different agency. Although the trend is for such codes to be uniform statewide, additional local requirements may also be applied. NAEYC believes that inspection, monitoring, and enforcement of all applicable codes should be coordinated to ensure that public personnel and fiscal resources are wisely used and to avoid undue delays, barriers to service, and unnecessary red tape (NAEYC, 1987).

Another legal requirement critical to child care is zoning, the regulation of land use by local planners under the state enabling law. Zoning restrictions have sometimes hindered the opening of new child care services. NAEYC concurs with the American Planning Association (1987) that center programs and family day care should be regarded as a needed community service rather than as a commercial use and should be permitted in any residential zone. Center programs are essentially no different from elementary schools in terms of traffic and usage, except that it is rare to find a center as large as the smallest of schools. Rather than rule out early childhood programs, city planning should work to include these essential services as they develop new housing and commercial uses.

Family day care homes have even less impact on the neighborhood, particularly if regulated. More than half the states (29) limit the number of children who can be cared for in family day care to six or fewer (Morgan, 1987), no different from a large family in terms of neighborhood impact. There is no reason to prohibit family day care services in any zone in which families are permitted to live or in which working families might need child care services. This reasoning also applies to condominiums and apartment complexes. A recent tragedy in Virginia demonstrates the consequences of restrictions on family day care. A mother who stopped providing family day care because it was not allowed in her apartment complex found another job but could not make the child care arrangements she needed for her school-age children. Left with an 8-year-old babysitter on a school holiday, her children burned to death when their home caught fire.

Fiscal Regulation

Although the standards that form the basis for legal program operation are essential, they are not the only regulatory systems used to assure quality services for children. Money is seldom given out without some strings attached. This is essentially what fiscal regulation is all about: setting certain standards that must be met in order to receive funds. For the most part, fiscal regulation is carried out by the federal or state government, although it is conceivable that other funders may also set standards as a condition of funding. As one would suspect, fiscal regulation provides a powerful motivating force.

The federal Head Start program provides an excellent example of fiscal regulation. This program is extremely prescriptive in the standards that it sets for program operation. In fact, the provision of such high standards is one of the reasons for the program's success, because when there has been a need to reauthorize funds, evidence of the results of compliance in terms of student outcomes has been most convincing. Several states that have recently instituted Head Start–like prekindergarten programs are also requiring programs to meet standards often higher than their state licensing codes.

Fiscal regulation may or may not impact programs other than those directly receiving funds. One example of a broad effect occurred recently in Massachusetts. A serious problem for early childhood programs is the difficulty in recruiting and retaining qualified staff, because of the low wage scale in such programs. As part of the Governor's Day Care Initiative, Massachusetts instituted a wage initiative in state-funded programs that significantly raised teaching salaries. As one would expect, private sector programs were soon forced to raise their salaries and benefits in order to remain competitive. The primary source for the additional salary money (particularly in unsubsidized programs) was parent fees, heightening problems of affordability. Projects are now underway to try to address this problem as well.

Fiscal regulation, although an important tool for assuring good programs for children, cannot function in isolation. When higher standards are required only of public sector programs, what often results is a two-tier system of program quality. Often trapped in programs of lesser quality are those children of low- and moderate-income families who do not qualify for (or cannot receive) subsidized care and who are unable to afford other programs.

Accreditation

Typically accreditation is a voluntary system. Several states offer accreditation processes; specialized groups, such as Montessori organizations, also accredit programs. NAEYC's accreditation system, operated by the National Academy of Early Childhood Programs, is unique in that it is a nationally recognized system open to all center-based early childhood education programs, including before- and after-school programs for children ages 6 to 8.

Although the Academy and its accreditation system officially began operation in September 1985, the development of the system extends back to the early 1980s. It grew out of the recognition of the tremendous growth in the number of early childhood programs and the need to support the quality of services provided to increasing numbers of young children. It is important to note that the Academy was not originally conceived as an accreditation system only. First and foremost, the goal was to develop a system that would stimulate and support lasting, ongoing improvements in the programs available to young children and their families. We were not just looking for a system that would identify the top 100 programs throughout the country; we were trying to develop a system that would encourage all programs to improve the level of services they provided. An important—and intended—benefit of the system is that it provides a way for consumers and the general public to recognize high-quality programs, but this goal is secondary to that of achieving real and lasting improvements in programs serving young children.

Much of the initial effort in developing the accreditation process revolved around building a consensus as to what characteristics define high-quality programs, which became the Academy's Criteria for High Quality. This process occurred over several years and drew upon the knowledge and practical experience of thousands of early childhood educators throughout the country. The Criteria address all areas affecting program provision: interactions among staff and children, curriculum, staff-parent interaction, staff qualifications and development, administration, staffing, physical environment, health and safety, nutrition and food service, and evaluation (NAEYC, 1984).

The Criteria are applied in a three-step accreditation process. The first and most important step of the process is the *self-study*. During the self-study process, programs judge their activities in relation to the Criteria, determine their particular strengths and areas needing improvement, and go about making needed changes. This process is designed to be collaborative and requires input from the director, teachers, and parents. It is time consuming, but directors invariably report that it is a worthwhile investment because of the increased communication, sense of teamwork, and direct benefits for children that result from the process.

The self-study process is self-initiated and self-paced. Programs determine how quickly they proceed through the self-study and how they will go about making needed improvements. Because changes are self-determined, they tend to be more lasting. Time after time, directors report to us that changes they have tried to initiate for years are now occurring as staff themselves determine what changes are needed.

Once improvements have been made and staff believe that the program is in substantial compliance with the Criteria, an extensive program description is completed and submitted to the Academy. The program description provides a uniform procedure for programs to report their compliance with each criterion.

Following the submission of the program description, the second stage of the accreditation process begins. This is the *validation* stage, during which specially trained early childhood educators work with directors to verify the accuracy of the program description. Validators make sample observations of several classrooms, consider samplings of written records and policies, and collect additional information from the director. Validators do not make the accreditation decision; their function is to provide a second objective view of the program, compare that with the submitted program description, and then discuss the results of the validation with the center director. This process allows the director to provide clarifying or additional information and gives explanations for nonvalidated criteria. Directors sign a release form signifying that the validated information is an accurate portrayal of the program and that the visit was conducted properly.

The actual accreditation decision is made by a three-member commission. Commissioners review validated program descriptions and must reach consensus as to whether accreditation is granted or deferred. Each commission is made up of a diverse group of early childhood professionals—program administrators, teacher educators, researchers, and others whose training and experience give them a national perspective on early childhood programs.

Accreditation does not require programs to achieve 100% compliance with each criterion. Rather, the process is based on professional consensus as to whether the program substantially complies with the Academy's Criteria. Experience shows that some of the Criteria are weighted more heavily than others; especially stressed are the areas of interactions among staff and children and the nature of the curriculum (Bredekamp & Apple, 1986). These areas are difficult to stipulate in a legal mandate. Accreditation criteria, reflecting professional consensus, can and do give very specific guidelines as to what these areas should look like. Licensing standards, establishing legal limits, generally stipulate that a curriculum must exist but do not give specific guidance as to what it should be. Essentially the difference is one of legal versus professional requirements. Although licensing establishes a floor of acceptability, accreditation recognizes program excellence. Because they do not provide legal permission to operate, accreditation criteria may be applied more subjectively than licensing standards. The two systems work in tandem to assure the quality of programs for children.

Accreditation does set a floor for excellence, as evidenced by the fact that not all programs achieve accreditation. The floor of excellence is not a rigid line, because accreditation decisions reflect professional consensus and not a certain percentage of points on a scale. There are clear and consistent differences between accredited and nonaccredited programs, however (Bredekamp & Apple, 1986), and the reliability and validity of the classroom observation scale that provides the bulk of the information on which the accreditation decision is based have been established (Bredekamp, 1986).

To date, approximately 85% of the programs that have applied for accreditation have been accredited in their initial consideration (S. Bredekamp, personal communication, November 1987). Deferred programs are given specific guidance in the areas needing improvement and are encouraged to reapply for consideration once changes have been made. The deferred programs are, in fact, following that process, demonstrating that the goal of the accreditation system—to stimulate real and lasting improvements—is being achieved. Accredited programs are also given suggestions as to how they might improve, although obviously the need for improvement is not as extensive as in the deferred programs. During the 3-year period of accreditation, programs submit annual reports documenting that these improvements have been made and that there is continued compliance with the Criteria.

Now that this system is almost 2 years old, the first annual reports have been assessed (Bredekamp & Berby, 1987). Not only have the suggested improvements been made, but additional ones have been made as well. Several programs have instituted career ladders and salary scales with regular pay increases. This is a real testimonial that the system is in fact working to increase professionalism while addressing a serious problem confronting the field. Children are clearly reaping the benefits, too. Programs report that the commitment to provide a high-quality program has remained high and that this enthusiasm is shared by directors, teachers, and families. It truly appears to be a system that works.

One of the initial concerns was that accreditation might be perceived as an elitist activity, open only to a select part of the early childhood community. Happily that has not occurred. As of November 7, 1987, nearly 2,000 programs from 48 states are involved in some stage of accreditation, representing every type of early childhood program—private, public, for-profit, nonprofit, part-day, full-day, Montessori, even public school kindergarten programs. This diversity is also represented among the 400-plus accredited programs, which come from 47 states.

THE REGULATORY CONTEXT

How do these different regulatory systems work in conjunction with one another? How are they alike, and how are they different? An important point to bear in mind is that each type of regulatory mechanism plays a somewhat different role, although their functions do overlap.

The systems work best together when they are planned with coordination in mind. Frustration is high for providers who are trying to establish a program, and for parents who are desperately awaiting the service, if the licensing code says one thing whereas zoning regulations say another. Zoning codes should not make additional requirements for the protection of children; that is the responsibility of the state licensing system. Coordination is further enhanced when zoning and municipal codes use definitions consistent with those in state licensing law.

It is useful to think of the various types of regulation on a continuum of objectivity. Licensing, because it grants public permission, must be strictly objective. At the other end of the scale are personal standards. Parents' personal standards are clearly the most subjective, whereas practitioners' personal standards are ideally influenced by professional knowledge and practice and are applied using both objective and subjective decisions. Accreditation, because it is applied to a self-selected group and because it relies heavily on professional judgment, includes both objective and subjective decisions. The application of professional judgment is particularly important in this regard and demonstrates an essential difference between licensing and accreditation. The state's role is not to assess the program's compliance with professional standards; the state decides whether the program is providing at least acceptable service. Licensing codes often refer to professional standards, but the standards are set by the profession.

In closing, let us look at a fictional situation in which all these regulatory systems might be combined. Assume for the moment that John and Mary Smith live in a state with very stringent licensing standards for child care and in a community with a number of accredited programs. Their child attends an accredited program for several years. One day the Smiths move to another state, which unfortunately has much less stringent licensing requirements. None of the early childhood programs in their new community have gotten involved in the accreditation process.

Mary and John are quite dismayed by the level of quality in the programs they visit. So they take action. They start writing letters to the editor of the local paper about the quality of child care they are finding. They talk to local reporters and convince them to write stories about the harmful situations that young children are being exposed to. Enrolling their child in the best center in town, Mary and John convince the director to start working toward accreditation and convince other community programs to get involved, too. Both Mary and John lobby their state representatives to strengthen the licensing standards. They work on building statewide support until stronger licensing standards are considered and adopted. A few years pass, and a new state legislator is elected. This legislator proposes deregulating child care and is voted out of office in the next election, because everyone agrees that the children's well-being in child care cannot be compromised.

A dream? For now, but there are glimmers of hope that this may come to pass. As a result of large-scale public education efforts by groups like NAEYC, the Child Care Action Campaign, the Children's Defense Fund, and the Public Television Outreach Alliance, to name just a few, we are seeing the advent of a new awareness about the need to assure the quality of and access to programs for young children. Nearly all the states (41) have revised their licensing requirements for centers since 1982, 19 of them since 1985, and in nearly every case the change is an improvement (Morgan, 1987). New legislative efforts at both the state and federal levels to provide financial support and strengthen state licensing provisions look promising. Interest in accreditation—among centers and parents seeking programs for their children—is high and continues to grow. These are glimmers, but nonetheless they suggest that there can be and will be a public commitment to assuring quality for young children.

DISCUSSION

Dr. Willer was asked to elaborate on the concern that the accreditation process might play into the increasing divide between parents who can afford to pay for quality care and those who cannot, further separating the levels of care within the child care system. She replied that this had been a fear throughout the development of the accreditation process, particularly because there is so little money in the early childhood field and although accreditation fees are low, they may seem high to a low-budget program. The Academy is finding, however, that accreditation is "a very fundable idea"; it is a low-cost item that allows a potential funder to make a really lasting improvement in the the quality of services that are being provided. Some of the major funders of subsidized programs are looking to accreditation as a means of supporting the quality of care. She noted again that accreditation is being used by all segments of the early childhood community.

One participant expressed reservations, stemming from her experience in training, about the ability of child care providers to be objective and honest about their own performance. Dr. Willer pointed to the collaborative nature of the self-study. In evaluating staff-child interactions, for example, first the teacher does the assessment, then the program director does a separate assessment and the two compare notes. The parents also are involved, so there is multiple input. Moreover, the evaluation tool is a very specific instrument that breaks down staff-child interactions into a number of different variables that are addressed individually. Dr. Willer acknowledged that there is room for ongoing improvement in the accreditation process, however. Terms like *developmentally appropriate* mean different things to different people, so the Academy has had to develop position papers and more specific guidance about what is intended. The Academy is also developing videos as training material, to help people implement what they say they want to do.

11
Enforcement of Child Care Regulations

Earline D. Kendall
Belmont College

Child care regulation, plagued by controversy, continues to be a hot potato for politicians and an unresolved issue for parents. Consequently, the question of whether regulation should be in the hands of federal or state agencies goes unanswered. State licensing is based on minimal standards, which vary tremendously from state to state. Morgan (1987) found that 15 states apply general program requirements to all age groups, whereas 9 states provide detailed requirements for infants and toddlers. Half the states set staff/child ratios for 6-month-old infants at 1:4; South Carolina has a 1:8 ratio for this age group. Federal regulation, which is frequently resisted by both child care providers and clients, has been no more promising than state licensing and has proved difficult to implement at the state level. Fiene and Nixon (1985) estimated that there are 118,000 licensed child care providers, who serve 1.2 million children daily at an annual cost of $6.3 billion, but that less than 1% of state day care funds is spent on monitoring child care. The current debate on child care licensing differs little from debates in the past except for specific issues being discussed: the increasing numbers of mothers returning to the workplace during the first few months of their babies' lives, the role of voluntary national accreditation, and the scandals over alleged sexual abuse in day care. The debate over unchanging problems in licensing continues, but these new considerations have an impact on the solutions that can be found.

Individualism continues to be a salient characteristic of the national posture, and Americans' belief in the right to rear their children without government intervention fuels a debate that reflects competing ideologies in day care. As one study notes, "Our society has been deeply influenced by the traditions of modern individualism" (Bellah, Madsen, Sullivan, Swidler, & Tipton, 1985, p. 303). Many Americans are reluctant to let government decide what is right and what is wrong for children. But even while they seek deregulation of child care, Americans clearly expect a reasonable level of care and seek to prevent such problems as sexual abuse in child care settings. Differences such as those between the competing ideologies of proprietary and nonprofit programs (Dublin, 1984) plague child care. Suspicion on both sides interferes with cooperative efforts of proprietary and nonprofit child care agencies. During the Reagan administration, calls for deregulation and distancing of the federal government from child care regulation have been backed by cries for parental freedom of choice (Lehrman & Pace, 1985). Nonprofit and proprietary child care programs serve different populations, with different philosophies and different support. Federal dollars for child care virtually disappeared during the 1980s, and proprietary child care increased during the same period. As federal support for nonprofit child care evaporated, so did federal regulation of child care. As a result, day care licensing efforts have suffered.

AN OVERVIEW OF CHILD CARE LICENSING

The State Role

Gwen Morgan (e.g., as cited in Fiene & Nixon, 1985) emphasizes day care licensing as a foundation for quality. As agencies attempt to improve services for children, families, and child care providers, licensing sets minimum standards for health, education, and safety. However, as Sciarra and Dorsey (1979) pointed out, "requirements are usually minimal and measurable, but they do not guarantee either quality of care or protection to the child" (p. 30). Historically, child care licensing was "jammed" into existing statutes regulating 24-hour child care (Class & Orton, 1980).

State social service agencies are generally the regulators of child care. In a few states, such as Maryland and Kansas, the health department licenses day care. Utah has a new Office of Licensing. A few states, including Massachusetts and South Carolina, have special offices for children; these states license child care through the same offices that handle other child-advocacy activities (Morgan, Stevenson, Fiene, & Stephens, 1987).

States revise their licensing standards periodically, adding or subtracting the dictates of ad hoc committees or current administrations. Exemptions made under such circumstances tend to be based on whims or political needs. For instance, states may exempt church-sponsored programs in one revision and rescind their exemption in the next (Blank, 1984). "Presently, 12 states exempt church-run child care programs from state child care regulation. While half are Southern states . . . an equal number are concentrated in the Midwest" (Phillips, 1987b, p. 9). Esoteric or inappropriate licensing issues sometimes become part of state standards in spite of widespread participation in the process. Public hearings held on the draft give providers and clients the opportunity to respond to proposed changes or to lobby for others. However, as Phillips noted, "Policy issues are often characterized as a moving target. They seldom are resolved with any finality, but rather reappear in different places in different forms" (p. 11).

When licensing regulations are finally promulgated, "standards become lawlike" (Morgan, 1984a, p. 168), carrying the weight of statutes and reflecting whatever biases are operating in that state's committee at the time standards are reviewed. Licensing regulations are backed by the power of law, with limits to this power. "A license is legal permission to operate" (Terpstra, 1985, p. 283); licensors issue or refuse to issue licenses based on their investigations of the child care settings.

In 1984, Kendall and Walker surveyed state licensing offices. Responses to their survey indicated that licensing dollars were dwindling and fewer staff members were being assigned to licensing units at the very time when the number and types of complaints received about day care were on the increase. Fiene and Nixon (1985) also reported that even in a period of allegations of sexual abuse in child care settings, when parents need assurance that state licensing programs provide protection for their children, fiscal cutbacks have caused staff cuts and workload increases. They noted that some states are registering family day care homes instead of licensing them, a cheaper system that shifts the locus of control in meeting registration requirements from the licensor to the provider. Many states have simplified their monitoring procedures to make them less onerous for providers, particularly those in the private sector. Moreover, the pressure to reduce the general level of state regulation and to encourage private market forces has further reduced the federal government's role.

In 1984, the Child Care Action Campaign (Morgan, 1984b) pointed out that the publicity surrounding the sexual abuse allegations underscored the importance of public policy efforts to address child care issues Kearney found in 1984 that 34 states were considering or had adopted changes in policies regarding child care, but these revisions reflect regulatory efforts that are fragmented at best.

National Regulation Efforts

During World War II, programs often operated around the clock to accommodate mothers working in war-related industries. After the war ended, hours of operation were shortened. Curtailed schedules continued during the 1960s and 1970s, when day care served two basic purposes: assisting welfare mothers in holding jobs or in obtaining job training and providing compensatory education and intellectual stimulation for their children. As a part of the War on Poverty during the Johnson administration, the federal government encouraged the provision of high-quality child care for low-income children.

Federal Interagency Day Care Regulations. During the period of focusing on compensatory education, the Federal Interagency Day Care Regulations (FIDCR) were developed, in part out of a sense that state day care licensing was "hopeless" (Class & Orton, 1980, p. 9). FIDCR soon became the subject of heated political controversy. Even to require federally funded agencies to meet FIDCR guidelines was regarded as an intrusion of the federal government into an area that could be state regulated (Grotberg, 1980).

When FIDCR enforcement failed, efforts to examine state licensing enforcement increased. In 1976, the Administration for Children, Youth and Families (ACYF) launched the Comparative Licensing Study (U.S. Department of Health and Human Services, 1982). In an update of that study, Collins (1983) reported little change from 1978 to 1982 except for greater emphasis on group size and infant care. Regulation revisions had responded only slightly to societal changes such as the number of mothers returning to work soon after childbirth or to increased research findings related to child care. Weintraub and Furman (in press) reviewed day care initiatives from WPA in the 1930s and the recommendations of the Children's Bureau for minimal standards in the 1940s, through the publication of FIDCR in 1968, the National Day Care Study (NDCS) in 1974, the Title XX amendment to the Social Security Act in 1975, and the Appropriateness Study of FIDCR in 1978, to the suspension of FIDCR in 1980.

NAEYC's Position on Licensing. Realizing that the individual states are not likely to seek uniform standards and that the federal government's attempts at child care regulation have generally failed, the National Association for the Education of Young Children (NAEYC, 1987) developed a position statement on licensing of center and family day home programs, predicated on the belief that regulation is necessary as consumer protection for parents and their children. NAEYC bases its voluntary national accreditation system on the requirement that only early childhood programs meeting applicable state regulations will be considered for NAEYC endorsement. NAEYC opposes any exemption, regardless of sponsor, number of children served, or length of the program's day. This strong position statement is expected to be useful to child care advocates in supporting strengthened child care standards and legislative efforts.

BARRIERS TO REGULATION

Child care regulation faces several barriers involving longstanding American traditions, including personal liberty, individualism, and the separation of church and state. The enduring right of parents to determine what is best for their children and the prerogative of churches to sponsor programs without government intervention continue to impede regulation in the child care field. Deregulation in other areas of public concern, such as the airline industry, has also established a climate in which regulation is perceived negatively in general, and some specific concerns in the child care field can be identified as barriers to regulatory efforts.

Barriers to FIDCR Implementation

When the federal government undertook the regulation of programs receiving federal funds, numerous problems resulted. Grotberg (1980) cited seven barriers to compliance with FIDCR: (a) changes in the day care market; (b) the absence of agreement regarding the purposes of day care; (c) federal regulations having no federal administration; (d) the absence of a federal implementation plan or clear delegation of responsibility; (e) an absence of procedures for monitoring and enforcing standards; (f) an absence of agreement regarding the purposes of standards; and (g) differences in philosophy and attitudes toward regulation.

Morgan (1984a), in suggesting reforms of the child care regulatory system, has emphasized the importance of removing these barriers to child care development. Unless the barriers to both compliance and day care development are overcome in the implementation of the ABC bill, the problems that plagued FIDCR will also plague ABC, even though the present climate surrounding child care differs in that child care is now seen as a societal issue, not a women's issue, and regulation is viewed as responsible practice, not an infringement of parental rights or an indictment of families who use child care. Perhaps we can, and will, learn from past experiences. Current efforts toward federal child care legislation may offer the best chance in a number of years to attack child care problems across the 50 states.

The Roles of Licensing Counselors as Barriers

The structure of the licensing system itself can function as a barrier to effective regulation of child care.

Role Conflict. State licensing agents generally function as both monitors and resources to child care programs, thus attempting to regulate and advise at the same time. Generally, they prefer to consult with providers rather than to enforce standards. Unless they are health or fire-safety officials, licensors typically have few prescriptive powers, and then only in the area of facility improvement.

Although licensing counselors represent a broad range of back-grounds, experience, skills, and training, their training is often acquired on the job. The result is an absence of coherent and coordinated preparation. The licensing counselor frequently feels conflicted in role, frustrated in practice, and inadequate in providing means for program improvement.

Case Overload. A related barrier to child care regulation is insufficient staff to monitor the programs. As individual states have provided fewer child care funds, the number of staff members in licensing agencies has also decreased. State departments have required licensing counselors to oversee other aspects of agency work in addition to child care licensing (Kendall & Walker, 1984). As a result, the caseload of licensing counselors often has become too large to manage more than a cursory overview of monitored programs. NAEYC recognizes this problem as a barrier to sound regulatory practice and addresses oversized caseloads in its position statement on licensing (see the recommendations at the end of this chapter).

Morgan (1984a), in reviewing needed reforms, indicated that the poorly staffed regulatory agencies in most states pose barriers to effective licensing practices. She viewed licensing as part of a systems approach, with regulation a function of agencies engaged in licensing, zoning, building and fire safety, and health and sanitation inspection. If problems in the system are to be addressed effectively and the regulatory maze in day care licensing is to be improved, an integrated approach is needed in all four of these areas.

Special Licensing Cases

Another barrier to enforcement of child care regulations is the variety of program options operating in most communities. Individual states find that group care standards do not adequately address the myriad child care programs currently in operation. States have been adding standards to address the particular needs of programs offering therapeutic, crisis, and night care for the last couple of decades, and it is likely that an increase in special care standards will continue into the next decade.

Registration. Voluntary registration of family day homes (FDH) is regarded in several states as a method to reduce licensing costs and to avoid resistance to child care regulation. The increasing numbers of women returning to the workplace soon after childbirth have caused enormous growth in the use of family homes. FDHs appear to be the most appropriate day care choice when children are under the age of 3.

Registration is a regulatory reform mechanism, used by several states, that transfers registration and certification responsibility from the licensing agency to the child care provider. Investigation of child care settings occurs only when consumers complain that a provider is not meeting the list of requirements or if a home is selected for a spot-check by the licensing agency. Turnover in family day care is such that registration cannot be kept up to date. Self-monitoring cannot possibly provide necessary safeguards, but registration "may affect the quality of better providers" (Morgan, 1984a, p. 170). Registration is feasible only for FDHs where small numbers of children are in care, usually no more than five in a home.

Infant and Toddler Regulations. Some form of mandatory regulatory oversight is required when larger groups of children are involved. States did not pass infant and toddler standards until the 1970s, when increasing numbers of mothers returned to work soon after childbirth. Group care of infants and toddlers presents particularly significant licensing concerns, because of the overwhelming evidence in a number of studies (Kendall, 1983) that children in diapers are particularly at risk for the spread of disease through day care contact. Hepatitis A and diarrhea outbreaks connected to day care have been tracked by the Centers for Disease Control in several states. According to Klein (1987):

> Infectious diseases, often occurring in epidemics, are to be expected in group day care because of the susceptibility of infants and toddlers to infection and the ready transmission of infection in the day care setting. Children in day care have more respiratory and gastrointestinal infections and are at higher risk for meningitis. (p. 9)

Zigler and Muenchow (1987) suggested implications for policy related
to controlling the spread of disease, including the same improvements in
day care that have long been indicated—smaller group size, sufficient staff
with specialized training in child development and hygiene, and reduced
staff turnover—and indicate the need for a total overhaul of the entire
process of day care licensing by redefining both state and federal roles. Kendall, Aronson, Goldberg, and Smith (1987) suggested procedures for training both child care providers and licensing personnel in preventing the
spread of disease. In several studies (see Osterholm, Klein, Aronson, &
Pickering, 1987), it was found that appropriate handwashing procedures
have markedly reduced the spread of disease in day care settings. States
have rushed to add handwashing guidelines to standards. Clearly, policy
changes and training procedures are needed to protect children, their
parents, caregivers, and the community at large from the diseases spread
through day care contacts.

Corporate Child Care. One of the fastest-growing sources of child care
is that provided as an employee benefit. At least six states now offer tax incentives for businesses providing child care services to employees (Kearney, 1984). Along with improving public schools, states are attempting to
provide incentives to companies that shoulder some costs of initiating child
care or that bear part of the ongoing costs. As corporate and state initiatives
increase, there is also an increase in the number of resource agencies working with industry to determine the child care option best suited to a particular company's needs and resources. The business community tends to
resist the traditional licensing quagmire, and its participation may provide
the needed catalyst for reform in some areas.

School-Age Licensing. As school systems make changes to accommodate educational reforms, before- and after-school child care needs also
are being explored. Church, neighborhood, day camp, and other programs
are inadequate in most communities to satisfy holiday and vacation needs
of elementary school children. Child care regulations written for day care
centers do not necessarily provide adequate guidelines for school-age
programs.

STATE SURVEY OF LICENSING

The special needs mentioned here serve to underscore the necessity for
licensing standards that better address a variety of situations. As society requires better provision for all its children, child care licensing becomes in-

creasingly complex. What we know about children and caring for them is not reflected in most state licensing standards and procedures.

In order to determine what states are doing currently to address changing day care regulation needs, I asked the 50 state agencies responsible for child care licensing: (a) whether the number and nature of complaints related to licensing have changed in the last 2 years; (b) how states address complaints; (c) whether different types of child care programs respond differently to day care regulation; and (d) whether state licensing agencies expect to increase or decrease child care standards in the future. Although the survey I report here did not attempt to cover all questions related to the current licensing concerns, 40 of the state agencies responded, and their comments enrich other findings reported here.

Complaints

The complaint reported by the largest number of states (22) was child abuse, followed by complaints related to staff-child ratios (reported by 18 states), supervision (18 states), and sanitation (14 states). These items were listed twice as often as the concerns of nutrition, discipline, overenrollment, and illegal operation (all of which received about equal mention, 5 to 9 states). Topics mentioned 3 or 4 times included equipment, facilities, unqualified staff, and program requirements. One licensing chief noted that parents are increasingly well informed, a factor that probably increases their complaints to licensing offices. The variety of complaints indicates a client awareness of what a high-quality child care program should provide.

When asked whether there was a difference in the nature of complaints over the last 2 years as compared with earlier periods, most (23) respondents said no. Those who saw a difference cited more child-abuse complaints (except for one state that received fewer complaints than 2 years ago). Four states indicated that the number of complaints "soared" or more than doubled in the last 2 years. Although California reported more than 10,000 complaints received last year by state and county offices, this number represented only a slight increase over the previous year. The increase in complaints related to illegal operation, overenrollment, and unlicensed family day homes may indicate renewed interest in mandatory regulation of child care.

States indicate uniform procedures for dealing with complaints, including immediate investigation, a stated time frame and plan for correcting problems, and fines or license revocation, followed by court action if the problem cannot be resolved. Legal-system delays and red-tape difficulties pose barriers to enforcement of standards in many states.

Responses to Regulation

Churches and for-profit programs are viewed as the sponsors most reluctant to comply with licensing regulations. Church programs continue to seek special status and view licensing as governmental intrusion, but states are allowing fewer exemptions to child care regulation. Increasing numbers of states are requiring church programs to comply with the same standards that other child care programs follow, or, in the case of two states, to register church programs rather than licensing them.

Family day home providers express feeling the least need for regulation. Large centers are more responsive to regulations than directors of small centers, who may have a more idiosyncratic view of childrearing, often related to the ways they reared their own children. Child care chains are seen as less likely to violate standards, more likely to have ample materials and equipment, but more apt to cut corners on staff. Employers offering child care want less red tape. Nonprofit programs correct problems quickly for fear of losing funding.

About half (21) of the respondents were willing to estimate the percentage of complaints related to type of sponsors (nonprofit, proprietary, employer-sponsored, day care chains, church programs, and family day homes). Of these, 7 stated that family day homes generated many more complaints, or from 40% to 85% of all child-care licensing complaints. In 7 states proprietary programs were negatively ranked, with as many as 40% to 85% of all complaints; in 6 states nonprofit programs received from 20% to 80% of all complaints. In 3 states child care chains have only one facility and thus generate few complaints, but in 3 other states child care chains reflect 40% to 60% of all complaints. Church programs account for 1% to 46% of the complaints, with fewer than 20% usual.

From state to state no pattern of problem programs emerged. In most states, however, complaints are not compiled according to the type of program investigated. These estimates indicate that any type of program can received scrutiny and that, depending on the area of the country, some program types generate more complaints than others. One respondent noted that the key to program quality is the quality of the program director, regardless of the type of sponsor.

Trends

When asked whether they saw a trend toward an increase or a decrease in child care regulations, twice as many respondents from the state licensing offices felt regulations were increasing. One respondent noted, however, that recent revisions were so comprehensive that the next changes would likely reduce the number of requirements. Another respondent stated that the next draft would come primarily from a panel of providers; therefore, a new code could be expected to have fewer regulations. Some states are attempting to write clearer standards, clarify record-keeping tasks, and include criminal-record checks.

The greatest number of changes is in the category of additional standards for options not currently covered by the state's code—sick-child care, crisis care, therapeutic care, night care, infant and toddler regulations, and school-age care. Public schools will likely assume a greater role in child care during the 1990s. Michigan's licensing officer noted the need for regulations addressing public school child care.

RECOMMENDATIONS

As states address new child care program standards, update fire and health regulations, and add standards for specialized programs, research findings that have implications for child care should be emphasized. For example, we know from the National Day Care Study (NDCS) that smaller class size improves the quality of the program and that individual children's needs are better met there than in large classes (Ruopp, Travers, Glantz, & Coelen, 1979). Further, the NDCS found that teachers with training in child development and early education provide better care than teachers who do not have appropriate training.

We also know that if diarrhea and hepatitis are to be avoided, infant and toddler programs require intensified hygiene practices. If substantial improvements in infant care are to occur, training for caregivers, administrators, and licensing counselors is imperative. Children in diapers can receive the care necessary for them to thrive at home or in family day homes. Because these problems are well documented and a small percentage of infants are in center care, licensing standards should prohibit center care of children under the age of 3.

A decrease in staff loads and an increase in staff training could make a major difference in the effectiveness of licensing counselors. The NAEYC position statement (1987) suggested a licensing counselor caseload of 50 centers, with never more than 75, in order to make a sufficient number of program inspections. If registration is used, NAEYC recommends that spot checks should be made in at least 20% of the homes, on a rotating and random basis. A program inspector might handle 500, but never more than 750 registered homes. NAEYC's position statement can serve as a standard. It concludes, "Licensing provides the necessary foundation of acceptable quality upon which all other efforts are built" (p. 68).

DISCUSSION

Much of the ensuing discussion focused on Dr. Kendall's controversial recommendation that child care for children under age 3 be limited to family day homes. Participants questioned whether any systematic research had been done on the health effects of different types of child care settings. The Centers for Disease Control have reported that the major problems with hepatitis A occur in larger centers with the longest hours, rather than in family day homes. Although their research has been conducted on a spotty basis, in response to outbreaks, and although outbreaks at large centers are more likely to receive attention than problems in family day homes, there has been a 20-state study that confirmed the higher risk to babies in states where licensing standards permit large numbers of children in care. Other studies have shown that group care for children in diapers is detrimental not only to the health of the children but to the health of the caregivers, the parents, and the community at large.

Some participants pointed out that individual child care settings vary widely in quality. Some family day homes are very poor, and some large centers are excellent places where infants thrive. It was generally agreed that the key is sanitation and that training of caregivers, especially in handwashing, is crucial. Dr. Kendall felt that given the high turnover in caregiving personnel, training and monitoring can never be adequate. She acknowledged that turnover is higher in family day homes than in centers but stressed that in such settings only a small number of infants is affected. Others persisted in the need to identify the characteristics of those centers in which infants do well and to look for ways in which center care for infants can incorporate the features that make family day care safer. Centers can be designed so that spaces for small groups of infants are partitioned off, with separate facilities for each group of four infants. New state standards requiring handwashing facilities adjacent to diapering facilities will also help.

Joseph Perrault, of Save the Children, pointed out that one of the reasons for the increase in complaints about child care may lie in the support system provided by child care resource and referral agencies. To the extent that parents are becoming better informed about what constitutes quality care and more comfortable with making complaints, the increase in complaints is a positive thing, if painful in the short run.

He also commented that the registration model for family day care functions not only as a regulatory system but as a community support system as well, through the Child Care Food Program. The food program has served to get family day care homes registered or licensed, and the financial reimbursement, training, and monitoring have resulted in improving the quality of family day care.

Nancy Travis, also of Save the Children, noted that although in some states there are many more complaints about family day homes than about centers, there are also many more family day homes than centers. She expressed a need to know more about how the complaints relate proportionally to the kinds of child care settings.

ACKNOWLEDGMENTS

The author expresses appreciation to Sharon M. Innes, Mozelle Core, and Betty Sherman for assistance with this chapter and to the many state licensing officers who responded to the survey reported here.

12

Insuring Child Care's Future:
The Continuing Crisis

Sharon Kalemkiarian
Insurance for Child Care Project

Although insurance may be the fourth largest single expenditure in the American family's budget, few Americans have any understanding of how this industry really works. Most of us have never read through an entire insurance policy. We see the industry as wealthy and powerful, and we hope that some of that money will be there for us when we need to file a claim.

For many years, child care providers found that insurance was there when they needed it. It was relatively cheap, easy to find, and rarely an area of attention or concern. A comprehensive general liability insurance policy could be purchased that covered injuries to the children while under the supervision of the program, whether on or off the premises. Family day care providers were often covered through their basic homeowner policies or through an inexpensive commercial policy. Insurance was just a part of doing business, a manageable expense that protected the program and the children.

In 1985, however, insurance premiums skyrocketed and policies were cancelled. As one cartoon depicted the crisis, the boat of child care was set adrift as insurance company executives jumped ship. Many causes for the crisis were alleged: profit gouging on the part of the insurance industry, a downturn in the insurance cycle, increasing claims paid out by the insurance companies, and the publicity about child abuse in child care programs. In each claim, there was some kernel of truth.

In fact, the crisis stemmed from a cause much more fundamental. America's financial and social institutions have not caught up with the changes in the American family. As more and more children are cared for outside their homes, the relatively new industry of child care has had to establish itself in our national economy and national psyche. The insurance industry, by its nature conservative and cautious, does not understand this new industry. It is afraid of any activities involving children, particularly children in great numbers. For the most part, the insurance industry has been unwilling to face the reality of children being in care, and it has been afraid to play its responsible role in helping people provide quality child care to America's families.

Yet child care programs need insurance. As managers who must meet the bottom line, whether in the public or the private sector, child care providers must protect their programs from catastrophic losses. And as professionals whose lives are dedicated to serving young children, child care providers want to be sure that injured children are compensated. Unless the need for child care is going to fade away, policymakers in government and industry will have to figure out how to insure this new service industry.

The experience since 1985 provides important lessons for insuring child care's future. This chapter summarizes the forces within the insurance industry, the insurance markets, and the child care profession that led to this unprecedented insurance crisis for child care. It assesses the long-term impact of liability insurance on the provision of child care services. And finally it outlines a plan of action that can assure a stable insurance future for our nation's children.

THE INSURANCE CRISIS: WHAT HAPPENED

To illustrate the chain of events since 1985, California is a useful case study. It may be a "worst-case" scenario, as California's child care programs were among the hardest hit in the nation. But the collapse of California's market and the various attempts to reconstitute that market through regulation or voluntary efforts are instructive of what works—and what does not work.

The first warning of trouble hit California's child care providers overnight: Mission Insurance Company cancelled over 6,000 family day care policies midterm. Mission was insolvent for reasons having nothing to do with these policies, which were a very small percentage of their total business. The company had a virtual monopoly on these policies in California; without Mission, these 6,000-plus family day care providers had no other insurance options. A lawsuit was filed successfully by the California

Federation of Family Day Care Associations to reinstate the policies (California Federation of Family Day Care Associations v. Mission Insurance Co., 1985). Pressure was also applied to Mission by the state regulators, who urged the company to offer temporary extension on the cancelled policies. Eventually another company picked up Mission's business, but at four times the price. This astronomical increase in price was never justified, but either you paid the bill or you went without insurance.

The fourfold increase in the price of family day care coverage was only the beginning of troubles for child care. Soon thereafter center-based programs began to experience price increases, cancellations, and restriction in coverage. Beginning in early 1985 and continuing through 1987, insurance companies either increased the premiums charged to centers or refused to renew these policies altogether. A 1987 survey of centers in the Los Angeles area revealed increases averaging from 400% to 800% (Kalemkiarian, 1987). Child care insurance policies are generally not payable on an installment basis, so these new, increased premiums were due up front at the beginning of the year.

As the premiums increased, most child care providers discovered they were paying for less coverage. The limits of liability on many policies dropped from $500,000 to $300,000. And a host of underwriting restrictions placed in the new policies either limited the types of activities covered or established arbitrary program guidelines. A survey by the California Department of Insurance (1986a) revealed that most companies responding would not write insurance for programs that served "special needs" children. Many required adult/child ratios that were more stringent than licensing standards and that most programs could not possibly meet. There were exclusions for programs that had pets, even if the animals were caged. Very few companies would insure centers that cared for infants. And most companies would not even consider a family day care policy but would write only for centers. One company required that a family day care provider have a nursing degree.

In discussions with insurance company representatives throughout 1986 and 1987, it became clear to child care advocates and even to some of the insurance industry spokespeople that many of these policies had no basis in rational risk reduction. There was nothing behind many of these restrictions but hunches of the underwriters. How many claims had been paid because of rabbits in cages, or because of care for infants versus preschool children? There were no claims figures given to justify such discriminatory policy guidelines. Such restrictions not only limited the pool of eligible programs for these policies but encouraged programs either not to tell the truth on their applications or to change their services.

Perhaps the most serious and consistent restriction was the exclusion of coverage for any claim arising out of allegations of abuse by a staff member. California insurance law provides that no one can be insured for committing an intentionally harmful act. So even before the crisis there was no insurance coverage for a staff member who abused a child and was sued by the parents. However, under the old policies if the director or the program itself was sued because a staff member abused a child, there probably was coverage. The parents would allege negligent supervision or even negligent hiring of the staff member.

Today, most insurance policies exclude coverage for any claim arising out of child abuse, no matter who is being sued. If this exclusion sticks, there are potentially two disastrous results. First, a program could be bankrupted just defending itself in court against a claim. The number of groundless claims of abuse appears to be on the rise (BMF Marketing, 1986), and although almost all these claims are withdrawn or closed as being without foundation, the lack of coverage for legal fees creates real anxiety for child care programs. Second, if a child is abused in a child care setting and there is no coverage, that child could well go uncompensated if the program lacks revenues to pay for the child's injuries.

A recent California appellate court decision gives some hope that this in fact will not be the case and that the insurance policies would be read to cover the director, owners, or corporation involved. But the law is developing in this area, and no one can be sure how these provisions would be read in various circumstances. In the meantime, the exclusion continues to be spelled out in black and white in most policies sold in California.

In summary, policies in California in 1988 have higher premiums, less coverage, and fewer choices. Premiums have risen by at least 100% when compared with 1984, 1985, and even 1986 prices. It is very difficult to find a policy for over $300,000 of coverage, compared with earlier limits of up to $1 million in coverage. Family day care providers still have essentially only one choice for commercial coverage. There are two companies that offer a homeowner's policy tailored for family day care, but only for up to six children. Despite dozens of companies writing homeowner's policies in California, no others have publicized the availability of such a policy. Centers have four companies to choose from if they wish to purchase from a regulated carrier and one company that will write policies but is a "surplus line" carrier and not regulated as closely by the state. Of the four regulated carriers, one has more stringent adult/child ratios than licensing, one has set an informal limit on the number of policies it wants to write and makes them available only to members of the private preschool association, and one has variable prices based on where in the state the center is located.

Why these increases, cancellations, and restrictions? Everyone involved in resolving this crisis has a different answer. Eventually even the insurance industry agreed that bad investments and a "boom and bust" way of doing business had contributed significantly to the general crisis in liability insurance. The industry compensated for losses in their portfolio investments by drastically increasing rates (National Insurance Consumer Organization, 1986). But this does not explain child care's continuing problems. The market should now be softening as the insurance industry recovers from its investment practices and reports record profits ("Crisis Is Over," 1987; National Insurance Consumer Organization, 1986). But for child care the picture has not changed. As the deputy commissioner for the California State Department of Insurance stated, the companies seem to have little appetite for this business (California Department of Insurance, 1987).

The reason for this lack of appetite lies in the perception of child care as a very risky and unpredictable line of insurance. When the crisis first began, the insurance companies claimed that child care had an extraordinarily bad claims record and that losses had simply outpaced premiums. Yet in 1986, when this cry of crippling losses was first asserted at public hearings, the industry's own figures did not support their claim (Insurance Services Office, 1986). Surveys by child care organizations showed that on the contrary, 9 out of 10 providers had never filed a claim. Of those claims filed, one survey showed that the average claim was for less than $500 (National Association for the Education of Young Children, 1986). When the Department of Insurance reviewed insurance company data, they reported that some increase in premiums over the allegedly underpriced policies of the early 1980s was needed but that the "sudden drastic increase in premium ... is not a responsible way of doing business" (California Department of Insurance, 1986b, p. 9).

Testimony by insurance representatives and correspondence to potential insureds reveals that it was not the actual claims that worried the industry so much as the potential for claims. In one letter of rejection to a child care center with an unblemished claims record, an insurer stated that the refusal was based on the media attention to a very well-publicized child abuse case, the McMartin case, and "not specifically reflected on you" (Weaver & Associates, Inc., letter to Carol Lancey, Cal Nursery Schools, Inc., July 30, 1986). Even though the policies now explicitly excluded coverage for sexual abuse, and even though data have shown that only 2% of reported abuse occurs in an institution of any type (Birch, 1985), the companies continued to be scared by the potential for abuse allegations. So the premiums jumped up, ostensibly to ease the worried minds of insurer actuaries.

This fear of claims continues to dominate the extremely cautious posture that the insurance industry has taken toward child care liability insurance. It results in a noncompetitive market, with policies on the open
market being written by a very few companies and all priced at about the
same arbitrary rate. It is impossible to shop around for coverage, for there
is no real choice for most programs. What is the long-term impact of such
a market, and why should that impact be of concern to child care policymakers?

THE IMPACT OF INSURANCE
ON THE DEVELOPMENT OF CHILD CARE SERVICES

It is still too soon to see any permanent shifts in child care services as a result
of the insurance crisis. But certain long-term developments can be anticipated from the preliminary impact of rate increases and policy restrictions.

Higher premiums eventually increase the cost of care. Initially, many
programs absorbed the increased premiums by holding back on teacher
salaries. But wages in child care are low, usually hovering around the minimum wage (National Commission on Working Women, 1986) With the
quality of child care closely linked to the quality of staff, holding back
teacher salaries is not a long-term solution to paying bills. Unless programs
are going to rely on bake sales or spaghetti dinners to raise insurance
premiums (a temporary solution for many programs in 1986), insured
programs will have to increase tuition as insurance premiums rise.

Passing the costs on to the consumer is ultimately how all businesses
have to deal with premium increases. But child care costs already are
prohibitively expensive for many working families. Those that can afford
the increases will pay them. But those that cannot may eventually choose
other, uninsured facilities, which can keep their child care fees lower. If a
child placed in an uninsured facility has medical coverage from the parent's
job, then at least physical injuries can be treated. But children from lower-
income working families are less likely to be covered by a health insurance
plan than their higher-income counterparts. The children most needing
coverage for medical expenses in case of injury may be those children most
likely to be placed in uninsured child care programs.

Many small providers, particularly family day care homes, have
chosen to go uninsured rather than to increase their rates. Estimates are that
up to 50% of the licensed, operating providers in California do not have
liability insurance. No figures on pre-1985 coverage have been released, but
leaders of the family day care organizations in California conclude from

their personal experience that many more providers are not purchasing insurance. The reason is almost always the high cost (Kalemkiarian, 1987). Although some California policymakers have claimed that these providers just do not want to be insured, advocates have argued that it is not good public policy to discourage insurance coverage by failing to take action to regulate this area of insurance.

The cost of insurance also may serve as a deterrent to the establishment of new child care programs. It was very difficult in California to get any definitive numbers on the programs that closed down because of insurance costs; there was no way to tell how many failed to open up at all. We do know that high insurance costs and requirements for high levels of coverage had slowed down many child care projects in the City of Irvine, a wealthy community in Orange County with a great need for child care. Small providers in other parts of the state reported that they did not expand their programs or add on second sites because they could not find coverage.

As more and more people shop for child care services, someone will eventually fill the need, but the cost of operating may encourage programs of a certain type and only in certain neighborhoods. New programs in the future may be more likely to be part of larger for-profit chains, which tend to serve upper-income clients (Ann Muscari, personal communication, 1987). The large for-profit child care companies have also had difficulty finding coverage, but in the end they have more bargaining power because they can purchase for the entire chain at once. The trend for licensed child care slots to be located in more affluent areas may simply be accelerated by insurance problems (see Hill-Scott, this volume). The need for child care in lower-income areas may increasingly be met by unlicensed, uninsured providers.

Restrictions in the policies also will impact the future supply of child care. Depending on their age or disability, some children may not be able to find care because they are excluded from insurance coverage. After-school programs in California have not been able to find coverage tailored to meet the needs of their afternoon-only programs. As a result, a modified "workfare" program called GAIN, which establishes a great need for school-age child care slots, in some areas will not require children to be placed in insured programs (letters to the Insurance for Child Care Project, 1987). A center serving sick children in San Diego almost did not open when the owner could not find a company that would offer insurance. There is a critical need for services for special-needs children, yet centers have eliminated their services to these children so that they could keep their insurance for the "normal" children at the facility. Other programs serving only special-needs children reported months of searching before they could find a company that would write a policy. Although most of these specialty programs eventually found coverage, it took the perseverance of a director fueled by a commitment to serving a particular group of children who needed care. New providers looking for ways to enter the business are not likely to be so persistent in seeking to offer care to children who cannot be easily insured.

Any scenario points to the very real possibility of inordinate influence by the insurance industry over the development of child care services in this country. In 1985, no child care advocate was anxious to know very much about insurance. That attitude has now changed; the question being asked is, what can be done? The behavior of the insurance companies in California leaves no doubt that the answer to the crisis will not come from within the industry. It lacks the vision, the will, and most importantly the understanding of child care services to come up with viable solutions. The action agenda outlined here is a survey of some of the measures that would give child care control over its insurance future.

AN AGENDA FOR ACTION

Child care providers make one request: They want reasonable access to comprehensive policies of liability insurance at fair rates. Each of these components is essential to a stable insurance future for child care. Rates should be fairly priced, so that premiums combined with earned investment income on the policies can cover claims. The policies must be comprehensive, without extensive restrictions on who is covered and what is covered. And there must be reasonable access: It should not take months to locate a decent policy.

There are two fundamental lessons that we have learned in our work in California on this issue. First, a solution can be found if there is the will to find one. And when you are looking for help from legislators, having the will means being ready to buck the very considerable political power of the insurance industry. The insurance industry maintains this power with substantial campaign contributions, constant lobbying, and claims that the insurance business is too complex for the average citizen to understand. Child care must also lobby, and although we cannot usually offer large campaign contributions, we can offer some relatively simple solutions that make common sense.

The second lesson is that there will have to be either some governmental intervention in the insurance market or a self-generated source of insurance if the problem is to be solved. Child care is not a large market when compared with other lines of insurance. And our aggregate premiums, even after the price increases, are relatively small when compared with those from other lines carried by the major insurance companies. This structural marketing problem, combined with the demonstrated fear that the insurance industry has of this business, almost guarantees that the forces of a free market will not work to create a solution through competition for our business.

The plan of action initiated by child care advocates includes reforms in the following areas: governmental regulation of the insurance industry, direct state subsidy of child care insurance, voluntary action by the insurance companies, and self-initiated insurance pools. A fifth area of reform—tort reform—has been urged by the insurance industry and is also discussed here.

Governmental Regulation

Since the Great Depression, the insurance industry has not been regulated at the federal level (Tobias, 1982). There have been recent attempts to pass legislation at the federal level that would remove the industry's exemption from antitrust laws. The National Insurance Consumers Organization (NICO) has been leading this fight. Any changes of this type should eventually benefit child care, and it is always a good idea to keep our eye on the big picture. But significant help from government is more likely to come at the state level.

In 1986, many state legislatures undertook extensive investigations after insurance companies cancelled policies or drastically increased premiums for local business and governments (Coalition for Consumer Justice, 1986). Florida and West Virginia enacted stringent rate regulation statutes. (The insurance industry threatened both states with withdrawal of all insurance from the state if these laws were not changed.) New York and California explored a variety of laws that would subject premiums to review or subject the insurance industry to state antitrust laws. Child care advocates should become acquainted with these general reform proposals and find out how these laws would affect child care policies.

But there are more specific measures for child care that should be pursued independent of any general insurance reform proposals. There is both a practical and a strategic reason to ask legislatures to consider child care separate from other insurance problems in the state. Practically, a measure just for child care can be tailored to meet the needs of our unique industry. The problems of our market are very different from those of other difficult lines, such as trucking or urban auto insurance. Strategically, legislators may be more willing to vote for reform measures if those reforms are limited to child care. It is easier to stand up to the pressure of the insurance lobbyists when you are voting for children. There is a growing awareness by legislators that child care services are essential to the lives of their constituents. The following state regulatory measures would in different ways subject the insurance industry to greater scrutiny while helping to stabilize the child care insurance market.

First, states should require that data be submitted to a state regulatory body. The insurance industry arguments are always based on their "actuarial data." These data include premiums collected, actual claims paid, and claims the companies anticipate they will have to pay. Getting this information is usually a major battle, as the companies do not want it released. The yearly data should be submitted to an appropriate regulatory body by every company writing child care insurance in that state. Beware: Data collection is no panacea. The old adage that "figures can lie and liars can figure" is nowhere more true. The problem does not stop with data accuracy; understanding insurance computations is an art in itself. But with the help of sympathetic insurance personnel, the data can become very useful in analyzing the premiums and fighting against claims of high losses.

Second, states should regulate the rates charged for child care liability insurance. This can be done in either of two ways: through regular review of the rates by a regulatory body before the rates are charged to customers or through a state-administered insurance pool. In the first method, the appropriate regulatory body could be charged with approving rate increases to child care whenever they rise more than a specified percentage in one year. Twenty-five percent is often pegged as the point beyond which review of premium increases is required. Public involvement in this rate review and approval process greatly enhances its effectiveness. A review of the policy guidelines, with authority to require broader coverage, should also be included.

In the second method, the state could mandate insurance programs regulating rates and policy guidelines. There are a variety of state programs that meet this goal. The most common are assigned risk pools (often used for auto insurance) and joint underwriting authorities (JUA). The basic concept is that the state requires every insurance company in the state to contribute toward a common pool, which insures people whom the market is not serving. Each company then shares in the risk and helps to finance the pool with initial capital and by backing the policies. Ultimately, the premiums charged still have to support the claims submitted to the pool. Both the policyholders and the insurance companies are held responsible if the pool comes up short from a major claim. The advantage of these programs is that they can regulate both rates and policy guidelines, as a managing board of the program sets a uniform standard for all policies issued by the pool. The disadvantage is that often rates will not come down, as the policies are issued on a conservative estimate of losses. A major claim could also the leave the state, the companies, or the policyholders with a loss that would be difficult to recoup from premiums.

Direct State Subsidies for Child Care Insurance

In most states, this is the most difficult type of assistance to get. State legislatures are always hesitant to spend money, and they do not want to be in "the insurance business." But there is a precedent for state governments to offer insurance to certain groups of people and to back those policies with the considerable resources of the state treasury. California has a worker's compensation program that not only sets the rate for worker's compensation in the state but offers policies directly to employers. Most states have risk management offices that insure government programs or offer packaging of insurance for local governments.

Child care advocates could ask for help directly from the state in numerous ways. The state could set up an insurance fund for child care, funded by state revenues but eventually designed to be self-sufficient from premiums and investment income. Or the state could provide seed money for child care programs to set up their own insurance fund, an option explored in more detail later. The licensing process could be used to enroll providers in an insurance program, subsidizing the program in part from licensing fees. Like all spending proposals, these ideas will be controversial. But depending on the severity of the problem and the precedents within the state, direct subsidies may be a viable plan.

Voluntary Action by the Insurance Companies

It is very difficult—some would say impossible—to negotiate with the insurance industry. Child care advocates are not in a good negotiating position. We have neither large numbers of policies nor high total premiums to offer any individual company. There have been a few notable efforts to encourage companies to get back in the market voluntarily, with mixed results.

New Policies. In 1986, the Child Care Action Campaign mounted an extensive campaign to find a company that would step into the vacuum left by exiting companies. After an arduous search, Continental Insurance agreed to write the policy. Negotiations then began between the company and numerous national child care organizations to decide what the policy would contain. Although an agreement was eventually reached, certain controversial provisions of the policy caused some state insurance commissioners to ban the sale of the policy in their states. One such provision deducted defense costs from the policy's total liability limits (Child Care Action Campaign, 1986).

Expanded Coverage. Many family day care providers could be covered by an endorsement (an additional coverage) to their homeowner's policies. Although this type of endorsement is very easy for large homeowner insurance companies to offer, after 1985 such policies could not be found. With the help of the state commissioner of insurance, California child care advocates were able to get two of the major homeowner companies, Allstate and State Farm, to offer homeowner's insurance that includes family day care coverage. Although we had been urging this expansion for months, no action was taken by the companies until a request was made directly by the insurance commissioner. With a precedent now in California and other states, these national companies should be offering that policy in every state in the union.

Voluntary Market Assistance Programs. In at least three states, voluntary programs have been set up by the insurance industry to assist child care providers in locating insurance coverage for their programs. In California, a program called Cal-Care was set up with the help of the Department of Insurance. Child care providers needing insurance fill out an application and mail it to the Cal-Care office. The application is mailed to at least three of the member companies, who can either reject the application or give a quote. The program brought more companies into the child care market—but only through the Cal-Care program. It was to be a "last resort" source of coverage. Although the idea as noble, Cal-Care has failed to be an important factor in the California market. As of the spring of 1987, out of 3,300 applications submitted, 2,163 were rejected without a quote (Committee on Finance and Insurance, 1987). And because each company set its own rates and policy guidelines, one provider could get a good quote and a ridiculous quote from the same application, because many of the Cal-Care companies have very little experience pricing child care policies and some are simply pricing the policies out of reach.

As of the end of 1987, only a couple of hundred policies have been written by Cal-Care. The chair of the Cal-Care board, representing Aetna, was concerned enough about the effectiveness of the program to write to the Department of Insurance, "We have a lot of 'paper' participants but very few real ones." Child care advocates have noted repeatedly at public hearings that the basic problem of Cal-Care has been that no one is in control and that the companies have no real enthusiasm for the program.

Self-Initiated Insurance

Child care could generate its own insurance. Two different approaches have been taken by other businesses.

Purchasing Groups. Although not really self-insurance, purchasing groups offer their members more control over their insurance future. A purchasing group is composed of people who have a need for the same type of insurance and have a similar profile as an insured. The goal is to get a group together that could assure a potential insurer that it was a good risk. The group then negotiates as a whole with a company for essentially one policy that covers everyone in the group. Although members pay their own premiums, they benefit from a uniform rate and, it is hoped, from a discount made possible by the size of the group. This is very different from policies that are offered to members of an association, which are usually still priced individually and are likely to carry less discount, since the insurer is not guaranteed any particular number of policies from the association.

Self-Insurance. When a business or other entity self-insures, money is set aside to pay for anticipated injuries or lawsuits. Child care programs could do this by either posting a bond or putting aside the cash. But with most programs wanting at least $300,000 of coverage, it is not realistic to expect an individual child care program to have this type of cash in reserve.

Group self-insurance could be managed either by actually starting a licensed insurance company or by forming what is called a risk-management group. A risk-management group is like an insurance company but usually has more lenient capital requirements. In 1986, the federal government passed legislation making it easier to form risk-management groups, and since then many states have passed legislation that mirrors the federal laws. The Washington State Family Day Care Association has done some pioneering work in trying to form such a group. The problem for most child care organizations is gathering enough providers with enough capital to make the group economically viable. In the short term, a self-insurance group will usually not reduce premiums, so that the members have to be willing to wait a few years before they receive the financial benefits of decreasing rates.

Tort Reform

Tort reform proposals basically change the rights of some people to sue other people in whatever areas and in whatever ways are specified by the reforms. The insurance industry has worked very hard to put their version of tort reform on the legislative agenda all across the country (Insurance Information Institute, 1987). These proposals have led to major confrontations among the insurance industry, trial lawyers, consumer groups, and other interests. The impact and scope of any tort reforms go far beyond the single issue of child care liability insurance.

At various times, the insurance industry has suggested specific reforms they would like to see for child care. They have suggested making child care programs immune from suit altogether. A less drastic proposal has been to shorten the period of years over which a child may bring suit. Currently, children can sue for previous injuries anytime before their 18th year. There are serious ethical considerations for any child care provider that must be taken into account when we discuss taking away the potential for a child to be compensated for legitimate injury. Some advocates have been willing to look at whether this period should be shortened, but only if in exchange the insurance industry is willing to offer guarantees of lower rates and comprehensive policies. The discussions have not gotten any further once such a guarantee is mentioned.

Another possible approach to tort reform in child care is no-fault insurance. No-fault policies assure compensation, usually also limiting the rights of the insured party to sue. Many states allow no-fault auto insurance policies, and the concept has spread into areas of insurance involving children (O'Connell, 1985). A new program for high school athletic programs, described by O'Connell (1985), provides compensation for very serious injuries. Many child care programs have no-fault accident policies for minor injuries. The California commissioner of insurance has proposed a modified no-fault scheme for child care that would establish a state fund to compensate for simple types of injuries according to a set compensation schedule, leaving more serious injuries to litigation in the courts. This and other no-fault proposals have not been seriously considered by either policymakers or child care advocates, but they offer a very promising area for further study.

CONCLUSION

It is ironic that the insurance industry can change the entire market for insurance overnight, yet child care advocates are advised by regulators, legislators, and insurance executives to be patient and wait for the crisis to disappear. The fact is that the crisis in child care liability insurance will not disappear. It may seem to be less acute, but fundamentally the insurance industry doesn't really want our business. If the future of child care in the United States is going to be the success story that we hope it can be, part of that success will be finding a way to insure child care's future. Nothing less than the safety of our children and the existence of our child care programs is at stake.

ACKNOWLEDGMENT

This chapter embodies the work of the Insurance for Child Care Project (IFCC). IFCC was started by a group of dedicated activists, who set out to make a difference in child care insurance policy. The work of the IFCC steering committee and countless other volunteers across California made a difference in California. Readers who want more specific information on any of the programs discussed may contact the author c/o Insurance for Child Care Project, P.O. Box 880433, San Diego, CA 92108.

13

No Room at the Inn:
The Crisis in Child Care Supply

Karen Hill-Scott
Crystal Stairs, Inc.

It has been almost 10 years since the last major study of child care supply was published. This landmark field research, which consisted of two large multipart surveys (Ruopp, Travers, Glantz, & Coelen, 1979; Travers & Goodson, 1979) gave us "state-of-the-moment" knowledge about how much and what types of care were available and what components of care seemed most associated with good child outcomes. It even provided a glimpse into the netherworld of unlicensed family child care. The perfect companion piece to these studies of supply would have been a national demographic analysis of child care demand, but this research was never seriously contemplated, let alone implemented. The 1980 election of President Ronald Reagan cheerily closed the door on any federal consideration of child care issues. Child care advocates as well as researchers spent the years from 1981 to 1987 hunkering down and working as hard as ever for what victories were to be had in child care policy; just getting through a year without budget cuts or lowering of standards was an accomplishment.

In these gloomy days for publicly supported child care, however, one phenomenon has seemed relatively impervious to the lack of federal interest. Mothers of children of all ages have continued to increase their participation in the labor force. The pressure for child care space that these families put on the marketplace is perceived by the private sector of child care, which is expanding. It is felt by resource and referral agencies, which are trying, often unsuccessfully, to match families with child care. It is felt by employers, particularly those who depend on a nonexpendable, highly skilled work force for whom child care is an issue. And it is felt by policy makers, who are being pressured by constituents and advocates to adopt public action that will increase child care. The policymaker, in turn, weighs such decisions against other public priorities, personal ideology on the issue, and estimates of the consequences on the next bid for re-election. None of these groups, however, knows just how severe the child care problem is or whether the available care is, in fact, keeping up with the demand for service.

On the one hand, many legislators look at maternal labor force participation with the inherent assumption that "if the mother is working, she's got child care somewhere, so it's not a public policy problem." On the other hand, advocates pull out statistics on waiting lists and quote a litany of newspaper stories and personal testimonials to show that much of the care that is available is hardly adequate and, in many cases, hardly child care.

Both groups are probably right. A large number of working families do find adequate, safe child care within the family, in the private sector, and in government-supported programs. But a large number do not have adequate or stable arrangements (including the many families in licensed but substandard programs). That is where the pressure for child care cannot be contained by the existing supply.

Just how many families cannot find care is the great unknown in child care planning. Unmet need is the seemingly bottomless pit that advocates are trying to fill with the piecemeal bits of child care progress embodied in numerous state, federal, and municipal policies.

The purpose of this chapter is to describe a methodology for estimating unmet needs by considering child care supply against demand and quantifying the difference. Such information, derived through a careful research process, provides a valid base for child care planning as well as advocacy. Using these data, it is possible to illustrate patterns of need across geographic areas, by age, ethnicity, and income groups. Moreover, when the data show where and how much expansion is needed, a cogent and compelling case for certain types of financing becomes obvious. The results of research conducted in 1985 on child care supply and demand in Los Angeles show that the magnitude of unmet need is so great that child care planners must consider the development of public finance mechanisms other than categorical grants as the next imperative. To this end, the chapter offers a description of financing alternatives, possibilities that might be "the ones that get away" in a fishing expedition in the streams of public finance. In a field where expertise is necessarily focused on child development, economic efforts have primarily been directed to obtaining subsidy to make child care accessible to the poor. But the economic issues are much broader than this, and other funds in addition to subsidy must be found.

DETERMINING WHERE WE STAND

The model for calculating unmet need is quite simple to understand:

CHILD CARE DEMAND – CHILD CARE SUPPLY = UNMET NEED

However, quantifying and describing each variable in the equation involves some fairly complicated research.

Overall Supply

For the study in Los Angeles, summarized here but described in detail in another report (Hill-Scott, in press), all licensed child care in the county was identified by combining and purging lists of child care homes and centers from licensing authorities, school districts, and city and county agencies. From this master file, two random samples of centers and homes, stratified by location, were drawn and a market survey of the facilities was conducted. This survey gathered data on a number of variables, including current business activity, occupancy rates, enrollment and costs by age of child, and wages and education of child care workers.

The study showed no particular pattern of location for child care supply. Of 261 zip code areas, some had very little care (200 or fewer spaces per zip code), others had a lot (2,000 or more spaces per zip code), and many were in between. If one were to rely on supply patterns alone, some low-income areas appeared to be well served, whereas middle- and upper-income areas had short supplies of child care. In fact, the location pattern of child care seemed to bear little relationship to income patterns for the county as a whole.

The amount of care, in terms of raw numbers, seemed to be abundant. There were almost 7,000 facilities, serving over 133,000 children (Table 13.1).

Of these spaces, 19% were subsidized, typically with state funds. Close to 26,000 children received subsidized care in a variety of day care types:

TABLE 13.1
Supply of Child Care in Los Angeles County

Type of Facility	Number of Facilities	Number of Spaces	% of Total
Child-care centers	1,749	103,257	77
Family day care homes	5,206	30,501	23
Total	6,955	133,758	100

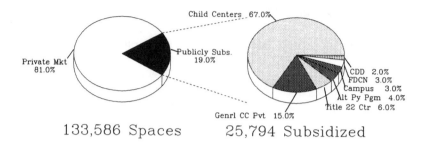

133,586 Spaces   25,794 Subsidized

FIG. 13.1.   Subsidized child care Los Angeles County, 1985.

homes, school-based centers, community centers, and voucher-type programs (Fig. 13.1).

Overall Demand

When supply was compared against demand, the picture changed dramatically. A complex method was used to determine demand, which was restricted to children with mothers in the labor force. With birth statistics adjusted for mortality and migration, child population was calculated by age, race, and location, so that the population could be aggregated by one or more variables or disaggregated by the same variables to the zip code level. There were a little over 1.4 million children in the county, with a stable birth rate—about 100,000 in each age cohort from 0 to 12 years.

The maternal labor force participation (LFP) rates presented other methodological challenges. LFP varies by race of mother, income of family, and age of child. The Bureau of Labor Statistics reports these rates by each of these variables by year. Using 1980 census data as our base year, we estimated, for each zip code, how many children of each age had mothers in the labor force in 1985. On the average, 48% of the children under 5 had mothers in the labor force, and 62% of the children between 6 and 12 had working mothers (Table 13.2). In fact, the most striking phenomenon was the generalized distribution of working mothers of school-age children, with only very poor and upper-income zip codes falling below the average level.

These LFP rates yielded almost 800,000 children with working mothers. It was not conceivable that all these children would need to use care in the licensed market, so the next step was to perform a sensitivity

TABLE 13.2
Children with Mothers in the Labor Force, Los Angeles County

Age Group	Number of Children	Number with Working Mothers	County Average %[a]
0–1	271,887	116,630	43
2–5	475,249	245,396	52
6–12	715,181	433,136	61
Total	1,462,317	795,162	

[a]Each zip code has its own average LFP, resulting in the total presented here. The county average is given to present the aggregate picture.

analysis to estimate what the shortage of child care would be at different levels of availability of informal, family-based care.

Sensitivity analysis is a technique used frequently by economists to project outcomes based on different sets of assumptions. In the case of child care, if the availability of informal care is high, demand for licensed care will be low; if availability of informal care is low, demand for licensed care will increase accordingly. Different studies of child care usage were reviewed to determine what proportion of the children with working mothers needed licensed care. These studies ranged from a Gallup Poll conducted in California (1985) to the U.S. Bureau of Census reports on children of working mothers (1982, 1987b). The census reports used the best sample and question sequence and were roughly comparable over time, so those findings were applied to the sensitivity analysis.

In all three census reports, free informal care was available to at least 25% of the working mothers. This care is not likely to be replaced by a formal caregiver, because it has no cost and reflects family preference. On the other hand, center care increased from 14% to 23% during the 1982–1985 period. (This finding held true in our market study in Los Angeles, where 24% of all preschoolers with working mothers were in centers and an additional 3% were in licensed family day care homes.) Finally, in 1985 about 50% of all families were in some form of unlicensed care but were paying a regular fee for service, just as though they were in the private licensed care market (Fig. 13.2).

Just how many of these families who are in unlicensed care really need to get into the regulated market? Returning to the concept of sensitivity analysis, a highly imperfect market would assert that because 25% get free care, 75% are in the market for licensed care, producing the largest unmet need. In a perfect market, 75% would be served by informal sources, leaving just 25% to use licensed care, and there would be no unmet need (Table 13.3).

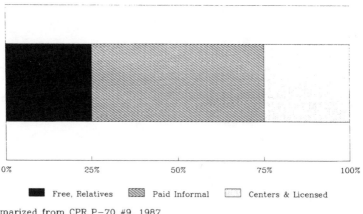

Summarized from CPR P–70 #9, 1987
(Proportions rounded for presentation)

FIG. 13.2.   Child care arrangements, working mothers preschool children in 1985.

Reality lies somewhere in between. Referral statistics, waiting lists, high center enrollments, and research on parents using informal care strongly indicate that the pressure is there to change from informal to organized child care arrangements. Yet we must assume that some of these families are well served and satisfied with their purchased informal child care. In the findings reported in this chapter, the midpoint was taken as a reasonable assumption. In other words, about half the families in paid informal care would not change if other care became available, and the other half would.

Without definitive national research on user preferences, any proportion of the families using and paying for informal care could be taken as the pressure on the licensed market. For example, there were 362,026 infants and preschool children with mothers in the labor force in Los Angeles County. If 25% receive free family-based care and another 25% have purchased satisfactory informal care, the demand for licensed care for the rest of the families would be for 181,013 spaces. Of the total spaces for child care (see Table 13.1), 110,425 are available for infants and preschoolers. That means that there is an unmet need of 70,588 spaces. One could hypothetically minimize the need substantially and assume that 65% receive free family-based and paid informal care; in that scenario, the unmet need is still roughly 15% more care than the present inventory of spaces. That small

TABLE 13.3
Sensitivity Analysis on Need for Child Care

If:	Then:
25% have free care	75% need licensed care
50% have free and satisfactory informal paid care	50% need licensed care
75% have free and satisfactory informal paid care	25% need licensed care

15% is 16,284 spaces, the equivalent of 2,700 family child care homes or 150 large centers.

A similar process using the census findings was applied to school-age children with working mothers. Here only 10% of the children were reported to be self-supervising, another 30% were in some form of relative, neighbor, or center care, and a full 60% were reported to be in the care of their own parents. There are many reservations regarding parents' self-reporting about leaving their children alone after school; in the California Gallup Poll conducted during the same period, 20% reported their children as latch-key children, a difference of 10% (Table 13.4).

The census data on school-age children do not differentiate between paid and unpaid informal arrangements, so it is difficult to discern what proportion of those children in some form of informal care would use a licensed after-school program if one were available. In this case, the sensitivity analysis had much different thresholds (Fig. 13.3).

At least 50% have free parental care and are not likely to change their arrangements at a financial cost. Another 10%–20% have latch-key care, which, because it is free, might not be replaced by paid child care if it were available. This is not to suggest that latch-key care is acceptable. This leaves from 30% to 40% in need of formal organized child care services. Because latch-key care is not a socially responsible alternative, however, the final form of the sensitivity analysis includes that group and appears in Table 13.5.

Here the midpoint between parental care and latch-key care is at 75% parental and other informal care and 25% needing licensed care. The result of the sensitivity analysis indicates that of 433,136 school-age children with working mothers, 108,284 need licensed care. There are only 23,333 spaces for school-age children, leaving an unmet need of 84,951 spaces.

TABLE 13.4
Child-Care Arrangements for School-Age Children

	Gallup Poll (1985)	Census Report (1987)
Parental supervision	50%	60%
After-school program	5%	n.a.
Other care	25%	30%
Latch-key	20%	10%
Total	100%	100%

Sources: Gallup Organization, *California Child Care: Final Report* (GO 84229), Princeton, NJ: 1985; U.S. Bureau of Census, Who's Minding the Kids: Child Care Arrangements Winter 84-85; *Current Population Reports*, ser. P-70, no. 9, 1987b.

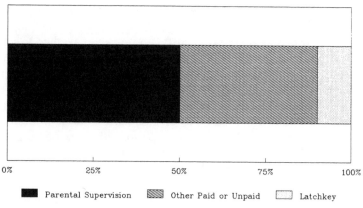

Summarized from CPR P–70 #9, 1987
(Proportions rounded for presentation)

FIG. 13.3.   Child care arrangements, working mothers school age children in 1985.

For each age group, the estimates of actual need are summarized in Table 13.6.

Overall, the methodological process of estimating unmet need proceeded as illustrated in Fig. 13.4. Close to 300,000 children need licensed child care, resulting in an unmet need for the county of over 150,000 spaces.

Where Care Is Needed

Because of greater population density in the central city, the high LFP rates of Black mothers, and the immigration of Latino children, low-income minority areas had the most severe shortages of care, despite the fact that supply alone appeared to be plentiful. These areas would also need subsidy to make the care affordable. The second largest segment of need was the area of the county where middle-class migration to affordable housing

TABLE 13.5
Sensitivity Analysis on Need for After-School Care

If:	*Then:*
60% have free parental care	40% need licensed care
75% have free parental and other informal care	25% need licensedcare
90% have free parental and other informal care	10% need licensed care

TABLE 13.6
Child Care Shortages in Los Angeles County

Age Group	Number of Children Needing Care	Spaces Available	% of Need Met	Shortage
0–1	58,315	12,926	22.2	45,389
2–5	122,698	97,499	79.5	25,199
6–12	108,284	23,333	21.5	84,951
Totals	289,297	133,758		155,539

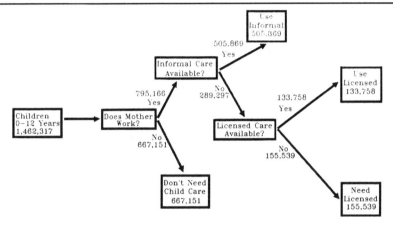

FIG. 13.4. Child care need Los Angeles County, 1985

has signaled the steady increase of two-paycheck marriages and the increased need for child care.

Another finding of import had to do with the distribution of child care subsidies, illustrating how the absence of market analysis has resulted in areas with lower need receiving subsidy and areas with high need receiving none. For example, two of the zip code areas with the highest need for subsidy had not one subsidized space. Conversely, two moderate-income areas had high-density subsidy of over 300 spaces each. We also found patterns of usage of homes versus centers and of licensed versus unlicensed care that seem to be associated with culture and/or age of child. Centers remain enrolled at 102% of capacity, although to some extent part-time children contributed to this appearance of overenrollment. Homes tend to be underenrolled by one child, on the average. In the Latino community, there is very little licensed child care in relation to need, and it is an obvious inference that families are using informal care. This fact is attributed both to the barriers created by the licensing process and to the reluctance of culturally intact communities to interact with public agencies responsible for child care licensing. Infant care constituted only 9% of the care in the county and was predominantly in family child care homes.

DECIDING WHAT TO DO

It was clear from this analysis that there is a need for more child care in Los Angeles County. Translating knowledge to action is not that simple, however. There are three broad questions that remain to be answered:

- How much money will it cost to meet the need?
- How would the resources be distributed, if they became available?
- How can resources be developed to finance child care expansion?

These three questions really confront the most fundamental issues of planning: providing for equity, yet responding to diversity. In other words, the distribution of new child care resources to user groups must be fair. At the same time, diverse user groups with special needs will require quite different levels of investment.

Achieving Equity

Equity pertains to the acquisition and distribution of resources. Often, child care advocates are so grateful for increments of child care progress that insufficient attention is paid to who pays and who benefits and to the long-term policy implications of each policy choice. For example, because child care subsidies are direct categorical grants, the revenues are drawn from the general tax base; everybody pays. But the benefits are distributed to relatively few, the most needy. Such redistribution of resources is intended to correct for structural inequities that may exist among income groups and to increase access to opportunity so that the needy will become self-sufficient taxpayers.

The problem with this kind of vertical distribution is that many taxpayers and legislators do not perceive a direct benefit to society from subsidy programs. They also want to contain the growth of categorical aid in any form to prevent the creation of costly entitlements. Thus, subsidy programs remain so small that even the majority of the needy are not served, as is the case with child care. In California, for example, which has the largest state-supported subsidy program in the country, only 10% of the eligible population are receiving a benefit (Hill-Scott & Pally, 1986). These few, however, receive free or reduced-rate child care for as long as the family remains eligible for service. When the eligible receive such high benefits but not all the eligible can be served, the program achieves high vertical target efficiency.

In order to achieve the equitable distribution of a benefit to those who pay the taxes and are therefore least likely or ineligible to receive direct subsidy, other approaches to equity are devised. With child care, a reduction in tax liability gives all those who pay for care the opportunity to receive an indirect subsidy for their child care costs. Currently, the indirect subsidy is received through the child care tax credit and the tax-sheltered Dependent Care Assistance Plan (DCAP). In these cases, the government does not spend money for child care; it forgoes income from every taxpayer who uses the credit. Neither the credit nor the DCAP provide the same level of benefit as direct subsidy. Where subsidy might be $3,000 per capita, the maximum returned to the taxpayer with the credit is $800 for 1 child and $1,400 for 2 children. The indirect subsidy is really a backhanded acknowledgment that there must be a national commitment to child care. It is estimated, however, that 6.4 million claims for the credit cost the government over $3 billion in forgone income in 1986 (Kahn & Kamerman, 1987). Because the eligibility for this program is so broad and the use of the credit so widespread, this program has high horizontal target efficiency. In other words, many of the eligible benefit, but the level of the benefit is small.

When the high vertical target efficiency of the subsidy overlays the high horizontal target efficiency of the tax credits, a bifurcated "system" of supporting child care results in which millions of income-eligible working poor families are shortchanged. A model of this bifurcation is illustrated in Fig. 13.5. Theoretically, using the present sliding-scale subsidy guidelines, direct subsidy should decline as family income increases, intersecting with the tax credit at or about the median income level (adjusted for family size). At this juncture, parent fees pay the full cost of care and any subsidy would be derived indirectly from the tax credit. However, the curve that should exist from direct subsidy to indirect subsidy is a vast gray area that remains a political hinterland yet to be explored by child care advocates.

The primary reason for not examining the current subsidy model and thereby exposing the severe inequity faced by the working poor is to avoid a negative revamping of child care subsidies. That is, rather than increasing the availability of subsidy to more low-income families, policymakers are likely to suggest lowering the current per capita benefit, thereby spreading the existing subsidy to more families. It is considered politically untenable to take away from whatever benefits the poor have received.

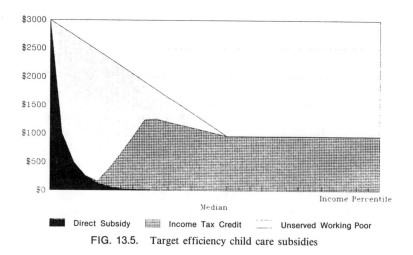

FIG. 13.5.   Target efficiency child care subsidies

The basic target efficiency problem can be compounded with other forms of distributional inequity. For example, because there is not enough subsidy to go around, serving an eligible person is more important than serving a geographic area with high need. Therefore high-need, low-resource areas without the agency infrastructure to obtain a grant get less than their share of child care funds. Of the 10 resource and referral service areas in Los Angeles County, the greatest penetration of need for subsidy is in the highest-income area, with 35% of need being met. The countywide average is 15% of need met by subsidy (Fig. 13.6). Similar patterns exist statewide, although legislation passed in 1980 (SB863, Child Care and Development Services Act) required the state administrative agency to allocate expansion funds in a manner that would correct for intercounty inequities.

A second type of distributional inequity is the result of emphasizing subsidy over capital outlay. Most categorical grants offer funds for services, not to build the facilities in which the service is offered. Therefore, areas without facilities already in business cannot apply for or use subsidy funds. Furthermore, areas that do not need subsidy but do desperately need facilities have no immediately available vehicle for capital financing. In some areas of Los Angeles, the primary need is for more licensed child care facilities, but land costs are so high that it is infeasible to get financing for a child care center. In the low-income areas of Los Angeles, the shortage of child care is manifested in both a shortage of child care space (new facilities) and a shortage of subsidy.

It would seem that these issues of equity need serious consideration whenever any plans are made to advocate for expansion of child care funding. Ignoring the equity question while supposedly solving the basic ineq-

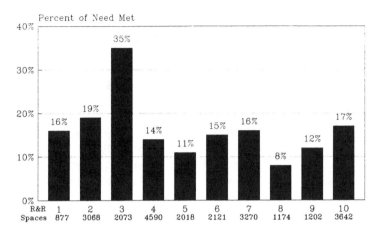

County Average: 15%
State Average: 10%

FIG. 13.6. Distributional equity of subsidy.

uity of child care shortages certainly seems contradictory. And gaining mainstream support for child care subsidy will be difficult without thinking of ways in which public assistance for child care can benefit moderate- and middle-income families as well.

Maintaining Diversity

Concurrent with the struggle to make child care more equitable are the efforts of diverse user groups and advocate groups to pursue their own agendas through child care legislation. These groups include children of various ages, ethnic minorities, teenage parents, student parents, migrant farmworkers, "yuppie puppies," special-needs children, and welfare recipients in mandatory work programs. Although all need child care, each group may have its own priorities that are reflected differently in the content of a child development program. Thus, in addition to getting a fair share of child care resources, meeting program content and program type priorities is important to interest groups.

For example, the unmet need for subsidized care in Los Angeles is greatest in the Latino and Black areas of the county. Fortunately, California guidelines for subsidized programs require cultural and linguistic appropriateness. These guidelines also permit a variety of sponsoring organizations to be eligible for funding, from family child care homes to school districts. This diversity has been the hallmark of the California experience (Hill-Scott, 1986).

In many states, however, both from the public at large and most recently from the ranks of child care advocates, there has been pressure for center-based models, preferably operated by school systems (Zigler, 1987b). A groundswell of support for a unilateral model of child care would definitely be in opposition to the official positions of the National Black Child Development Institute (NBCDI), various infant care groups, and family child care home associations. The NBCDI has issued a report basically opposing child care in the public schools unless specific safeguards are taken to protect the interests of Black children (NBCDI, 1987). And in heavily Latino East Los Angeles, fully 50% of the licensed care is provided by community-based organizations, not public institutions. In this community, distrust of public agencies and enclave politics create a requirement that direct grassroots efforts be undertaken to get providers licensed and to get children to licensed facilities.

Another area of ethnic diversity has to do with program content, as it is manifested in curriculum, dominant language used for communication and instruction, and adult styles of interacting with children. There are many ethnic groups permeating the culture of Los Angeles. White children are a minority in the school system, and there is one child care center where 26 languages are represented in the enrollment. In most cases, however, ethnic diversity pertains to either Black or Latino concerns.

Generally speaking, Black parents and providers are very committed to programs with strong discipline and control as well as heavy academics. This orientation is rooted in West African cultural heritage (Hale-Benson, 1986) as well as in the experience that education is a means to social mobility for ethnic groups. By contrast, typical White standards for developmentally appropriate child care programs would put far greater emphasis on exploration, freedom, and socialization. Olenick (1986), for example, used widely accepted standards of good developmental practice to assess 100 centers in Los Angeles County. He found that even the best programs in the Black community were more structured and controlling than the typical nursery school. Sometimes the adult control appeared arbitrary, uninformed, and developmentally inappropriate. It was clear, nonetheless, that a different standard of child behavior was expected in these programs. To judge them inferior or unacceptable without considering their cultural context (Hale-Benson, 1986) may be far more inappropriate and may display far more ignorance of culture than the programs display of child development.

Similar issues prevail with Latino concerns, particularly over language usage, language adoption, and cultural assimilation. The meaning of the term *bilingual* is, in itself, a controversy. The various strategies to achieve bilingualism are smothered in such strong pro-American sentiment that in

1986 the voters of California amended the state constitution to make English the official language. This sentiment contrasts with the reality faced by many child care programs, in which children come from monolingual families and a large monolingual culture that exists like an amalgam of Latin American countries within the English-speaking region. Simply insisting that English is the official language does not move these children closer to being able to function and speak in both their culture of origin and culture of context. And not publishing licensing regulations in Spanish does very little to lower the barriers for Latino providers to become a part of the child care system.

Increasing Availability

If the dilemmas of achieving equity and maintaining diversity could be resolved, the magical moment will have arrived when sufficient resources to meet child care needs have finally been obtained. Getting to that point, however, will require that the three questions posed earlier in this chapter can be answered. Public policy makers cannot be expected to support child care without target figures on the amount of care needed and the cost of developing that care, as well as a serious consideration of strategies to finance those costs in ways that are acceptable to the taxpayer. Child care experts, even child care policy experts, tend to be developmental psychologists, educators, and the like, whose expertise is rightly focused on the child. The primary barriers to increasing the availability of child care, however, are lack of funds for capitalization, inconsistent and contradictory regulation, and lack of funds for subsidy. The field of child care therefore needs to engage experts in land-use planning, public finance, and regulatory law in any efforts toward expansion. In other words, the biggest impediment to alleviating the shortage of child care is not our knowledge of child development or caregiver training or care modalities. The problem is financing and securing a broad social commitment to resolving the child care crisis. With the proper resources, child development experts could design and implement many different types of child care programs.

Despite the high per capita cost and low per capita "profit" associated with child care, this service sector employs many people and puts a lot of money (taxable income) into the economy. In 1985, based on actual market rates for care, an estimated $300 million was spent for licensed child care in Los Angeles County. This revenue represents only the fees that can be documented; close to twice as much is spent in the underground economy of unlicensed care and not taxed. These fees are more than the subsidy for the entire state and probably more than was spent on children's clothing,

or television sets, or hundreds of other consumer goods and services that
are touted as strong contributors to the economy (Table 13.7).

Rather than presenting child care as a drain on resources, advocates
would be well advised to emphasize the flow of funds into the economy as
a reasonable basis for future investment. The extent of that investment, particularly for capital outlay, is quite large. But given that fees do flow
through the child care sector and that some costs are recoverable, investment in child care is not a giveaway nor a total loss economically on a direct
basis. Certainly, when advocating for subsidy, child care advocates have
developed expertise in describing deferred and indirect benefits of
childhood supervision and intervention; this has been a major contribution
of Weikart's High Scope Project (Schweinhart & Weikart, 1983), from which
advocates have crafted articulate arguments. Capital outlay to alleviate the
shortage of space, however, could go to fund private, fee-for-service
programs as well as subsidized centers and homes.

From the findings for Los Angeles, estimates of the capital and subsidy requirements to solve the county child care crisis were developed.
Using the income data, the number of spaces that would require subsidy
was calculated. As we have seen (Table 13.6), there is a shortage of 155,539
spaces. Of these, 92,323 need some level of subsidy. Using present average
rates per subsidized child in the system, an additional $290 million in sub-
sidy funds would be required.

Assuming new facility space would be developed in centers and
homes in roughly the same proportions as in the existing supply (80:20),
cost projections would be roughly as shown in Table 13.8. The cost of
financing capital outlay for approximately 1,200 centers and 5,000 homes
at current reasonable costs in Los Angeles County totals over $1 billion.
Capitalization for centers can be amortized over at least 15 years at a cost
of only $567 per child per year in present-value dollars. Homes, on the other
hand, experience high rates of turnover, so that about half the costs for
homes would recur; over a 15-year period the cost would be $337 per year
per child. These rough projections should convey an appreciation of the
magnitude of need as a total cost, while illustrating that the actual cost per
child is really quite small.

TABLE 13.7
Revenues for Child Care in Los Angeles County, 1985

	Number of Children	Average per Child	Total
Fee for service care	107,792	$2,859.75	$308,258,120
Subsidized care	25,966	3,130.00	81,277,651
Total	133,758		$389,535,771

TABLE 13.8
Estimated Costs of Meeting the Need for Child Care in Los Angeles County

	Number of Children	Cost per Child	Total
Subsidy	92,323	$3,130	$ 290,909,773
Capital			
Centers	124,431	8,500	1,057,665,200
Homes	31,108	692	21,516,228
Total	155,539		$1,079,181,428

It is undoubtedly wishful thinking to assume that such a large commitment could be obtained over the short term. However, the successes of other public service sectors may serve as examples of precedents in public finance that child care planners would do well to understand. After all, if the National Football League team owners can get cities to build rarely profitable football stadiums in the name of the public good (Flanigan, 1987), advocates in child care should be able to make some headway with exploratory forays into the area of public finance. In 1987, in a matter of weeks the city of Irwindale, California issued $97 million in revenue bonds to build the Los Angeles Raiders a football stadium on an abandoned gravel pit. On November 5, 1987 *USA Today* reported, quite routinely, that 15 senators and 1 member of Congress paid a visit to baseball commissioner Peter Ueberroth to beg him to bring baseball franchises to major cities in their states. The cities would finance the ballparks. If child care advocates could grasp these same techniques, the field could use these approaches to provide long-term financing, which is superior to categorical grants, especially for the purpose of increasing availability.

Four possible approaches to financing the expansion of child care are discussed here. The criteria used to determine their appropriateness were prior use for financing in a related sector, such as education, recreation, or social and health services; prior use for projects that involved private sector participation; and "relative feasability." For example, there is a constitutional limit on spending in California and a limit on the power to increase property taxes, so no mechanisms that relied on tax increases are suggested. The four approaches are (a) issuing state and/or municipal bonds, (b) creating community facility districts, (c) encouraging tax-increment financing in redevelopment areas, and (d) imposing developer exactments. The feasibility of using any or all of these approaches in particular states or municipalities depends on the local environment.

Bond Issues. A bond issue would be a true test of the assertion that the taxpayers really do want child care. Of the many types of bonds, general obligation bonds would be the most favorable to the child care community, but revenue bonds appear to be the most feasible (Horler, n.d.).

The general obligation bond is backed by the full faith and credit of the issuing state. Therefore, it would be repaid through the collection of state taxes, in the event that loans made from the fund were defaulted, or if the funds were used exclusively for publicly owned facilities such as schools. General obligation bonds constitute about one third of all government bond issues.

The revenue bond is issued to support a particular project and is usually repaid out of revenues from that project. Revenue bonds are used to finance all sorts of projects. Because bondholders do not have to pay taxes on the interest earned from such bonds ("tax-exempt municipals"), the funds can be raised at lower than market rates and the user fees, which repay the loan, in turn are lower. Revenue bonds can therefore create favorable financing for "public services" provided by the private sector. About two thirds of all government bonds are revenue bonds.

There are also special tax bonds that are issued to finance a particular project and that are paid back from the collection of a special tax. This approach seems less feasible for child care, because users and nonusers would be directly assessed, and new taxation in any form is considered objectionable.

Community Facility Districts. A community facility district (or special assessment district) may be created by a local agency, such as a city, county, school district, municipal corporation or district, or a joint powers entity. The district develops services that are needed by that community. Such community facility districts have been created for libraries, recreation, and schools. In California, a proposed amendment to the Mello-Roos Community Facilities Act of 1982 could specifically name child care as an eligible service. In this approach to financing, the residents of the area vote to become a community facilities district, and through a voluntary special tax (not a property tax) pay off the debt incurred to build the facility desired. The local agency that created the district is responsible for the management of the facility and the collection of revenues. The facility may be leased and the lease payments used to offset the burden of the special tax.

Tax-Increment Financing. Redevelopment agencies, authorized under state or community redevelopment laws, are usually public entities established to revitalize economically depressed or blighted areas in the community. They are created by cities or within unincorporated areas of counties. The redevelopment agency, by improving the community, increases tax revenues to the locality through increased property taxes as the redeveloped property increases in value. The increase of tax revenue over the base revenue collected is called tax-increment revenue. The tax-increment revenue belongs to the redevelopment agency for its own uses for up to 30 years or until the redevelopment project is complete (Horler, n.d.).

The Hollywood Redevelopment Plan in 1987 called for the use of tax-increment financing to create both child care centers and child care subsidies. Most recently Mayor Tom Bradley, in his 1988 State of the City address, suggested that the Los Angeles Community Redevelopment Agency consider tax-increment financing as a method of creating what will be the largest city-sponsored child care program in the country.

Developer Exactments. In most municipalities, whenever large commercial or residential real estate projects are undertaken, the developer pays a fee for or pays directly for a variety of infrastructure improvements. These improvements are needed because the development creates an increased demand on existing systems such as schools, parklands, parking, utility lines, and sewers. Such an exactment could be used to offset the increased demand for child care created by thousands of workers or new residents moving to the developed area. Since 1986, three cities in California have put such ordinances on the books, and two of the three have started new child care centers as a result.

Other Approaches. There are many other approaches, such as "sin" taxes and other excise taxes, tax-refund donations, lottery fund appropriations, and donations of public lands for child care. They are not discussed here in detail for several reasons. General tax increases were excluded because they are infeasible in California. Tax refunds have not generated huge revenues for other services, and the schools are the priority service for the California lottery (Commission on California State Government, 1987).

Donating or prioritizing unused public land for child care is not discussed because these approaches do not generate revenues directly. Government at all levels is a huge landlord, however, and access to publicly owned space or land for child care facilities would provide immense cost offsets. In Los Angeles, if all the land for needed child care space were in the public sector, the cost savings on capitalization would be $466 million, almost half the total cost. California law (Child Care Facilities for State Employees, SB764, 1980) recognizes this benefit and requires that all new state-owned buildings have space set aside for licensable child care centers.

Regulatory changes and their enabling legislation often pave the way for finance initiatives to follow. For example, a regulatory change that required municipalities to include child care elements in local general plans might compel a city to consider child care, at least in concept, as a public concern. The legitimacy of the place of child care on the public finance agenda would be established.

Whatever approach is taken, it seems clear that without understanding broad-based methods of public finance, advocates will continue to experience difficulty in bringing child care as a public good into the American social conscience. Child care will remain a service that receives dribbles of public funding for relatively few low-income families. Lip service will continue to be paid to the middle class through the well-deserved but small tax credit. And we will enter the 21st century still lamenting the child care crisis in America.

14

Cultural Context for Child Care in the Black Community

Janice Hale-Benson
Cleveland State University

Since the 1950s, educational reform designed to benefit Black children has focused on desegregation, despite a declining pool of White children to integrate with inner-city Black children. The critical issue now being raised by Black scholars is how to create schools that will educate Black children effectively wherever they are found.

In my view and that of others, a central issue in improving educational outcomes for Black children is the recognition of their culture. The education of White children is more successful than that of Black children because the schools have been designed for White children. Hakim Rashid (1981) noted that children from non-European, lower socioeconomic status cultural groups are at a disadvantage in the schools because the American educational system has evolved out of a European philosophical, theoretical, and pedagogical context.

The failure to conceptualize Black children within their cultural context has created the expectation that they are really White children in black-face. Educational change will not occur until we devise educational strategies that are appropriate for Black children. We must create interrelated learning environments in which African-American culture in all its diversity is integrated throughout the curriculum and the politics of the classroom. And because early childhood is when learning and caregiving settings begin to have their influence, educational change must begin there. Early childhood education can play an important role in closing the achievement gap between African-American and White children.

BLACK CHILDREN IN WHITE SCHOOLS

W. E. B. DuBois (1903/1961) described the Black person in America as
having two warring souls. On the one hand, Black people are the product
of their African-American heritage and culture. On the other hand, they are
shaped by the demands of Euro-American culture. Unfortunately, the
Euro-American influence has always been emphasized to the exclusion of
the African influence. Said another way, despite the pressure of 400 years
in America, African-Americans have not melted into the pot.

One explanation for the difficulty Black children experience in school
lies in their participation in a culture that is very different from the culture
that designed the school (Hale-Benson, 1986). I locate myself clearly among
the theorists who trace the genesis of Black culture to the African heritage,
while acknowledging that there are other theories; the evidence supporting each theory is inconclusive. Whatever the origin of the Black culture,
the mismatch between between it and Euro-American culture has serious
educational consequences for Black children, for they are required to
master two cultures in order to achieve upward mobility in school and the
workplace.

It is possible, in fact, that African-American male children may have
to master three divergent cultures. African-American males have a culture
that is distinct not only from White male culture but from Black female culture. This Black male culture is not recognized and may even be assaulted
at school because it is not understood.

Most elementary school classes are taught by women, with the result
that a female orientation is created in the classroom. As we enter the 21st
century, we will increasingly find that most inner-city classrooms contain
a majority of minority children being taught by White female teachers.
White female teachers tend to be more comfortable with and knowledgeable about the behavioral characteristics of White female children and, to a
lesser degree, White male children. Cornbleth and Korth (1980) provide
support for this contention in a study of teacher perceptions and teacher-
student interaction in integrated classrooms. Teachers in their study rated
White females as having the most desirable personal characteristics and the
highest potential for achievement. White females were rated highest on
descriptors such as *efficient, organized, reserved, industrious,* and *pleasant,* and
lowest on descriptors such as *outspoken, aggressive,* and *outgoing.* Generally, Black males were mirror reflections of the White females; they were rated
lowest on the former characteristics and highest on the latter. White males
and Black females were rated in between.

These data suggest that there is a cultural configuration in classrooms.
They also lend support to the notion that in order to achieve, Black males

must acquire behavioral characteristics that are incongruent with the culture they bring to school. It is important to acknowledge this dual socialization that is required of Black children, because by fostering biculturalism, we can reduce the conflict within the child that depletes his or her energy and clouds his or her perceptions. Early childhood education can play an important role in this process.

Social scientists commonly engage in a type of chauvinistic ethnocentrism that perpetuates an image of normality in describing White children and an image of pathology in describing Black children. If Johnny cannot read, educators generally suggest that there is an inappropriate match between his level of development and the curriculum or instructional strategies. If Willie cannot read, the appropriateness of instruction is generally not questioned. The explanation offered is that he is either genetically inferior or culturally deprived.

The "intervention" strategies of the 1960s, which grew out of this view, are passé. Recent research by Black scholars (Hale-Benson, 1986; Rashid, 1981) has rejected the notion that African-American children are culturally or cognitively deprived. They are seen as members of a culture endowed with specific modes of cognition. In place of intervention, early childhood educational and caregiving settings therefore must search for cultural continuity.

Achieved Failure

How does the dual socialization I have described function to produce poor educational outcomes for Black children? Recent scholarship has examined the specific interethnic code conflict that takes place between Black children and White teachers and that over time results in failure for Black children.

Black Americans are a "pariah group" (McDermott, 1987) in American society, "actively rejected by the host population because of behavior or characteristics postively condemned" by group standards (Barth, 1969, p. 31). McDermott observed that in each generation, children renew the lifestyles of their parents, oblivious to the oppression that the host group brings down upon their heads. According to the traditional thesis of structural inequality, the host population works actively to defeat the efforts of each and every pariah child to beat the cycle of degradation that is his or her birthright. Racial markers, low-prestige dialects, school failure, occupational specialties, and lifestyles tag each new generation for low ascribed status.

For McDermott, however, inherited disadvantage as simple tagging is a simplistic explanation. Overt ascription, he pointed out, is frowned upon legally and in popular ideologies, yet the pariah boundaries remain firm

throughout the society and in school systems. Even without formal institu-
tionalized ascription, pariah status survives into each generation. Mc-
Dermott offered an alternative explanation, the thesis of *achieved failure*. He
suggested the following:

> The host population does not simply slot a child on the basis of its
> parentage and then keep a careful eye out for the child so that he never
> advances a slot. Rather, it seems as if the child must learn how to do it
> himself; he must learn a way of acting normally which the host popula-
> tion will be able to condemn according to the criteria the hosts have
> learned for evaluating, albeit arbitrarily, their own normal behavior.
> Pariah status appears almost as achieved as ascribed. (1987, p. 176)

Rather than regarding themselves as blinded by prejudice, the hosts
maintain that they are utilizing standards of evaluation that are used
uniformly for all people regardless of race or ethnic identity. And each new
pariah generation affirms the soundness of this classification system, because the children learn and exemplify the behavior essential to the
system's maintenance. It is this process that McDermott examined.

Pariah groups do not enter school disadvantaged; they leave school
disadvantaged. Ascription of status does not account for all of this disadvantage; nor do the inherent characteristics of the pariah population account for it. Clearly, the pariah group regards the host behavior as oppres-
sive. Similarly, the host group regards the pariah behavior as inadequate.
McDermott suggested that the central problem lies in the way the two
groups find this out about each other.

Misunderstandings take place very often in the early grades. Interethnic code differences cause miscommunication between the teacher and the
child, and the results are disastrous. According to McDermott (1987):

> Once the host teacher treats a child as inadequate, the child will find
> the teacher oppressive. Often, once a child finds a teacher oppressive,
> the child will start behaving inadequately. After such a point, relations
> between the child and the teacher regress—the objectionable behavior
> of each will feed back negatively into the objectionable behavior of the
> other. (p. 178)

This miscommunication results in a deterioration of relations until the
children begin to form alternatives to the teacher's organization of the classroom. In an attempt to become visible, the children construct a new social
organization, which results in more condemnation of their behavior. The
teacher then becomes the administrator in charge of failure.

In this way, McDermott said, school failure becomes an achievement,
because it is a rational adaptation made by children to human relations.

Children produce pariah-host statuses in their interactions with each other and with their teachers. In very subtle ways, pariah children in host classrooms learn to behave in new, culturally appropriate ways that involve learning to attend to cues produced in the peer group and to disattend to teacher- and school-produced cues, such as calls for attention or the introduction of new tasks such as reading.

McDermott suggested that these attention patterns are deeply programmed in the central nervous system. When the child attempts to attend to cues that are outside of his or her normal perceptual patterns, he or she fails. In this way, when many Black children fail in reading, it appears to be the result of a neurological impairment. The children are not actually impaired at all—they have merely learned over time to attend to different stimuli in a school situation—but they are categorized as disabled and treated as inferior.

Several researchers (Alitto, 1969; Fishman & Leuders-Salmon, 1972; Hostetler & Huntington, 1971) have noted the success of educational settings in which teachers are members of the same ethnic and dialect minorities as the children. By contrast, when the classroom is divided into two separate worlds, with teachers and children playing different games, the result is a social reorganization of the classroom in which the teacher's authority and information transfer is challenged.

Communicative Code Differences

Spindler (1959/1963) has demonstrated that middle-class teachers attend to middle-class children and label them the most talented and ambitious children in the class. School success follows parallel patterns. Lower-class children over time give up trying and amass failing "institutional biographies" (Goffman, 1963) as they move through school, because they are unable to give evidence of their intelligence in terms of the limited code that teachers use for evaluating children.

Black children are particularly at risk for being overlooked because of a nonrecognition of Afro-American culture and the strengths that emerge from that culture. I have pointed out elsewhere (Hale-Benson, 1986) that Western social science overly emphasizes linguistic and logico-mathematical skills in assessing intelligence. Even these skills must be demonstrated in patterns that approximate those used by Anglo-Americans to be recognized by the educational system. Cazden (1970) has described Black children who do badly on language tests in formal situations and very well in informal situations; the opposite is true for White children.

There are subtle but significant changes in the use of language among Black children as they move through elementary school. Pariah children code switch when addressing pariah people and host people. The job of code switching is difficult, however, when the teacher regards you as ignorant for using one code and your peer group rejects you for using the other.

William Labov (1964) has delineated stages in the acquisition of nonstandard English:

1. Up to age 5: Basic grammatical rules and lexicon are taken from parents.
2. Age 5 to 12, the reading years: Peer group vernacular is established.
3. Adolescence: "The social significance of the dialect characteristics of his friends become gradually apparent."
4. High school age: "The child begins to learn how to modify his speech in the direction of the prestige standard in formal stituations or even to some extent in casual speech." (p. 91)

Skills that emerge from Black culture are recognized only when they are extraordinary and marketable to the capitalist ecosystem, such as the athletic skills of Michael Jordan or the musical skills of Michael Jackson. When these skills are exhibited in early childhood as a part of a pattern that if nurtured could support the self-esteem and achievement of Black children, they are virtually ignored.

Consequences of Code Differences

Young children are very vulnerable to messages of relationship. Black children are adept at nonverbal communication and sensitive to affective cues (Hale-Benson, 1986). McDermott (1987) pointed out that young children, upon entering school, are more sensitive to relational messages than to information transfer.

Rist (1970) analyzed the effect of dividing a kindergarten classroom into three "ability groups," the fast, slow, and nonlearners at Tables 1, 2, and 3 respectively:

> The organization of the kindergarten classroom according to the expectation of success or failure after the *eighth day of school* became the basis for the differential treatment of the children for the remainder of the school year. From the day that the class was assigned to permanent seats, the activities in the classroom were perceivably different from previously. The fundamental division of the class into those expected to learn and those expected not to permeated the teacher's orientation to the class. (p. 423; italics added)

The teacher's subjective evaluations were shown by Rist to be rooted in the teacher's evaluation of the children's physical appearance and interactional and verbal behavior. At Table 1 were children with neater and cleaner clothes, more clothes on cold days, and lighter skin, as well as class leaders and direction givers. The children at the low tables spoke less in class, used heavy dialect, and seldom spoke to the teacher.

By the time the children were in the third grade, the ones who started out at the lower tables were still at the lower tables. Once a child is tracked, it is difficult for him or her to break loose. The lower the table, the less instructional time the child receives. This child is well on the way to amassing the institutional biography that will follow him or her year to year through the school. The sorting process continues as each year more and more are sorted out, until a select few reach college. McDermott (1987) stated that the "select few make it to college on the basis that they are most like their teachers" (p. 198).

Given Labov's (1964) speech data, the children at Table 3 are not neurologically impaired slow learners. McDermott predicted that by sixth grade the children at Table 3 will talk the most, be the most popular, and be the best dressers in the class. There is nothing wrong with their native ability. They will just be directing their achievement efforts away from the school.

The reason these children were not selected for achievement in their early years has to do with the communicative code differences between them and their teachers. If they are not able to work out this code conflict in the early years, the children at the lower tables take flight into their own subculture, which becomes oppositional to the classroom culture constructed by the teacher.

A key to the construction of this alternative classroom culture is the fact that children are assigned to the lower groups together. This arrangement creates larger numbers to construct the revolt, which becomes more powerful. There is a normal developmental shift away from the teacher and toward the peer group in fourth, fifth, and sixth grades. Therefore the achievement gap between Black and White children becomes most apparent in late elementary school.

The children in the host classroom have three choices, according to McDermott (1987). They can take the school as a source of identity, as do the children at Table 1, or they can take the peer group as a source of identity, as do the children at Tables 2 and 3. Of the latter, many are transformed into gangs by late elementary school. The third and worst choice is represented by the children at the lower tables who accept the teacher's definitions of them and their abilities and passively fail through school into pariah status. These children not only fail in school but also fail in their identity work. Children are better off who dispute the messages of relationship sent by the teacher and cause disruption in the classroom, because they have a better chance of constructing a solid ego in their community that could lead to achievement by an alternative route. The children who passively accept subordinate status do not disrupt the calm classroom status quo but emerge from the educational experience with weak egos. McDermott (1987) summed it up: "In either response, learning is blocked; in the first case by active selective inattention and misbehavior, in the second case with motivational lag and selective inattention. Neither group learns to read" (p. 199).

McDermott pointed out that the host group teachers do not create this code difference. Both the children and the teachers participate in ethnic group traditions that they bring to school. In the early years, teachers make the difference because they are not as adaptable as children. However, in later years, as the peer group gains strength, the children force the distinction between their code and the teacher's code. In *making their code make a difference*, they are learning how to produce pariah status for themselves vis-à-vis the host group.

Ethnic Group Identity and Mobility

McDermott (1987) pondered the question of why Blacks do not fare as well as other ethnic groups in working out the politics of the classroom. A possible explanation is found in the work of Robert Havighurst (1976), who suggested a compatability between the White Anglo-Saxon protestant American middle class and the ethnic cultures of European Whites, Jews, Chinese, and Japanese. It seems that Blacks and Hispanics must shed more of the beliefs, values, attitudes, and behavioral styles associated with their ethnicity in order to acquire the somewhat divergent culture of the middle-class mainstream.

As noted earlier, I have developed the theory that at the root of disciplinary difficulties and problems in achievement by Black children is a lack of understanding of Afro-American culture and childrearing, as well as a lack of recognition of the mismatch between this culture and the Euro-American oriented culture of the school (Hale-Benson, 1986). The research of Donald Henderson and Alfonzo Washington (1975) is an example of investigations of Afro-American cultural patterns that may have implications for educational practices. They affirm that Black children mature in communities that are culturally different from the communities of the broader society and that these differences are often regarded by the school as deficiencies.

Given the vulnerability and family turmoil, particularly of lower-income Black youth, the shift from school toward the positive strokes and affective support of the peer group can be seen as a flight from the failure and ego damage of the school. Bruce Hare (1987) defined Black youth culture as a *long-term failure arena.* On a short-term basis, Black youths exhibit competent, adaptive behavior and achieve in the arenas that are open to them. They demonstrate street wisdom and they excel in playground sports, sexuality, domestic and childrearing chores, supplementing family income, and taking on other aspects of adult roles at an early age. But even though this youth culture provides alternative outlets for achievement, it offers little hope of long-term legitimate success. Rather, it carries with it the danger of drafting the youths into the self-destructive worlds of drugs, crime, and sexual promiscuity. This is what my father called "majoring in a minor."

Hare observed that the collectively negative schooling experiences of Black youth produce this antischool sentiment. The accompanying availability of positive peer-group experiences and the inability of youths to perceive the long-term consequences of adolescent decisions cause the youths to make what appears to be a logical decision to shift from the school to peers.

EARLY CHILD CARE: CONNECTING
BLACK CHILDREN TO THE FUTURE

The implications of the consequences of negative schooling experiences are clear for those who are the first teachers and care providers for Black children. The National Black Child Development Institute (1985) has raised serious questions about the trend toward placing the preschool care of Black children in urban public schools:

> Are existing public school–based programs serving the Black family adequately and fostering Black children's growth and development? Can public school–based child care models be developed that will not maintain the discriminatory tradition of our public schools? And can the momentum toward public school–based child care be slowed long enough to allow a much needed and long overdue analysis of the record and implications of continuing this experiment? (p. 3)

Asa G. Hilliard has observed that the movement toward early child care in the public schools may serve to identify and isolate nonachieving Black children at an even earlier age. He pointed out the cultural bias that is implicit in the designation of a disproportionate number of Black children as educable mentally retarded (National Black Child Development Institute Report, 1985):

> There are more Black children placed in EMR (educable mentally retarded) than there are White children, nationwide. EMR is a "soft" category, whereas a look at "hard" categories of assessment, like visually impaired, hearing impaired, or mentally retarded, show almost no disproportion between Black children and White children. EMR is the category where there is perhaps the greatest imprecision in assessment, and this usually works to the disadvantage of Black children. (p. 22)

Visions for Children is an early childhood education program I have designed to demonstrate the recommendations outlined earlier and in *Black Children: Their Roots, Culture and Learning Styles* (Hale-Benson, 1986). This program, funded by the Cleveland Foundation, operates in Shaker Heights, Ohio and is delivered in a day care format. This demonstration program is designed to articulate a pedagogy that begins in early childhood and includes an interrelated learning environment drawn from African American culture, teaching strategies that complement African American learning styles, and materials relevant to the African American experience. This model, seeking cultural continuity, addresses a number of important questions:

1. What unified approach can be found to create an interrelated learning environment that achieves cultural continuity?

2. How can an educational program be designed that moves Black children away from a poverty/remedial track toward an academically oriented preschool experience?

3. How can Black children be connected to the future and acquire experiences with computers that are embedded in their learning styles?

4. How can the Black community achieve a holistic education for Black children in which they are educated about Afro- American culture and heritage in all its diversity throughout the curriculum at the same time that they learn about other cultures?

5. How can standardized testing be demystified for Black parents so that they can facilitate their children's performance on such measures?

6. How can the lower academic performance of Black male children be improved? How can the overriding feminine orientation of early childhood classrooms be reduced and more tolerance of male culture, and specifically Black male culture, be introduced?

7. How can more information be provided to Black parents about how to provide a road map to achievement for their children? The high motivation to achieve that Black parents provide for their children has been well

documented by scholars. What seems to be missing is the ability to identify the mechanisms for achievement and resolving stumbling blocks along the way.

8. How can parents and teachers assist Black children in coping with the world in which they live as well as changing the world around us?

9. How can existing patterns in teaching children to handle aggression be improved so that aggression works for them instead of against them? How can parents and teachers teach social skills so that children learn nonviolent techniques of interpersonal conflict resolution? How can social skills be taught in such a way that children are able to negotiate mainstream institutions as well as Afro-American culture?

The schools, for cultural and educational reasons, need to accommodate instruction to the learning styles of Black children. Early child care settings need to build bridges between the culture Black children bring to school and the outcomes they must achieve in order to survive and become upwardly mobile in American society.

DISCUSSION

Dr. Hale-Benson was asked to address the argument that one task of child care and educational settings is to acquaint children with the majority culture, to socialize them in ways that will help them succeed in the mainstream culture. She replied that her primary commitment is to equal educational outcomes for Black children, and the educational processes that "throw the baby into the swimming pool" are not having success. The success models, she pointed out, are those in which Black children are educated in a cultural context, especially the Black colleges, which produce more Black graduates than the White colleges, even though the White colleges enroll more Black students.

Her approach is controversial, however, she noted. Particularly in a city like Cleveland, the prevailing notion for middle-class Blacks is that the goal is to move to Shaker Heights and get one's children into integrated schools. The idea that there might be something to be gained from a homogeneous educational setting geared to Black children would be less controversial in Atlanta, which has the history of the Black colleges.

The participants were eager to know more specifically how cultural differences are reflected in current classroom practice and how the Black culture can be acknowledged in ways that will improve educational outcomes. One example cited by Dr. Hale-Benson is the difference in disciplinary approaches used in the Black home and in the school. At home Black children are accustomed to receiving corporal punishment if they cross a certain line. White teachers who do not spank them for crossing the line at school are not behaving in the way Black children have come to believe that authority figures behave, and a cultural dissonance is created. Dr. Hale-Benson assured the group that she was not necessarily advocating corporal punishment but pointed out that in earlier days, when there were closer communications between teachers and parents, a child who misbehaved in school could be sure of being punished again at home. Today, this kind of close connection and agreement between parents and teachers does not exist.

Others agreed and pointed to instances in which this cultural difference necessitated re-evaluating instruments and modes of assessing both home environments and child care settings. Certain criteria have to be re-examined to determine whether they are culturally appropriate. A verbal threat, for instance, will not upset a child from a culture that uses such threats extensively. Other cultures have very different ideas about what is acceptable behavior on the part of a child and think that Americans have lost their grip on parental authority.

Questioned whether the prevalence of corporal punishment in the culture might not be a dysfunctional aspect of the Black culture that might explain some of the outcomes, Dr. Hale-Benson declined to assess it as such. She did, however, note that her program does try to teach children how to channel the strong affective orientation that comes out of the African heritage and how to engage in nonviolent conflict resolution.

In general, Dr. Hale-Benson believes that our notions for child psychology are drawn from what is normal for White children; we do not know what is normal for Black children. Black children, she thinks, and especially Black males, are more kinesthetic than White children and need more opportunity to expend energy. There is research (Boykin, 1978, 1986) suggesting that Black children learn better when movement is incorporated in the learning process, whereas for White children movement is deleterious to performance on tasks.

Language is another aspect of the Black culture that is not acknowledged in White schools. Schools measure linguistic skills by the number of objects and concepts one has words for, and White children have broader vocabularies than Black children. In the Black culture language is more closely related to the creative arts, as the rapping songs exemplify. Charismatic language and style are important; Black children are performers. White people appreciate the performance styles of the Black culture when someone reaches the stature of Michael Jackson, but they do not value them or encourage them in the Black child.

Dr. Hale-Benson was asked to describe how she creates an environment that takes advantage of Black children's inclination to focus on peer esteem in order to produce favorable educational outcomes. She stressed that in her program the children work in very small groups; there are almost no total class activities. The children are divided by age into groups named for African tribes, and they develop a great sense of identity with the group—sometimes a problem if a grouping must be changed because of shifting enrollment. The teacher/child ratio is high, but all teachers work with all groups, so that if a teacher leaves or is absent, there is continuity; it is, in her terms, an extended-family way of teaching. Teachers collectively evaluate the children as well.

A large question, of course, is what will happen when the children get into the local public schools. A longitudinal study is planned to follow the children; the first group of children entered kindergarten this year. The parents of children in the program would like to see the program extended, but there are no plans to do so at present.

The different experiences of other ethnic groups in White schools were brought up and contrasted with that of Black children. Asian children, although just as different physically, socially, and linguistically from their White teachers, are brought up with a cultural emphasis on obedience and hard work that makes it possible for them to function well in White classroom settings. Research by Havighurst (1976) and Sarason (1973) suggests that people from Asian, northern European, Scandinavian, and European Jewish backgrounds have a kind of cultural compatability with the White Anglo-Saxon protestant mainstream of American life, whereas people of Hispanic, African, and some southern European backgrounds must shed more of their culture of origin and acquire behavior patterns that are more divergent from their culture in order to achieve middle-class status in American society. The process of straddling the two cultures is therefore more difficult for Afro-American and Hispanic children.

The role of parents in this process was also debated. Asian parents tend to be more involved in children's schoolwork than Black parents. One participant wondered if that were simply because centuries of prejudice have turned Black parents off the educational system or if there was a deeper cultural reason, perhaps wanting to encourage independence in children. Dr. Hale-Benson stated that generally the behavior of lower-income Black parents becomes descriptive of Black families in general because little effort has been made to study Black middle-class families empirically. It is known that Black families in general place a high value on education and have high educational aspirations for their children. The vast majority of Black college students represent the first generation of their families to attend college. Black families make extraordinary sacrifices to obtain higher education for their children. However, Black lower-income families often have less information about the specific strategies to use in helping their children achieve their aspirations. Not knowing what to do could account for differences found between Black parents and parents in other ethnic groups in achievement-oriented activities such as helping with homework.

Dr. Hale-Benson reiterated her opinion that the schools are prepared to educate the children of White upper-income families and that those children are prepared to receive the education the schools are prepared to give. Children who differ ethnically, and to some extent those who differ from the "norm" of femininity, are at risk for school failure. The traditional focus has been upon blaming the child and family who differ rather than upon examining the instructional technology being utilized and being willing to adjust it to fit the population that the schools are called upon to serve.

One participant wondered whether a non-Afro-American teacher could be taught to deal appropriately with the cultural context of Black children. Dr. Hale-Benson felt that the answer was yes, once the components are understood, but she cautioned that at this point she is just beginning to study what the appropriate pedagogy might be.

The discussion turned to the broader scene of ethnic groups in American society. A participant pointed out that many communities have a large number of different ethnic groups, but none of them in a large concentration. How does one balance ethics and practicality, she asked, meeting the needs of various language groups with limited staff and resources? Dr. Hill-Scott spoke strongly to the issue, stating that America has a responsibility to meet the needs of its people. Unfortunately, she added, our public institutions do not function in that way; bureaucracies function to perpetuate themselves. She acknowledged the difficulties but felt that they had to be dealt with; if something has to be printed in 14 languages to reach the people who need it, then that must be done. Dr. Lopez agreed, noting that it may be necessary to go to court to force bureaucracies to provide bilingual programs or bilingual staff to help ethnic minorities gain access to services. Ms. Kalemkiarian felt, however, that there is a growing recognition in the education community that teachers are going to have to be trained to deal with the wide variety of ethnic children who are entering the schools, to adjust to them both linguistically and culturally in order to help these children become part of American society.

How will all this cultural diversity be reflected in child care for a heterogeneous population, they were asked. Will meeting the needs of various ethnic groups result in totally separate child care delivery systems? Dr. Hill-Scott noted that child care is largely a segregated service, because it is neighborhood based, but she advocates a bicultural model. The critical point, she stressed, is the unconditional acceptance of the child and the child's culture: "where you come from is okay, and you as a child are an okay person."

15

Aims, Policies, and Standards of For-Profit Child Care

Ann Muscari
Kinder-Care Learning Centers, Inc.

The topic suggested to me for this volume gave me pause at first, because I believe that the aims, policies, and standards of for-profit child care providers are much the same as those of anyone else in the child care business. But reality is what is perceived, and some do not perceive the similarities, so I spell them out here. Of necessity my frame of reference is Kinder-Care, but I believe that the examples I draw from our program have parallels throughout the proprietary segment of the child care industry.

AIMS

The aims of for-profit child care may be stated as:

- To provide a quality day of care for every child every day;
- To recruit, select, train, and supervise professionally competent staff;
- To manage the center operation in a professional manner; maintain compliance with state standards; achieve self-imposed quality levels; and operate within budget goals; and
- To communicate with parents in a way that inspires their trust and earns their confidence.

MARKET

The chain/proprietary sector today probably makes up over half of all child care services. The market for private-sector child care is generally middle-class families with incomes of $25,000 or above, 2 years or more of college, steady employment, probably 1.5 to 2 children, and a keen interest in their children's welfare. A substantial number of the parents are professionals: lawyers, managers, teachers, and health care workers. A smaller segment, but a significant one, consists of single parents.

Sociological changes, increased divorce rates, more women working, higher mobility of families, decreased domestic help, reduction in birthrates, and having children later in life have all contributed to the growth of the industry. In the 1980s, thousands of women have moved into managerial positions and other nontraditional jobs and careers. At the same time, the use of child care centers, particularly by educated families, has increased.

Proprietary child care meets the needs of this middle-class market niche, which is looking for quality, affordability, and accessibility. For a mobile working population, employment transfers are eased when children can be moved from one center of a chain to another that will be familiar in its physical arrangements, its curriculum, and its routine. Records can be transferred to assure continuity of care.

POLICIES

The policies and standards of for-profit child care reflect those established by the states in which we operate. Regulation is an essential part of doing business and is integral to the safety and well-being of children in child care. As an industry, we are supportive of reasonable, fair, and equitable regulation. We feel strongly that no group should be exempt from regulation and that all child care alternatives should be held to equal standards of quality. Our corporate policy on licensing is to be in compliance, to be familiar with the standards, and to maintain positive and professional communication with regulators regarding the licensing and inspection process.

We believe that regulators (and in many cases legislators and academicians) need to be more in touch with the real-world, day-to-day operation of child care before mandating regulations that impact negatively on business, children, and families. The child care business is labor intensive and price sensitive—both areas affected by regulatory changes. As a private sector, we have not been makers of public policy, but we welcome opportunities to inform policymakers of our point of view. We try very hard to serve on state advisory boards, task forces, and other groups reviewing standards for revision. For years, the proprietary sector has tried to serve on the NAEYC board, without success.

We do not perceive a need for federal standards or regulation, nor do we look favorably on a federal bureaucracy overseeing our business. As the "privatization" concept has grown within government, we believe our philosophy of management has been underscored: better management means more consistent quality and fiscal accountability. In our segment of the market, we must maintain quality to satisfy the customers we need in order to support the accountability that is ever present in the business environment.

STANDARDS

A primary concern is the health and safety of children and staff. Caregivers are trained in such areas as diapering procedures, fire and storm evacuation, recognizing potential hazards, and appropriate procedures for dealing with sickness or injury. We believe that the key to health and safety is prevention through awareness. In each Kinder-Care center, a health and safety coordinator, trained in first aid and CPR certified, is designated. She is responsible for conducting safety meetings and encouraging staff in following the guidelines of the "Safety Calendar," which gives staff daily routine health/safety tasks to perform.

Professional employees, recruited and selected carefully, impact on quality. Large proprietary chains have special advantages in their ability to develop highly competent personnel. They can offer a career path that includes not only upward mobility but geographic mobility as well. They have the resources to provide center directors with training and to assist them in becoming good managers and in developing their skills at hiring and supervising. They can also offer benefit packages and internal training programs that enable employees to meet credentialing and state licensing requirements. The labor pool of caregivers between the ages of 18 and 35 is shrinking, and many potentially fine caregivers and center directors are ineligible because of lack of credits in early childhood education. These people can be helped by tuition reimbursement and other educational programs.

Similarly, large proprietary chains can draw on high level expertise in designing the education programs for the children in their care. A central curriculum staff can develop age-appropriate learning materials to be used by all centers. At Kinder-Care, a PhD in early childhood education and her staff write a monthly outline or skeleton of curriculum plus considerable amounts of enrichment material to "dress" that skeleton. In each center, the director and staff enrich the program with their own creative ideas and materials, appropriate to the geographic locale and ethnic backgrounds of the children. A uniform system of recording developmental progress and sharing it with parents via reports and personal conferences assures that each child's language, cognitive, social, and emotional development are being closely followed.

Parental involvement is an important aspect of proprietary child care, just as it is of nonprofit care. Parents tend to feel most confident and experience the most peace of mind when they are informed and involved. We establish and maintain open communication through national newsletters and other materials as well as newsletters and notes emanating from the centers. In a chain, when there is a complaint that cannot be resolved with the center director, parents can take their appeal to a higher level.

Proprietary centers are expected to be involved with the community as well as with parents. Centers and parents work together at fundraising and other community activities. At Kinder-Care, for example, our centers raised $700,000 for the Muscular Dystrophy Association in 1987 and were involved as well with Ronald McDonald Houses, zoos, local food banks, and local charities.

SOME ECONOMIC CONSIDERATIONS

In recent years the insurance crisis has influenced the growth of the private sector of child care. Larger companies have paid the price of higher premiums, and with management skills in risk management they have been able to negotiate coverage. Smaller companies have not been so fortunate; many have experienced 500%–800% increases in premiums and have chosen to sell or merge. Many cannot grow because of the insurance expense. Tort reform may help, but the increased numbers of suits filed and the media attention to the negative are working against us. Our company has gone to great lengths to teach crisis management to our supervisors, and we have very detailed procedures for handling any potential crisis. The economic reality, of course, is that it is the customers who must pay for the increased rates.

Tax credits are a major concern to our segment of child care. Some states offer credits to consumers, and a few offer them to businesses that sponsor or subsidize care of employees' children. Recent headlines have implied tax problems with cafeteria plans, so we probably have a long hard row to hoe before tax credits are increased or improved. A thriving economy will go a long way toward helping American working families with improved tax credits and motivating business to underwrite more centers for employees' children.

Employer-sponsored child care has been visible in the proprietary sector for some time. Kinder-Care opened its first account in 1981 and continues to operate over 40 such agreements. The for-profit sector understands business and is well qualified to develop partnerships for child care benefits, offering a full menu of consulting, construction, renovation, management, and operation. But although the few visionary companies that are involved are very positive about their programs, most companies do not keep data on absenteeism and turnover that would help to prove to them the worth of such a program beyond good employee relations and public relations. This segment of the market is therefore growing slowly.

INTO THE 1990S AND BEYOND

What does the future hold for proprietary child care? Growth and expansion are inevitable to meet the needs of working middle-class families. Increased infant and toddler care and preschool programs are needed. After-school programs are also growing as parents recognize the dangers to the "latch-key" child.

At Kinder-Care, we have expanded our training programs for both staff and directors, and we are committed to working with licensing professionals toward realistic regulations for all providers. We have asked a number of state agencies to review our internal credentialing programs with a view to accepting graduation from these programs in fulfillment of state requirements. We have also been approached by academic and medical groups regarding opportunities for research projects. And we have put in place a Quality Focus project to serve as an evaluation tool to ensure standards of quality in our centers nationwide.

The challenge is great, the opportunities are many, and the future will be exciting.

DISCUSSION

Ms. Muscari was asked to discuss Kinder-Care's experience with infant care, especially with relation to the problem of contagion. She replied that infant/toddler care (so called because different states have different definitions of infancy, ranging from 6 months to 2 years) has grown considerably since the late 1970s and, she predicts, will continue to grow. At present about 20% of the children in Kinder-Care centers are under 18 months of age. Infant care has gone well, without "monumental disease problems." There are disease outbreaks, but they are not a major problem, and when they occur they are dealt with promptly.

Ms. Muscari was then asked a number of questions regarding Kinder-Care's policies on staff qualifications, staff/child ratios, and parent participation on center boards of directors. Staff members must be high school graduates, preferably with prior experience or education in the field. Some applicants who appear to have promise as caregivers may be hired without experience, however, and trained by Kinder-Care, after a careful background check. Centers also comply with state standards in hiring personnel. All new employees are given a 90-day probationary period during which they are closely observed.

Staff/child ratios vary from state to state. Nationwide the ratio for infant care is between 1:5 and 1:6. In states that require an extremely high adult/child ratio, such as Maryland, where it is 1:3, Kinder-Care generally does not operate infant care, because the cost would be prohibitive for most parents.

For other age groups, 1:20 is standard for school- age children; 1:14 for 4-year-olds; 1:10 or 1:12 for 3-year-olds; 1:8 for 2-year-olds. From state to state these ratios vary by one or two one way or the other. Mixed-age grouping can be a problem. If you want to put a couple of almost-3-year-olds in a class of 3-year-olds, you must use the ratio for 2-year-olds.

Kinder-Care does not have parent advisory boards, for which they see no need. Parents are free to come in and voice complaints or discuss programming. Very few parents are unhappy with the curriculum. Their complaints are more likely to concern financial policies, such as having to pay fees when the child is sick. Parents work out problems with the director or, if they are unhappy with the director's solution, with the district manager.

The role of Kinder-Care as a profit-making organization was on the minds of a number of the participants, who see child care as a marginal business in most places and clearly were wondering whether the profit is being made at the expense of the children in care. Specifically, Ms. Muscari was asked about the low pay for the lower levels of staffing, generally minimum wage for beginning workers, which results in high turnover among the teaching staff. Given the importance to the child of stability of the teacher, and given the continued growth of for-profit care, which will recruit less-qualified people to work at low wages, this was a cause for concern.

Ms. Muscari replied that only about 8% of Kinder-Care personnel are at minimum wage; competitive salaries and good benefit packages help reduce turnover. She pointed out that many nonprofit centers are expected to have a surplus and that many such programs pay minimum wage to start and have high turnover. Many low-level workers prefer to work in for-profit centers, where they can be assured of pleasant surroundings, adequate materials, good instruction, and good training. She stressed that highly developed management skills and economies of scale make it possible to run centers at lower cost than most other programs. Centers begin to make money when they are about half full, and occupancy now is around 73% nationwide.

Other participants acknowledged that people who run typical non-profit child care programs are not likely to be as knowledgeable about economies of scale, efficiencies of management, centralization of curricula, and centralization of training, which Kinder-Care has developed over 20 years of experience. Turnover and levels of pay are probably about on a par with the industry. Regarding parent involvement, it was suggested that there is currently an underground movement to do away with parent boards in community centers. Empowering people who are not trained to run centers has proved in some cases to be self-destructive, and some non-profits are rethinking parents as decision makers.

16
Issues and Obstacles in the Training of Caregivers

Jeffrey Arnett
Oglethorpe University

The level of training of child care staff is widely regarded as an important factor, perhaps even the most important factor, in determining the quality of the day care environment (Ruopp, Travers, Glantz, & Coelen, 1979; Scarr, 1984). Parents seeking day care for their children are often advised to make the level of training of the staff a high priority (Scarr, 1984). Child care activists have long focused on training as a target for regulatory efforts, in the Federal Interagency Day Care Regulations (FIDCR) and in state regulations. There is an equally broad consensus that the level of training of the typical caregiver in the typical day care center is unconscionably low. Many states require no more than a perceptible pulse and some basic literacy skills for child care staff other than the director—i.e., for the people who have the most direct contact with the children. This chapter presents evidence concerning the importance of training as a dimension of day care quality and explores the reasons for the discrepancy between the perceived importance of training and the actual level of training of most caregivers.

Several questions related to training for caregivers are examined. First, what does the currently available research tell us about behavior related to training, and what additional research is needed? Second, what is taught in a typical training program, and what should be taught? Third, is it important that caregivers have training specific to child care, or is overall level of education an adequate substitute? Fourth, is it reasonable or even possible to require a high level of training for an occupation that is among the least remunerative in our economy? Finally, what alternatives are there for

241

improving the level of training among people caring for preschool children?

THE IMPORTANCE OF TRAINING: RESEARCH EVIDENCE

There is a consistent and growing body of evidence that training is related in a number of ways to the behavior of caregivers in day care centers. The National Day Care Study (Ruopp et al., 1979) found specific training in early childhood education, child development, or day care to be associated with caregiver behaviors toward children such as praising, comforting, responding, questioning, and instructing. Also, caregiver training was associated with characteristics of the children in their care, such as cooperativeness, greater attention to tasks and activities, less social isolation, and higher scores on standardized tests of cognitive development. Tizard, Philps, and Plewis (1976) also found training to be related to caregivers' behavior, in particular to their verbal interaction with children. Training was positively associated with caregivers' overall level of verbal interaction with children and with the cognitive content of caregivers' speech. The language skills of the children were in turn related to the level of verbal interaction of the caregivers.

In addition to studies such as these, which subsume a wide variety of training types and lengths under the term *training*, there are studies that have involved the evaluation of a specific training program. Kaplan and Conn (1984) evaluated a 20-hour training program that entailed classroom instruction on a broad range of topics, including child development, behavior management, nutrition, and special-needs children. This study was notable for having pre- and posttraining evaluations of the caregivers. In the posttraining evaluation, caregivers were observed to have made significant gains in facilitating social development and providing physical care, and they also improved the physical condition of the classroom and the materials available to the children. More direct teaching behaviors such as facilitating language development or cognitive development were not altered by the training.

Arnett (1987) evaluated another specific training program, entailing four classroom courses over 2 years and a brief practicum. Courses in communication and child development were taken in the first year of training, and courses in child care and preschool activities, plus the practicum, were taken in the second year. Caregivers fell into one of four discrete levels of training: those with no training, those who had completed half the training program, those who had completed the entire training program, and those who had obtained other, more extensive training elsewhere (i.e., 4-year degrees in early childhood education). The caregivers with 4-year degrees were clearly different from the other three groups; in global observations they were rated significantly higher in positive interaction with children and significantly lower in detachment and punitiveness. But the briefer specific training program did have demonstrable effects; those who had completed half or all of the training program were rated higher in positive interaction with children than caregivers with no training, and their childrearing attitudes were less authoritarian.

Most studies of training have been conducted in centers. A rare study of training among family day care providers (Ristau, Gardner, & Hodges, 1976) involved the training of advisors who would in turn make biweekly training visits to family day care providers. Caregivers who had received training were compared with untrained caregivers, also working in family day care settings, in interactions with the children in their care. Those who had received the training engaged more often in interactive play with the children, and there were trends ($p < .10$) in the direction of a decrease in criticizing and warning statements. Similarly, Howes (1983) observed family day care providers caring for toddlers and found those with more training to be more likely to play with the children and to respond positively to children's social bids.

These studies represent an important beginning in examining the effects of training on the behavior of caregivers. Nevertheless, at this point the body of research in this area is thin. In fact, the great majority of programs intended to enhance the competence of caregivers have failed to conduct more than a cursory evaluation of whether the program succeeded in its goal (Peters & Kostelnik, 1981), and even the best of the studies cited here leave a number of questions unanswered.

What, then, would an exemplary study of training for caregivers include? First, the study would involve direct observations of caregivers in interactions with children. That might seem self-evident, and all the studies cited here meet this criterion, but many other training program evaluations rely only on caregiver self-reports. The few available studies evaluating the Child Development Associate (CDA) credential, which has received considerable attention from policymakers considering state training requirements (Collins, 1983), are unfortunately in this category.

Second, the study would include caregivers with a variety of levels of training. Currently, there is a lack of evidence concerning the amount of training necessary to produce significant changes in caregivers' behavior and concerning the differences among caregivers with different levels of training. Four discrete training levels might be evaluated: (a) no training; (b) one or more day-long or weekend-long workshops; (c) a longer training program, extending over 1 or 2 years (training to prepare caregivers for the CDA credential is often of this length); (d) a 4-year degree in a child-related major. Thus far only one study (Arnett, 1987) has compared caregivers with differing levels of training.

Third, such a study would include pre- and posttraining evaluations. It is not sufficient simply to include an untrained control group for comparison. The possibility of pre-existing motivational and/or cognitive differences between trained and untrained groups is a confounding variable and makes it difficult to establish with assurance that the training is responsible for any behavioral differences between them. Of the studies mentioned here, only Kaplan and Conn (1984) included this feature.

Fourth, follow-up evaluations should be conducted to determine whether behavioral changes observed immediately after training become an enduring part of the caregiver's behavior. Studies of the effects of training in contexts other than day care (Cooper, Thomas, & Baer, 1970; Katz, Johnson, & Gelfand, 1972) provide a warning of the kind of backsliding that can occur over time. No study conducted thus far has included a follow-up, although for caregivers in studies that examine training as a heterogeneous variable (Ruopp et al., 1979; Tizard, Philps, & Plewis, 1976) a number of years may have passed since the caregivers completed their training.

Finally, pre- and posttraining evaluations of children's behavior should also be included, to see whether any changes in caregivers' behavior are reflected in the behavior of the children in their care. In the research currently available, associations noted between caregiver training and children's behavior provide little evidence that the differences among caregivers cause the differences among children, because the associations could easily reflect characteristics of the parents. For example, bright parents are likely to be in a middle- to upper-income bracket and therefore are likely to be able to afford day care of the highest quality for their children. A correlation between caregiver training (or any other indices of quality) and children's cognitive development therefore proves very little, because bright parents would be likely to have bright children, independent of the children's day care experience.

THE ISSUE OF CONTENT AND THE CHILD
DEVELOPMENT ASSOCIATE CREDENTIAL

Discussion of the effectiveness and importance of training is often based on the assumption that the content of training is uniform, that "training" can mean only one thing, and that what caregivers need to know is self-evident.

Is this a valid assumption? By way of answering this question, this section examines the content of the Child Development Associate credential (CDA National Credentialing Program, 1987).

The Child Development Associate (CDA) credential is a widely known credential of training, often cited in state regulations. In fact, however, the CDA program does not specify the content of training except in broad terms. Instead, the Child Development Associate Consortium, which is the agency that awards the credential, specifies a number of competencies and functional areas considered to be important (Table 16.1). The program is intended to be largely field based rather than classroom based, in the belief that training is most effective if it involves the direct application of the individual's skills in the day care environment, and also because the academic skills of caregivers are often limited. For the most part, the program is self-instructional. There is, however, a standardized CDA assessment system, on which the trainees are evaluated once training is completed.

In order to be eligible for the CDA assessment, the caregiver must have a minimum of 640 hours of experience working with preschool children and must have had at least three "formal or informal educational experiences," which may include anything from semester-long college courses to day-long workshops. The caregiver then compiles a portfolio containing a description of her activity concerning each of the 13 functional areas. When she decides she is ready, she asks to be evaluated by her advisor, who is often (although not always) the director of the center. This advisor observes her for a minimum of 12 weeks, evaluating her at least 3 times in each functional area, the three times spaced at least 3 weeks apart, and making suggestions for the improvement of her performance.

A parent also participates in the evaluation process, typically a parent with a child in the center but not in the direct care of the caregiver being evaluated. This parent observes the caregiver for an unspecified length of time and completes an observation form evaluating the caregiver's performance. The parent also distributes a questionnaire to parents who do have a child under the care of the caregiver, asking a number of questions concerning the parents' satisfaction with the caregiver's performance.

The last stage of the process involves a formal assessment by a CDA representative, who is typically an early childhood professional from the surrounding community, perhaps a professor of early childhood education or developmental psychology at the local university. The CDA representative observes the caregiver for approximately 3 hours during the course of 1 day and also interviews her to clarify any aspect of the observation and to learn more about her work performance. Then the CDA representative, the advisor, and the parent confer and decide whether or not

TABLE 16.1
CDA Competency Goals and Functional Areas for Preschool Caregivers in
Center-Based Programs

Competency Goals	Functional Areas
I. To establish and maintain a safe, healthy learning environment	1. Safe: Candidate provides a safe environment to prevent and reduce injuries.
	2. Healthy: Candidate promotes good health and nutrition and provides an environment that contributes to the prevention of illness.
	3. Learning environment: Candidate uses space, relationships, materials, and routines as resources for constructing an interesting, secure, and enjoyable environment that encourages play, exploration, and learning.
II. To advance physical and intellectual competence	4. Physical: Candidate provides a variety of equipment, activities, and opportunities to promote the physical development of children.
	5. Cognitive: Candidate provides activities and opportunities that encourage curiosity, exploration, and problem solving appropriate to the developmental levels and learning styles of children.
	6. Communication: Candidate actively communicates with children and provides opportunities and support for children to understand, acquire, and use verbal and nonverbal means of communicating thoughts and feelings.
	7. Creative: Candidate provides opportunities that stimulate children to play with sound, rhythm, language, materials, space, and ideas in individual ways and to express their creative abilities.
III. To support social and emotional development and provide positive guidance	8. Self: Candidate provides physical and emotional development and security for each child and helps each child to know, accept, and take pride in himself or herself and to develop a sense of independence.
	9. Social: Candidate helps each child feel accepted in the group, helps children learn to communicate and get along with others, and encourages feelings of empathy and mutual respect among children and adults.
	10. Guidance: Candidate provides a supportive environment in which children can begin to learn and practice appro-

TABLE 16.1 *(continued)*

	priate and acceptable behaviors as individuals and as a group.
IV. To establish positive and productive relationships with families	11. Families: Candidate maintains an open, friendly, and cooperative relationship with each child's family, encourages their involvement in the program, and supports the child's relationship with his or her family.
V. To ensure a well-run, purposeful program responsive to participant needs	12. Program management: Candidate is a manager who uses all available resources to ensure an effective operation. The candidate is a competent organizer, planner, record keeper, and communicator, and a cooperative co-worker.
VI. To maintain a commitment to professionalism	13. Professionalism: Candidate makes decisions based on knowledge of early childhood theories and practices, promotes quality in child care services, and takes advantage of opportunities to improve competence, both for personal and professional growth and for the benefit of children and families.

the caregiver should pass. She does not have to be found to have attained a high level of competence in all the functional areas in order to pass; the evaluators may pass her while recommending improvement in certain areas. Virtually all of the caregivers (about 98%) pass.

Table 16.1 describes the CDA competency goals and functional areas for preschool caregivers. For the assessment conducted by the CDA representative, more specific criteria are described for each functional area.

The CDA credential is an important beginning in establishing a minimum level of competence for caregivers, but some recommendations for change might be made. Of particular concern is the rigor of the assessment process. Any assessment with a passing rate of 98% has to be regarded with some suspicion, especially when the training itself is so independent and loosely defined. This concern is compounded by the fact that there is virtually no research evidence comparing the competence of caregivers with the CDA credential with that of caregivers with no training. What little research has been conducted has relied on self-report measures of dubious value and validity. Child care advocates who urge the establishment of the CDA as a national minimum credential should reconsider until the worth of the credential is verified by research.

Another change that might be recommended for the CDA program is that it focus more on training in behavior management—i.e., on techniques of discipline and control with groups of children or with individual children. In the current CDA program, only 1 of the 13 functional areas directly concerns behavior management (#10, Guidance). But 30 minutes in any day care center is enough to demonstrate that this is in fact the central occupation of people who work in day care centers and the area in which they are most in need of effective skills. How do you maintain control over 10 or so lively 4-year-olds during a time when it is important that they be self-controlled and cooperative, such as when you are reading a story to the group? How do you maintain your own self-control when the little boy whom you have already told 14 times not to try to pet the fish in the fish tank is doing it again? These sorts of conundrums are likely to be the most pressing ones for caregivers, and these sorts of skills on the part of caregivers, or the lack of such skills, certainly affect the quality of a child's day care experience far more than any other skills or knowledge a caregiver might obtain.

This analysis of the CDA illustrates the importance of considering the content of training when evaluating its effectiveness. Someone evaluating caregivers who had been trained in programs such as the one described earlier and expecting to find differences between trained and untrained caregivers in their disciplinary interactions with children would be likely to be disappointed. In point of fact, most studies of the effects of training focus on just these sorts of interactional variables, without considering that the caregivers being observed might have been trained to develop much different skills.

OVERALL EDUCATIONAL LEVEL
VERSUS TRAINING SPECIFIC TO CHILD CARE

Is it really training that is the important requirement for caregivers, or would it be enough simply to require that caregivers have a certain minimum level of education, perhaps a bachelor's degree, in any field? One might reasonably hypothesize that a university degree, even if not in a child-related field, might have connotations of intelligence, self-discipline, and reliability that would be useful qualities for caregivers. The National Day Care Study (Ruopp et al., 1979) seemed to indicate otherwise, however. Regression analyses conducted on those data led the investigators to conclude that education not specifically related to child care was unrelated to caregivers' behavior. However, educational level was confounded with caregiver race, which made it impossible to analyze independently the relation between educational level and caregivers' behavior.

Similarly, Arnett (1987) found overall education to be unrelated to caregivers' behavior. Education was used as a covariate to training in those analyses, and training specific to child care was found to be associated with various caregiver behaviors, as noted earlier. But education and training were highly correlated, as the caregivers with the highest level of training were those who had obtained 4-year degrees in early childhood education. As with the National Day Care Study, evaluating the independent influence of education was problematic.

A study that included caregivers with child-related college education and caregivers with college education unrelated to child care indicates that education unrelated to child care may be more influential on caregivers' behavior than was previously thought. Berk (1985) observed few differences between the two groups, while both differed from a high school–educated group. Those with 2 or more years of child-related college education were distinct from the high school-educated group in that they used more indirect guidance and less restriction with children, were more encouraging toward children, and displayed more behaviors considered to promote the development of children's verbal skills. Caregivers with 2 or more years of college education unrelated to children differed from the high school–educated caregivers in fewer ways—more indirect guidance and less restriction—but there were no significant differences in any category between college-educated caregivers with a child-related major and college-educated caregivers without a child-related major.

As Berk noted, however, this study had its own possible confounding factors. The findings may reflect differences in socioeconomic status (SES) rather than the effects of a college education. Studies of the relation between SES and parenting behavior have found just the sort of differences according to social class that Berk finds with regard to education: Parents' discipline is less restrictive and more indirect as SES increases (Hess, 1970). The precise relationship between overall education and caregivers' behavior with children remains an open question.

OBSTACLES TO TRAINING REQUIREMENTS

On the basis of the available evidence, it can be said generally that training does have demonstrable and desirable associations to the behavior of caregivers. Would it be a good idea, then, to have a nationwide minimum requirement for training for caregivers in day care centers—say, 2 years of child-related college education? Most investigators in day care would probably be inclined to answer this question affirmatively, but a close examination of the consequences of adopting such a requirement makes the wisdom of it seem questionable.

Adoption of a minimum requirement of 2 postsecondary years of training would raise the overall quality of day care in this country, if caregivers could be found to fill the positions. Several factors make that prospect unlikely. Most obvious is that the average pay in the field is abysmal. According to the 1980 census, the average wage for child care workers in the educational and social services that year was $3.22 per hour. To put that in perspective, people caring for animals had an average wage of $4.20 that year. In 1984, this same category of child care workers had a median full-time income of $9,204 (U.S.D.L., Bureau of Labor Statistics, 1985a); the poverty level for that year for a family of four was $10,610.

Low pay is the basis of two other problems that make training requirements problematic, specifically the problems of turnover and the low status of child care as an occupation. The estimates of turnover for child care workers range as high as 42% per year (Phillips & Whitebook, 1986); the most common reason offered for leaving is low pay. How likely are most caregivers to comply with a requirement that they obtain extensive additional training if they are planning to leave the field within a year or two? It is also hard to imagine many people becoming enthusiastic about investing time and money in extensive training for a field that we as a culture hold in such low esteem.

But the turnover rate would improve, and the status of the profession would rise, if the pay were higher. The low wages, then, seem to be the primary obstacle. Can the answer be found in simply raising the wages of caregivers, perhaps through state legislation or unionization? Again, that may seem attractive at first glance, but a closer examination shows this solution to be questionable. Child care providers already work on a notoriously tight budget, and staff costs are the largest single expense category for day care providers (Ruopp et al., 1979). On other side, most parents with children in day care already find that the cost of care puts a squeeze on the family budget, even with day care at its current cost. In summary, it would be difficult to find enough people who would be willing to obtain extensive training when the financial compensation for such training is slight. In an empirical demonstration of this conclusion, Peters and Sutton (1984) found that caregivers who completed the Child Development Associate training program received no pay raises or promotions as a result.

The problem of requiring a high level of training is equally formidable whether it concerns attracting new people to the field or inducing the people currently employed as caregivers to obtain training. Consider the situation of the typical caregiver currently working in a day care center. She works 8–10 hours a day in a strenuous occupation, for less than she could make working the drive-in window at McDonald's. Now day care regulators want her to take what little salary she has and pay to obtain training. They want her to expend her meager free time to attend night classes over a number of years. The attractiveness of that prospect to the average caregiver should be obvious.

ALTERNATIVE APPROACHES

Are there, then, any promising alternatives? Clearly it is unlikely that the current system will ever raise the level of training among caregivers to a point that would satisfy most of those concerned about day care quality. For infants and toddlers, some combination of parental leave and employer-sponsored day care may the most workable solution. Virtually every industrialized nation except the United States has some form of legally established parental leave (see Kamerman, this volume). And a number of studies attest to the benefits that accrue to employers who provide day care for their employees' children, especially lower turnover and absenteeism (Hiatt, 1982; Ogilvie, 1972; U.S.D.L., Women's Bureau, 1980). Despite the tax incentives included in the Economic Recovery Tax Act of 1981, employer-sponsored day care remains rare, perhaps partly because most corporate boards are composed largely of older males. Still, given the formidable costs of child care for infants and toddlers, because of the low child/staff ratio required, a combined public and private sector effort may be the most effective approach. Perhaps further inducements for employers to provide day care could be devised.

For preschool children, the most promising recourse may be for public schools gradually to include some child care functions in their programs, for children older than age 2.5 but younger than school age. A proposal of this sort, propounded by Edward Zigler, has been gaining attention in recent months (cf. Trotter, 1987). Zigler recommended that public schools be considered not only as educational institutions but as potential child care centers as well. Care would be available (not mandatory) for all children over age 3, but for 3- and 4-year-olds the care would be oriented toward play rather than toward education. At age 5, children would spend half a day in kindergarten and the other half in the child care part of the school, or at home if there is a parent at home. The school would also provide before-school and after-school child care for children aged 6 to 12 whose parents are working during that time and would even provide vacation care. The child-care portion of the school would be staffed not by teachers but by people who have the CDA credential; the program would therefore be more affordable, because the child care workers would not have to be paid as much as highly trained teachers. Someone with a degree would supervise the program. Local taxes would pay for some of the expense of the program, but parents would pay a fee for the child care services they use, adjusted according to their family income.

For children in disadvantaged neighborhoods, perhaps the program could be conducted along the lines of the Head Start program that currently exists. These children might benefit from educationally oriented child care at ages 3 and 4, but Zigler emphasizes that for most children, the program should be nonacademic, with the emphasis on play. Most children will learn all they need to know at this age through play, and subjecting them to an academic curriculum would be futile or even damaging, because of the potential for failure. It would also be unnecessarily expensive.

The plan is a reasonable and promising one. Two modifications might be considered. Making the program available at age 2.5 rather than at age 3 is one possibility. By 30 months most children are capable of spending long periods with their peers, and even eager to do so. They would have to be toilet trained, of course, as an entrance requirement. The other possible change in the program concerns staffing. The CDA requirement alone might not be a sufficient training requirement, at least not until it includes more extensive training in behavior management and until the effectiveness of the CDA training program is verified by research. Even if it is shown to meet its stated goals, it represents a minimum training program. Perhaps there could be one teacher with a 4-year degree in early childhood education for each staff member with a CDA credential. For example, for 20 to 25 children ages 3–4, there could be one of each.

Putting what is currently considered day care under the aegis of the public school system would have several advantages over the current system. First and foremost, it would ensure that the caregivers/teachers would be well trained, certified, and highly qualified, compared with most caregivers currently working in day care centers. Second, and not coincidentally, the caregivers would have much higher salaries. Third, there would be less disparity in the sort of care children from varying SES backgrounds receive. Obviously, there are differences in the quality of school systems according to the economic well-being of the surrounding community, but it is likely that even a low-funded public school program for 3- and 4-year-olds would be superior to the low-funded day care centers that currently exist. It may be prudent to direct federal support for child care especially to low-income communities.

Several bills supporting preschool education/child care in some form are currently before the Congress. One would provide $120 million for 60 demonstration programs at schools nationwide over 3 years, to test and refine the idea. Meanwhile, states are proceeding with their own programs.

The National Education Association reports that some 3,000 of the country's 15,000 school districts already provide some kind of preschool education ("U.S. Teachers," 1987). In 23 states, legislation is pending to establish classes for 4-year-olds in public schools. Already, New York City is in the process of instituting such a program for 4-year-olds (Molnar & Thompson, 1987). However, most of these current and proposed programs are education oriented. As such, they will almost certainly be more expensive than a nonacademic program would be and may for this reason undermine the constituency for providing less expensive play-oriented care for preschool children. Also, they are likely to cover only the regular school hours or even to be limited to half-day programs, which would still present a child care problem for parents who work full-time.

Several other objections to school-based child care need to be acknowledged and considered. One is that there may not be room for 3- and 4-year-olds in the public schools by the time this program could be developed and implemented. By 1995, the children of the baby boomers will have reached school age, and public school systems will be hard pressed to find room even for all the children who are at least 6 years old. A second objection is that children in many communities are bussed a half hour or more to school, a condition that is difficult even for 6- or 7-year-olds, and that many parents (not to mention bus drivers) may consider intolerable for younger children. Parents can choose a day care center for their child that is on the way to work or close to home; they often do not have that luxury with respect to the public school, because of interracial bussing or simply because schools are larger and less numerous than day care centers.

School-based care, then, is no panacea for our national child care problem. It may work very well in some communities, but in others it will not be an adequate solution. Ultimately, a diverse, multifaceted approach of which school-based care is only one element may work best. Another element may involve providing vouchers that parents can use to obtain child care of their own choice. The vouchers would not be intended to pay the entire cost of child care but to lighten the financial burden on the parents and enable them to obtain better care than they would otherwise be able to afford. This kind of program currently exists for low-income families, under Title XX of Social Security. One especially desirable feature of that program is that, in many states, the vouchers are valid only when care is obtained from a licensed program, thereby establishing at least a minimum level of quality. It would be wise to retain this requirement if the program were to be expanded to include families in higher income brackets.

Wouldn't the cost of public support for child care of *any* kind be prohibitive and widely protested? Perhaps not. Making it voluntary would hold down costs, and parents would still have to pay a substantial part of the expense. Besides, the idea of a public responsibility for children, even on the part of the childless, is already the foundation of the existing public school system. The current proposals involve an expansion of the currently existing public role in providing for the healthy development of children.

There are certainly those who will resist an expansion of that role, and they are right that it should not be undertaken without caution. Making it voluntary would minimize resistance from parents who may desire, quite understandably, to choose privately run care, or to care for their children at home during those years. The first colonists came to the United States to escape state intrusion into their personal lives, and that sentiment has endured and runs deep in this country. Nevertheless, a public role in child care may come to seem highly desirable if the alternative is a generation of children who receive inadequate care during their first years of life.

DISCUSSION

Dr. Phillips noted that the research literature on training child care staff reveals a number of contradictions, studies in which more training or more experience predicted negative outcomes for children, and several participants offered possible explanations. Dr. Phillips postulated that a worker who has had years of experience and received considerable training but who has not received rewards for her work may become frustrated or burned out. Dr. Arnett agreed that experience might in this way be related to negative outcomes, but not training; training and experience might be confounded in some of the studies. He also noted that his personal observations in Bermuda day care centers suggested generational differences in caregivers. The older women who had been working at the centers for many years had become used to doing things in certain ways, and short-term training programs were not likely to change their ways of dealing with children. Dr. Scarr pointed out that government-sponsored or subsidized programs, which tend to have higher standards for training of caregivers, are associated with children who have lower behavioral development because they are coming from disadvantaged families. Middle-class children may have less well-trained caregivers but perform better, making it appear that training is a negative.

Ms. Kalemkiarian stated that the nonprofit program for which she is a board member has found that teachers with little academic training but some classroom experience were often better prepared to teach than teachers with academic credentials and little experience. They believe that academic training is important, however, and they have instituted an incentive program that allows teachers to increase their compensation by obtaining more academic units. She suggested as an area of possible study the differential effects of training received on the job and pre-job training that is part of one's education. Dr. Kendall noted that educators are beginning to look more closely at the effects of teacher education, following up their graduates to evaluate the impact of their training, with a view to modifying their programs accordingly. Although college education is important, several participants agreed, there are arguments for the greater practicality of paraprofessionals with lower levels of training.

Ms. Muscari made the point that training matters little if the right staff has not been selected in the first place. In her view, there is a dearth of understanding of the selection process. Dr. Arnett questioned whether child care providers have much selection, given the problem of low pay, but others affirmed that promising workers can be identified and developed. There are many good people who may not have had a middle-class background and a 4-year education but who need work and who have the ability to relate to children. Moreover, there are many people who want to do this job in spite of the financial sacrifices. Senior citizens may represent a rich resource to be tapped.

The feasibility of locating large-scale child care programs in the public school system was also debated. Some participants questioned whether the public at large would be willing to support the costs of not only running such programs but building new facilities to house them; others felt that the principle of spreading the cost over users and nonusers is well established in the public school system, and that in many communities school buildings are empty or underutilized. Transportation is another obstacle; the prospect of bussing 2-, 3- and 4-year-olds was not looked on with favor.

Dr. Hill-Scott pointed out that a strong case can be made, and will be made, for a voucher system in place of plans to develop child care in the public schools. If the public school system handles child care, she said, the cost will escalate to the point where people won't be willing to support it. Child care can be provided more economically in the private sector, and with vouchers parents could go out to the private market and shop for their care. It would not result in equitable care, she noted, because parents who could afford to would be able to pay rates in excess of the voucher value to obtain higher-quality care. But vouchers, particularly on a sliding-scale basis, are a plausible option, one that will be supported by many policymakers. Child care advocates must understand all possible options as they explore various ways of developing adequate child care.

17
Future Directions and Need for Child Care in the United States

Deborah A. Phillips
University of Virginia

Over 20 years ago, the Children's Bureau held a National Conference on Day Care Services (U.S. Department of Health, Education, & Welfare, 1966) at which Mary Dublin Keyserling called for day care for every child who needs it. Two years later, the Children's Bureau and the Women's Bureau sponsored a follow-up conference (U.S. Department of Labor, 1967) at which a familiar plea was made: "The Children's Bureau must share part of the blame for the failure to look at reality in today's day care picture, when thousands of infants and young children are being placed in haphazard situations because their mothers are working" (p. 14).

With history as prologue, the themes of the preceding chapters take on an aura of déjà vu. We have been warned about haphazard and inconsistent child care policies; the tremendous gap between the demand for child care and the supply of available services has been documented; the threat to children constituted by inattention to quality in typical child care programs has been described; and, throughout the chapters, admonitions for child care policy to proceed from reality have been sounded.

The future of child care in the United States is the topic of this concluding chapter. Recent projections of the future demand for child care and trends in patterns of child care use are presented. These demographic realities provide the departure point for a broader discussion of several contemporary social, economic, and political pressures that may affect the shape of child care in the 1990s. I argue that a gradual shift is occurring from a traditional orientation that approaches child care as a marginal service for deficient families to debates that are increasingly framed in pragmatic investment terms. The chapter concludes by balancing this optimistic stance with a few cautionary challenges.

DEMOGRAPHICS IS DESTINY

Contemporary debates about child care are driven by demographic upheaval. The changing economic structure of American families, most notably the relentless entry of mothers into the labor force, is largely responsible for the resurgence of interest in child care. A significant threshold was passed in 1985 when over half of all mothers with children under age 3 were in the labor force (U.S.D.L., Bureau of Labor Statistics, 1986). In 1987, this 50% threshold was passed for mothers of infants age 1 year or younger (U.S.D.L., Bureau of Labor Statistics, 1987). In a society whose political system is premised on the concept of the majority, the significance of these watershed statistics cannot be underestimated.

Child care, previously allied closely with welfare services, has become a mainstream issue. Far from being a service reserved for poor and otherwise "inadequate" families, child care emerged in the mid-1980s as a normative aspect of rearing children in the United States. As noted in prior chapters, the proportion of children with working mothers has increased steadily and substantially since the 1970s. This trend characterizes children of all ages and races, and those in both single- and two-parent families at all income levels (Hofferth & Phillips, 1987; Kamerman, this volume). In summary, prior age- and class-based profiles of child care use are converging on a common social pattern of substantial reliance on child care.

The Future Demand for Child Care

The future demand for child care will depend, as it does today, on a panoply of factors, including parental preferences for and access to various types of child care, family structure and income, national economic and work force trends, and the availability of both public subsidies for child care and leaves for parents with infants and sick or handicapped children. Nevertheless, in the most immediate sense, the demand for child care depends on the number of young children who live in families in which all parents work. Traditionally, estimates of the number of children with employed mothers have served as proxies for projected child care needs (Hofferth, 1979; Hofferth & Phillips, 1987; Smith, 1979). These estimates are, in turn, a joint function of the size of the childhood population and the proportion of this population with mothers in the labor force.

Projecting the Child Population. As a result of childbearing among the large baby boom cohort, the population of children in the United States is now on the rise (Hofferth & Phillips, 1987). Although both the numbers of births and the fertility rate began to decline after 1960, the large number of adults who are now bearing children means a high number of births despite relatively low fertility rates (Hofferth, 1987). Accordingly, the number of preschool children began to increase as of 1980 and by 1990 is expected to reach 23 million children under age 6. This projected figure is only slightly lower than the 24.6 million children under age 6 at the height of the baby boom (Hofferth & Phillips, 1987).

Tracking this so-called "baby boomlet" over the life course makes it possible to predict growth in older age groups that also have child care needs. For example, the number of school-age children (5–17 years) started to increase in 1986 and is expected to reach 45 million by 1995 (Hofferth & Phillips, 1987). Demand for before- and after-school child care can be expected to follow a parallel course. These trends in the school-age population also have sobering implications for the availability of school classrooms for daytime child care use.

Children with Working Mothers. The figures concerning growth in the childhood population take on added significance when juxtaposed with trends in maternal employment. If current trends continue (and there is every reason to expect that they will), by 1995 over 75% of school-age children and over 66% of preschool children will have a mother in the work force (see Fig. 17.1 and 17.2). This will amount to 34.4 million school-age children with employed mothers, 37% more than in 1980. The number of preschoolers with working mothers will reach 14.6 million by 1995, 73% more than in 1980 (Hofferth & Phillips, 1987).

Based on current employment patterns (U.S.D.L., Bureau of Labor Statistics, 1985b), close to 70% of these mothers will work full-time, although they will not necessarily work year-round. Today about 66% of all working women with a child under 3 years of age, and 71% of all working mothers, are employed full-time. Even more striking are tabulations from the 1982 National Surveys of Family Growth, which reveal that 75% of employed mothers with children under age 1 work full-time (Hofferth & Phillips, 1987). It is important, therefore, to recognize that when we are discussing the need for child care, we are predominantly discussing a need for full-time care.

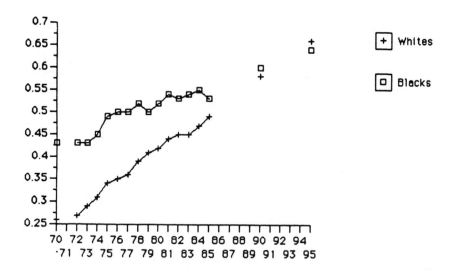

FIG. 17.1.   Percent of children under 6 with mothers in labor force (Hofferth, 1987. Unpublished tabulations from Hofferth & Phillips, 1987).

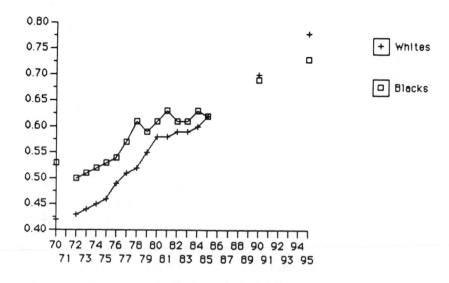

FIG. 17.2.   Percent of children 6–17 with mothers in labor force (Hofferth, 1987. Unpublished tabulations from Hofferth & Phillips, 1987).

Moreover, indications of a close association between early and later labor force participation (Heckman, 1978) suggest that this cohort of mothers, many of whom worked prior to having children, will remain in or rapidly re-enter the labor force following childbirth. Although policy changes that alter the availability of parental leaves may affect this trend somewhat, it is reasonable to expect that current shortages of infant day care will worsen over the next decade.

Racial and Marital Trends in Maternal Employment. Just as prior age-based distinctions regarding use of child care are breaking down, patterns of use for children of different races and different family structures are also coming to look more alike. The labor force participation rates of Black and White mothers appear to be converging (see Fig. 17.1 and 17.2). There has been a sharper increase in the percentage of White than of Black children with working mothers between 1970 and 1985. In 1970, 53% of Black and 42% of White school-aged children had mothers in the work force. By 1985, 62% of both Black and White school-age children had working mothers. For preschoolers, the percentage point difference has narrowed from 17 points in 1970, when 26% of White and 43% of Black preschoolers had working mothers, to 4 percentage points in 1985. If current trends continue, a larger percentage of White children than Black children will live in a family in which the mother works (Hofferth & Phillips, 1987).

Also converging are the labor force participation rates of single mothers and mothers who are married and living with their husbands. Just between 1980 and 1986, the rates for married mothers with children under age 6 rose from 45% to 54%. The 1986 labor force participation rate for single mothers with children under age 6 was 59%. Among mothers with children under age 3, 41% of married mothers and 45% of single mothers worked in 1980; as of 1986, 51% of married mothers and 49% of single mothers with children under age 3 were working (Kahn & Kamerman, 1987).

Summary of Demographic Projections. These data can be summarized quickly: Maternal employment is not a fad, and it does not discriminate. It is not a phenomenon restricted to older children, Black families, and single mothers, as many used to believe and in this way justified their view of child care as a marginal service for minority populations. This view was highly problematic at the time; today, in addition, it is grossly outdated.

Moreover, this baby boom generation of parents is a cohort that has grown accustomed to having society change to meet its needs. As children, they saw the schools expand, and as young adults they saw job opportunities expand. Women in this generation, in particular, are responsible for dramatic social accommodations to changing needs and attitudes. It is

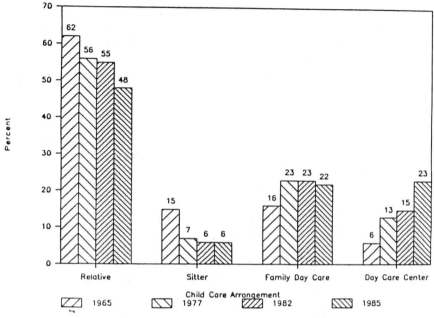

FIG. 17.3.   Care of preschool children, 1965–1985.

likely that their expectations about child care will be a potent influence on the future shape of our society.

Trends in Patterns of Child Care Use

Among the most basic policy issues in the area of child care is whether the supply of child care arrangements will keep pace with the projected growth in demand for care. The number of children with working mothers provides an estimate of the magnitude of the demand for child care, but it provides no information about where that demand will be directed. This requires an examination of trends in patterns of child care use.

Figure 17.3 presents trends from 1965 to 1985 in care arrangements made for preschoolers whose mothers work. Because families that rely on supervised care *not* provided by a sibling or spouse constitute the effective demand on the child care market, this population provides the base for the trends illustrated in Fig. 17.3.

The most striking trend revealed is the substantial growth in use of group care programs from 1965 to 1982. Across this 17-year span, there was a gradual decline in care by a nonrelative in the child's home (sitter/nanny), a modest increase in family day care (care by a nonrelative in the adult's home), and an enormous increase in care in a day care center or nursery school (Hofferth & Phillips, 1987). Recent data show continued increases in the proportion of children of employed mothers in child care centers, to over 20% of children under 5 with employed mothers in 1985 (U.S. Bureau of Census, 1987b).

Given that infants and toddlers are experiencing the most rapid growth in need for child care, parents' care choices for this population provide an important key to future demand for child care. For full-time employed mothers with infants and toddlers, reliance on relatives and family day care homes—the most commonly used forms of care for these young children—has declined in recent years, while use of day care centers has risen dramatically. Whereas only 5% of children under age 3 in 1965 (*not* in self-care or the care of a sibling or father) were in center-based arrangements, by 1982 this figure had reached 16%. In 1982, 21% of all children in child care centers were under 3 years of age (Hofferth & Phillips, 1987), and Muscari (this volume) reports that about 20% of all Kinder-Care enrollees are infants and toddlers.

Among part-time employed mothers with infants and toddlers, family day care homes—and, to a lesser extent, relatives—are showing the greatest increases in use. Thus, market forms of infant and toddler care are likely to experience tremendous pressures to expand. These are the scarcest commodities in the child care field, and as a result of the need for high staff/child ratios, the most expensive.

Will the supply of child care exist to meet the need? What will this child care look like? Who will provide it? And who will pay for it? These are the fundamental issues that will direct the future course of child care.

FUTURE DIRECTIONS FOR CHILD CARE

As with the future demand for child care, the direction taken by our nation's child care services over the next decade will be the product of numerous entangled influences. Actual patterns of child care use will vary with trends in the cost, supply, and "acceptability" of various types of care. The child care market itself will be affected by the changing involvement of government, businesses, churches, schools, and other sectors of our society, as well as by regulatory changes. The quality of the child care programs of the future will also be affected by trends in regulation, by the availability of a qualified work force of providers, and by the ability and willingness of parents to demand and pay for good quality care.

To lend coherence to this presentation, the three central components of child care that have provided the themes of prior chapters are used as an organizational framework: supply and availability, cost and affordability, and developmental quality. This section concludes with a discussion of what will perhaps be the most powerful determinant of the future direction of child care: social values and ideology.

Supply and Availability

Thus far we have discussed the demand for child care and the likely direction it will take based on current patterns of use for children of different ages whose mothers work full- and part-time. The actual landscape of child care use over the next decade, however, will substantially depend on the supply of different forms of child care.

Estimating the future supply of child care is a very tricky and imprecise business, but there are several ingredients to consider. First, and most important, is the availability of a work force of women (98% of child care workers are women; U.S.D.L., Bureau of Labor Statistics, 1985b) who will provide the child care of the future. This becomes particularly significant in light of trends toward growing use of market forms of child care.

Throughout history, a combination of "kith and kin" and more or less trained professionals have provided child care (Joffe, 1977). There is no reason to expect that a similarly mixed work force will fail to materialize in the future, although there are suggestions that child care may be becoming a relatively less attractive job option for women.

Child care workers are paid less than adults who tend our cars and parking lots, our washing machines, and our pets. In 1984, 9 out of 10 child care providers who work in private households earned poverty-wage levels (U.S.D.L., Bureau of Labor Statistics, 1985b). The same was true of over half of all market-based child care workers (Phillips & Whitebook, in press). The median annual earnings of full-time child care workers in 1984 was $9,204 for those employed in educational and social service positions. The poverty level in 1984 for a family of four was $10,610. Yet the average educational level of these child care workers equals that of the total U.S. work force (U.S. Bureau of Census, 1984).

Given contemporary growth in alternative service sector jobs, it is conceivable that the supply of child care providers will fail to keep pace with the growth in demand. Women who leave the child care field cite low wages, poor benefits, and stressful working conditions as the major reasons for their departure (Kontos & Stremmel, 1987; Whitebook, Howes, Friedman, & Darrah, 1982). Increased wages for women working outside of the home in somewhat higher status, less physically demanding and isolating jobs might, for example, encourage some women to move out of marginal employment as home providers. A more critical issue, addressed later in the discussion of quality, concerns the qualifications and commitment of the future child care work force. Although there may be adequate numbers of providers during any given month, significant questions about the preparation and consistency of this work force loom large as we approach the 1990s (Modigliani, 1986; Phillips & Whitebook, in press).

The future supply of child care is also likely to become increasingly diverse as growing numbers of employers, school districts, local governments, and other players become involved in child care provision. They will join the current conglomeration of churches, community agencies, for-profit centers, and home-based providers who constitute the major sources of nonrelative care. Schools and employers, although unlikely to alter the face of child care completely, constitute two sectors of society that are increasingly being looked to as additional sources of child care. Each also offers a unique opportunity: Business holds the potential for work-site care, and the schools have the advantage of a tax-based economic foundation.

Involvement of the schools in child care is a highly controversial topic. Some groups have voiced concerns about the age and cultural appropriateness of school-based child care programs (Bredekamp, 1987; Hale-Benson, this volume; National Black Child Development Institute, 1987). Some traditional child care providers harbor fears of being supplanted by the schools, which have the ability to pay higher staff salaries and also enjoy greater public acceptability as a social institution for children. Other child care advocates view the schools as a source of greater social legitimacy for child care and of more predictable care and therefore look to them as an obvious candidate for a truly national delivery system for child care.

The future shape of school involvement in child care will clearly be the product of a volatile exchange of opinions. But even those who are reluctant to approach the schools acknowledge that they *are* involved in child care and are likely to become more involved. A major new child care bill (S. 1995) places schools at the hub of a new national system of child care. More than 25% of the states have implemented part-day pre-kindergarten programs in the schools (Morado, 1986), which, although they cannot meet families' full-time child care needs, reflect a growing interest on the part of schools to extend downward the age groups they perceive as appropriate for educational services.

Increasing pressure is also being placed on employers to offer a variety of benefits that can alleviate the conflicts associated with combining family and career roles. Child care is prominent among these benefits (Friedman, 1985; Galinsky & Friedman, 1986). Presently, about 2,000 employers out of 6 million businesses nationwide provide some form of child care assistance, although direct provision of child care services is the exception (Friedman, 1985). As of 1985, 120 corporations and 400 hospitals provided child care centers at or near the workplace. Projections about the future of employer-supported child care typically adopt a middle-of-the-road stance (Friedman, 1985; Hofferth & Phillips, 1987), reflecting cynicism about the likelihood of major involvement by the business sector but some optimism about employers' growing receptivity to economic rationales for expanding their family benefits (Fernandez, 1986). In this context, the impact of the generational advancement of today's dual-career parents and single working parents into positions of corporate leadership should not be underestimated.

In summary, two major factors that are likely to affect the future supply of child care are the availability of women to provide child care and the increasing diversification of the child care market. These factors, in turn, raise major questions about the future status (and thus attractiveness) of child care work and the need for greater coherence in the byzantine array of child care arrangements that confronts parents in the United States.

Cost and Affordability

Families typically assign a high priority to cost, second only to geographic convenience, when selecting child care (Hofferth, 1987; Steinberg & Green, 1979; Unco, Inc., 1975; Yaeger, 1979). Issues of economic equity in child care choices, and of subsidization of costs for the poor, are thus extremely significant factors to consider in the future equation for child care.

High-income families pay more for child care than low-income families, all else being equal (Hofferth, 1987). Similarly, the more hours a mother is employed, the higher her wage, and the higher her education—each of which predicts income—the more likely she is to rely on "formal," paid forms of care such as a family day care home or a center (Floge, 1985). In contrast, low-income families spend a higher proportion of their total family income on child care than do high-income families. In 1985, families with a youngest child under 5 spent, on average, 11% of their income on child care. Poor White mothers, however, paid 20% of their income on child care, whereas White mothers with incomes above the poverty line used only 9% of their income for child care. Among Black mothers, the nonpoor spent 8% and the poor 26% of their income for child care (Hofferth, 1987).

The differential purchasing power of poor and nonpoor families, and the channeling of government subsidies to programs that serve predominantly subsidized (and thus poor) children, has created a two-tiered system of child care (Phillips, 1984; Scarr & Weinberg, 1986; Zigler, 1987a). Economic segregation has been a historical fact of life for child care in the United States (Grubb & Lazerson, 1982; Steinfels, 1973) and is so thoroughly entrenched that it is likely to characterize the child care programs of the 1990s. Growth in the for-profit child care market, which caters to a middle-class clientele (Muscari, this volume), coinciding with major funding reductions in federal programs that support the child care costs of the poor (Blank, this volume), may actually exacerbate economic stratification of the child care market.

With respect to affordability, data recently reported by Hofferth (1987) on the child care expenditures of mothers in their 20s show that the costs of center-based and family day care have stayed relatively constant in real terms over the past decade. In contrast, the costs of paid care by a relative and in-home care by a sitter have increased greatly. If these trends continue, the relative differences in demand coupled with what appears to be a rising disparity in costs among these various arrangements may add to the pressures for growth that are anticipated for the more formal, market forms of child care.

The availability of subsidies will also affect the future costs of child care. Child care costs are directly related to provider salaries, leading many to assert that the low wages of child care providers constitute the nation's largest child care subsidy for families (Modigliani, 1986; Phillips & Whitebook, in press). Thus, the future profile of child care staff will affect the future cost of child care; younger (or the retired elderly), less well-educated or prepared, less committed staff can be paid less.

Government programs, including tax provisions, constitute the second source of subsidy. Direct government support for social services has been very important to the growth of the nonprofit day care center. The future of these subsidies is held hostage to broad concerns about the federal deficit, to priorities in spending, and to broader social expectations about the responsibilities of the federal and state governments. As Blank (this volume) has noted, the major source of these direct subsidies—Title XX of the Social Security Act—is now funded at half its 1977 funding level in real dollars.

Tax support for child care, channeled primarily through the Dependent Care Tax Credit, has shown much greater resistance to change than have the direct subsidies. Lost revenues attributable to the credit have actually tripled from about $1 billion in 1980 to an estimated $3.4 billion in 1986 (Robins, 1988), marking a considerable shift of federal child care support from poor to nonpoor, taxpaying families (Phillips, 1984). Some pending policy proposals would actually pare back the tax credit for child care and redirect funds to more direct sources of child care support, but there are no indications that these proposals are garnering the political endorsements needed for passage.

In summary, indications that expenditures have shown little fluctuation over recent years suggest that families are paying about what they are willing and/or able to pay for child care. The relative costs of formal and informal arrangements appear to be less stable, although there are inadequate data available on which to base future projections. A major issue for the years ahead concerns the intractibility of economic segregation in child care programs, resulting in part from historical funding patterns, the neighborhood basis of most child care arrangements, and families' differential purchasing power.

Developmental Quality

The future direction of child care quality is perhaps the most volatile, and thus least amenable to prediction, of the three components of child care discussed in this section. Several factors, however, are converging to make issues of child care quality increasingly salient.

The first is the renewed visibility and sense of urgency around issues of child safety in child care that were prompted by recent allegations of sexual abuse in child care centers (Phillips, 1986). Although safety is only part of what developmental psychologists have in mind when they talk about quality of care (see Belsky, this volume; Lamb, this volume), it lies at the basis of child care regulation. And regulation is the only available mechanism for establishing a consistent baseline level of quality in child care.

Growing attention is now being paid to the coverage, monitoring, and enforcement of child care licensing laws, as distinct from the actual provisions of the laws (Kendall, this volume). If this attention serves to restore funds that have been cut from the regulatory arms of state child care offices, one might expect the future enforcement of regulations to be strengthened. Pressures in the opposite direction, however, continue to be exerted by "charismatic" churches that seek exemptions from child care licensing (Phillips, 1987c), and from some policymakers who believe that the supply of child care will be enhanced only if child care regulations are relaxed.

The second factor that is drawing attention to quality issues is the active public debate about the long-term effects of early childhood education (Berrueta-Clement, Schweinhart, Barnett, Epstein, & Weikart, 1984; Lazar, Darlington, Murray, Royce, & Snipper, 1982) coupled with the broader educational reform effort (see National Commission on Excellence in Education, 1983). Child care has typically been viewed as different from education, particularly when the impetus for its use derives from adult employment needs (the welfare model of child care) rather than from child-development needs (the Head Start model). But this distinction is now being blurred by the fact that families who are seeking early childhood education are also the ones who require full-day child care. The basic investment argument that lends the Head Start program its popularity—a dollar spent now will save at least a dollar of future spending—is gaining increasing prominence in the child care debate. That a good investment requires quality care is not questioned; whether we, as a nation, are willing to support the costs of a good quality child care system remains a very active controversy.

A third ingredient in the contemporary quality debate involves child care staff. There is a growing appreciation of the inconsistency, on the one hand, of research evidence that points to the training, stability, and expertise of child care providers as highly predictive of positive outcomes for children (Cummings & Beagles-Ross, 1984; McCartney, 1984; Phillips & Howes, 1987; Phillips, McCartney, & Scarr, 1987; Ruopp, Travers, Glantz, & Coelen, 1979), and, on the other hand, evidence concerning the low salaries and extremely high turnover rates of child care workers (Phillips & Whitebook, in press). As noted earlier, beyond the mere availability of adequate numbers of child care providers is the critical issue of how skilled and how stable this work force is likely to be in the coming years. Growing sensitivity to this issue can be seen in the fact that the Act for Better Child Care legislation (S. 1885, H.R. 3660), which is currently moving through Congress, includes efforts to enhance the compensation and training of child care staff among its allowable uses of federal dollars.

Whether these factors that are lending issues of quality a higher profile will produce a higher general level of quality in our nation's child care programs remains to be seen. Typically efforts to improve child care quality are traded off when posed against efforts to expand the sheer amount of child care or to hold down the costs of care (Phillips & Zigler, 1987). Quality is equated with stringent regulation and expensive child care, both of which are unpopular ingredients in the child care equation. Thus, although the quality of child care in the United States is under tremendous scrutiny, there are strong pressures that must be overcome before real improvements can be made. In the meantime, quality is largely in the eye of the beholder, making consumer education a vital need in the area of child care.

Attitudes and Ideology

Policy decisions are fundamentally expressions of social attitudes. This is particularly true of child care, which is among the most value-laden, controversial topics on the policy agenda. The controversy derives from two facets of the topic of child care: first, its direct association with highly value-laden issues, and second, the multiple and sometimes conflicting purposes served by child care, only some of which have to do with children.

The values that have traditionally infiltrated child care policy and research involve beliefs about the role of the state in family life, about the kind of mothers we like and particularly whether they should work outside the home, and about the kind of children we want to raise, and they are reflected in the prevailing wisdom about the best means of accomplishing our childrearing goals (McCartney & Phillips, 1988; Scarr, 1986). The contemporary debate about child care has added to this repertoire values about the schools and racial equity, about profit making in the context of child care, and about the status and remuneration of child care work.

With respect to purposes, there is no well-articulated framework for discussing conflicting views of child care as a social intervention or an economic convenience; as a service for children or a service for adults; as a comprehensive developmental program or basic caretaking; as a supplement to or substitute for parental care. Even more dramatic contrasts are provided by portrayals of child care as a hotbed of sexual abuse and as an effective source of respite care for abused children, and child care as a beneficial early intervention program and as a threat to mother-infant bonding.

Any attempt to speculate about the future of child care in the United States must address not only the tangible influences of demographic change, costs and supply, and labor force trends, but also the far less tangible factor of social ideology. Perceptions of whether child care is a social service, an educational service, or an economic necessity, perceptions of who uses child care, and views about who should provide and pay for it constitute the broad framework within which the future direction of child care will be charted.

In 1933, child care was linked to economic revitalization as a source of jobs for unemployed teachers and other women. In 1941, child care was integral to the war effort as a support for mothers who were needed in the war factories. During both periods, substantial federal funds and widespread public support were showered upon child care. But when the emergencies constituted by the Great Depression and World War II subsided, support for child care was withdrawn. Like rationing, it was essential but distasteful, and all were glad when it presumably became unnecessary (Joffe, 1977; McCartney & Phillips, 1988; Phillips & Zigler, 1987; Steinfels, 1973).

In between these heydays, child care reverted to its more traditional role as a social service for poor families who were viewed as either unable to provide their children with enriched learning environments or unable to provide for their own economic self-sufficiency without public intervention in the form of workfare and publicly supported child care. In both instances, recipients of public child care were viewed as nonmainstream, at best, if not deficient. Child care, as a result, was suspect, its use undesirable.

What is interesting today, and what is going to have a profound effect on the future direction of child care, is the weakening of this equation of child care with poverty, family deficiency, and temporary national emergencies. It is abundantly evident that social reality has deviated so thoroughly from the ideal family projected by the portrayal of child care as marginal and undesirable that a wedge has been created for other factors to begin shaping the future of child care.

Consequently, the public debate about child care is no longer about *whether* there will be federal support for child care, or whether families will continue to rely on child care. Instead it has focused on questions of who should be responsible for assuring that child care is available, affordable, and of decent quality. The contemporary debate about child care is being framed in pragmatic investment terms, whether in the context of welfare reform or of our labor economy.

The significance of this emerging reorientation for policy deliberations is, of course, vast. One illustration of its effect is provided by the thrust of the comprehensive child care legislation developed by the Alliance for Better Child Care (see Blank, this volume). The first need that is identified in the language accompanying the bill is the need "of *all* families for improved access to quality child care options." Child care has been mainstreamed. The growing legitimacy of child care is also evident in a report issued recently by the Committee for Economic Development (1987), titled *Children in Need: Investment Strategies for the Educationally Disadvantaged*. A central recommendation is made for "quality child-care arrangements for poor working parents."

These opinion makers of our society are genuinely concerned about the consequences of failing to provide adequate child care: loss of employees in whom companies have made substantial investments of time and money and, possibly, loss of an adequately trained future work force. Their driving concern is the "wasting of human capital." Their growing attention to child care is coinciding with new public opinion data (see Blank, this volume) that indicate broad social concern about the rearing conditions of young children. If, indeed, policy proceeds from public ideology, these indicators bode well for the future direction of child care in this country.

CONCLUSION

Margaret Steinfels (1973) characterized child care as having a "shadowy past and indecisive present" (p. 35). This chapter has speculated about the future of child care. The portrayal of child care that this crystal ball gazing has revealed includes many elements. There is likely to be continued and sizable growth in the demand for child care, particularly for center-based programs, from families with infants through school-age children. Indeed, prior distinctions in patterns of child care use by families of different races, of different household structures, and with children of different ages are merging into a common pattern of considerable reliance on child care.

The central question for the future, then, is how our society is going to respond to the growing need for child care. In this chapter I discussed likely trends affecting the supply, cost, and quality of child care and concluded by suggesting that there has been a significant shift toward increasingly practical, "reality-based," and even investment-driven public attitudes about child care.

There are many remaining challenges, despite this optimistic final note. The child care field is highly splintered. In the past, this divisiveness has worked against national efforts to improve our child care system. Areas of contention include the federal role in child care regulation, the place of the public schools in child care, and the appropriate relation between the nonprofit and for-profit child care sectors. Parents, who may constitute the most effective advocates for child care, remain to be mobilized. Their successful campaigns for Head Start and for education for the handicapped provide examples of their potential contribution to future child care policies. Other challenges are presented by continuing public ambivalence about infant child care, by pervasive concerns about the federal budget, and by the devaluation of child care work.

I opened this chapter with quotes that revealed hopes about the future of child care voiced two decades ago. I leave you with the unanswerable question of whether the portrait of child care's future that emerges from the speculations in this chapter will become historical reality or grist for the introductory comments of some speaker at a conference 20 years hence who wishes to illustrate the lack of progress on child care.

DISCUSSION

Dr. Phillips was asked whether her research had revealed any changes in the work styles of women who had been in the work force with young children for several years and were now having their second or third children. She replied that there is no research evidence on the labor force choices of this group of women. The discussion brought out several dilemmas for women that have not been solved by supposed solutions to child care problems. Dr. Scarr described what has happened in Sweden as a result of the liberal leave policies and availability of high-quality, subsidized child care. Parents there receive up to 1 year of parental leave, 9 months fully or nearly fully paid and the remaining 3 months paid at a low level. Parents may also take as many as 60 days a year to stay at home with a sick child. No one does that, she said, but a parent with a seriously ill child has that right. A parent may also take unpaid job-protected leave until a child is 18 months old and work a 6-hour day until a child is 8. As a result, most women work part-time and drop in and out of the labor force with each child, and there is serious concern about the lack of career investment and advancement for women.

The history of this phenomenon is ironic, she stated. In the 1930s, the number of women who were working and not having children led to concerns about population growth. Parental leave and child care were therefore provided so that women could work and have children. It was a true ideological commitment to equality between men and women, a realization that if women were to be given an equal chance, the children had to be cared for. But so far, the provisions for the children have brought about inequality for women, at least occupationally and economically.

Others recognized the problem as widespread, noting that women are making choices that result in this inequality. Perhaps the problem lies in inequality between husband and wife. Of the parental leave days taken in Sweden, 95% are taken by women. Part of the problem there is that the emphasis has been on parental leave rather than on child care; the cost of providing child care has proved very high, and there are actually not enough slots, especially for infants.

Maternal leave policies can also have a negative impact on job opportunities for women. An employer who is required to give a woman her job back after an unpaid leave may be reluctant to hire her in the first place. It may seem easier just to hire a man in the first place, rather than face the prospect of training someone to take her place. For that reason the National Organization for Women opposes maternity leave policy. Dr. Hill-Scott pointed out that, ironically, one of the reasons why women's wages have been kept depressed is that employers have relied on women as an expendable in-and-out labor force. She proposed that mothers be given "baby points"—similar to veterans' preference points—when they return to the work force after childbirth, thus reducing the implied penalty for taking time off for childrearing.

18
General Discussion

Public policy and advocacy issues dominate this general discussion. Perhaps the issue most difficult to resolve is the level of quality of care to which child care advocacy should aspire. There were objections to discussing minimum standards; these, some felt, are what licensing provides, and they are not enough. What we have now, according to Ms. Blank, is the minimum we can afford, and we must have more; if we cannot find the resources to ensure that children grow up to be healthy, sane, productive adults, "the minimum is going to create a maximum problem down the line."

Dr. Kamerman agreed but pointed out that to get the resources, child-development experts will have to be prepared to say what it will take to provide adequate care. Realistically, we know that it will not be possible to obtain the funds for the best possible care. The critical issue therefore is to identify the characteristics of decent care. The child care community must send to the policymakers a clear message about the level of care at which children are being harmed. Politicians understand what truly abusive care is, but the subtler nuances of what constitutes higher-quality care and its implications for children are harder to convey. Those who feel that high-quality care is very important have to provide evidence of the consequences of differential levels of quality above a certain minimum. At least one must begin with a clear definition of decent, adequate care and consider what that will cost.

Inseparable from the issue of quality and its cost is, of course, the question of affordability. Dr. Arnett called for realism about what standards to set and urged that research focus on what these minimum standards should be. Providers are struggling to provide the level of care they are now giving at prices that parents are barely able to pay, he pointed out. Dr. Scarr agreed, noting that increasing the caregiver/infant ratio from 1:5 or 1:6 to 1:3 doubles the cost of infant care.

Part of the problem, Dr. Kamerman commented, might be that there is not enough consensus in the child-development field about what constitutes decent care. Other participants disagreed and felt that adequate care can be identified; the problem is to convince people to spend money on it. Dr. Belsky advocated instilling a little fear in lawmakers, who need to be shown evidence that the system needs fixing. To him the most compelling argument is that we have an aging population that is becoming increasingly dependent on fewer young people to be productive and generate the taxes to care for these dependents. In the past, with an abundance of progeny, our society has been willing to waste human capital, but we can no longer afford to do so. He cited Peterson (1987), who contrasts the $9,000 "disbursement" spent annually per elderly person with the $900 "investment" spent annually per child.

In general, the contributors agreed that child care as a system is a societal issue and must be addressed as important to the public good. Just as states are recognizing that failure to fund public school systems affects the economy and quality of life in the state, they must be made to recognize the economic benefits to be gained from investing in child care. In the immediate future, child care benefits a state's employment force as large employers take it into consideration in deciding where to set up facilities. In the more distant future, it will help to provide the shrinking youth population with the skills they will need to run our society. The arguments for child care are strong, they agreed.

One problem with past child care initiatives has been lack of coordination, because they have been tied to welfare reform, labor force needs, population needs, and other adult issues. In Europe child care has grown out of multiple motives, the developmental needs of children, adult needs, and societal interests. Especially in the welfare reform area, there is a basic conflict, between those who see child care as a strategy for getting women in the AFDC program into the work force and those who see child care as a strategy for enhancing children's development. There may have to be trade-offs such as using welfare reform as one means to expand child care, but it is important to keep the focus of the policy debate on children's needs.

A major barrier to getting the resources needed for child care, Ms. Kalemkiarian pointed out, is the intense political and moral ambivalence that people have toward the child care issue. In providing child care, politicians see themselves as condoning behaviors that they may not really approve and accepting a whole new system of choices for mothers and fathers. It is important to keep the depth of these feelings in mind in planning how to mobilize forces for a child care campaign. The way around this ambivalence, Dr. Hill-Scott asserted, is to make child care an issue on which people will vote. The one thing senators, members of Congress, and state legislators care about is re-election; there has to be a clear message in the votes. Ms. Martinez agreed, adding that you must test the level of a lawmaker's commitment. They will all say they are for children; it is necessary to get a concrete commitment to a major piece of legislation such as the ABC bill (the proposed Act for Better Child Care). Regarding the ambivalence itself, she noted that increasing numbers of politicians have daughters in the work force and grandchildren in child care. This personal experience with child care may have an impact on the formation of public policy by Republicans and Democrats alike.

The need for activism on the part of parents was brought up by several people, who wondered how parents could be gotten more deeply involved in the political process. There is currently no organization of parents needing child care that could mobilize the parents behind legislative efforts, and there are no vigils or marches as there have been for other critical social issues. The importance of getting parents to write to their members of Congress and other politicians was stressed. Newsletters from child care centers can be an important means of keeping parents informed about pending legislative and regulatory measures, and child care providers need to be trained to become more active advocates through the parents at their centers. Dr. Hill-Scott pointed out, however, that working parents with children in child care are very busy and want to spend what free time they have with their children. Their advocacy has to be tailored to what they can do with limited time and must be directed to a specific issue. She cited two campaigns for a latch-key bill, in which parents mailed a door key to their legislators as a statement of support for after-school programs. The other approach was to mail a sample ballot, marked for the opposition, to the governor who had vetoed the bill. As a rule of thumb, she said, legislators count one letter as three hundred votes. Ms. Kalemkiarian suggested the possibility of setting up advocacy networks through which parents could work, specifically for the ABC bill, if the child care community agreed on that as a focus. Foundations might be willing to put up the money to train a group of young people to become organizers around the country.

Dr. Kamerman pointed out, however, that in this country families with young children are a small minority of the population, and those families with young children in which both parents work are a still smaller minority. Moreover, those who have the most concern about the issues and make up the natural political constituency are so overwhelmed by trying to cope with work and childrearing and child care that they are not going to be active political advocates.

In Dr. Kamerman's view, we must educate the public at large about the issue and make clear that what happens to children in child care is important to the entire society. She is encouraged by signs that the media are beginning to pay attention to children's issues.

References

Agar, M. E., & Mitchell, G. (1975). Behavior of free-ranging adult rhesus macaques: A review. In G. H. Bourne (Ed.), *The rhesus monkey: Vol. 1. Anatomy and physiology* (pp. 323–342). New York: Academic Press.

Ainslie, R. (1987, August). *The social ecology of day care infants with secure and insecure maternal attachment.* Paper presented at the annual meetings of the American Psychological Association, New York.

Ainsworth, M. D. S. (1973). The development of infant-mother attachment. In B. M. Caldwell & H. N. Ricciuti (Eds.), *Review of child development research* (Vol. 3, pp. 1–94). Chicago: University of Chicago Press.

Ainsworth, M. D. S. (1982). Attachment: Retrospect and prospect. In C. M. Parkes & J. Stevenson-Hinde (Eds.), *The place of attachment in human behavior* (pp. 3–30). New York: Basic Books.

Ainsworth, M., & Bell, S. (1970). Attachment, exploration, and separation: Illustrated by the behavior of one-year-olds in a strange situation. *Child Development, 41,* 49–67.

Ainsworth, M. D. S., Blehar, M. C., Walters, E., & Wall, S. (1978). *Patterns of attachment: A psychological study of the Strange Situation.* Hillsdale, NJ: Lawrence Erlbaum Associates.

Ainsworth, M. D. S., & Wittig, D. (1969). Attachment and exploratory behavior of one-year-olds in a Strange Situation. In B. Foss (Ed.), *Determinants of infant behavior* (Vol. 4, pp. 111–136). London: Methuen.

Alin-Akerman, B., & Nordberg, L. (1980). *Griffiths utvecklingsskalor I och II [Griffiths developmental scales I and II].* Stockholm: Psykologiforlaget.

Alitto, S. (1969). The language issue in communist Chinese education. In C. Hu (Ed.), *Aspects of Chinese education* (pp. 43–59). New York: Teachers College Press.

Alliance for Better Child Care. (1987a). *Child care: The time is now.* Washington, DC: Author.

Alliance for Better Child Care. (1987b). Public policy report. *Young Children, 42*(4), 31–33.

American Federation of State, County and Municipal Employees (AFSCME). (1987). *America's child care needs.* Washington, DC.

American Planning Association. (1987). *Policy implementation principles on the provision of child care.* Washington, DC: Author.

Anderson, C. O., Kenney, A. M., & Mason, W. A. (1977). Effects of maternal mobility, partner, and endocrine state on social responsiveness of adolescent rhesus monkeys. *Developmental Psychobiology, 10,* 421–434.

Andersson, B. (1987, April). *The importance of public day-care for preschool children's later development.* Paper presented at the biennial meetings of the Society for Research in Child Development, Baltimore.

Arend, R., Gove, F. L., & Sroufe, L. A. (1979). Continuity of individual adaptation from infancy to kindergarten: A predictive study of ego-resiliency and curiosity in preschoolers. *Child Development, 50,* 950–959.

Arnett, J. (1987, April). *Training for caregivers in day care centers.* Paper presented at the biennial meetings of the Society for Research in Child Development, Baltimore.

Barglow, P., & Vaughn, B. (1987, August). *Psychological and demographic variables associated with attachment security for infants of working mothers.* Paper presented at the annual meetings of the American Psychological Association, New York.

Barglow, P., Vaughn, B., & Molitar, N. (1987). Effects of maternal absence due to employment on the quality of infant-mother attachment in a low-risk sample. *Child Development, 58,* 945–954.

Barglow, P., Vaughn, B., & Molitar, N. (in preparation). *Day care and attachment quality.* Unpublished manuscript.

Barth, F. (1969). Introduction. In F. Barth (Ed.), *Ethnic groups and boundaries* (pp. 9–38). Boston: Little Brown.

Barton, M., & Schwarz, J. (1981, August). *Day care in the middle class: Effects in elementary school.* Paper presented at the annual meetings of the American Psychological Association, Los Angeles.

Bates, J., Maslin, C., & Frankel, K. (1985). Attachment security, mother-child interaction, and temperament as predictors of behavior problem ratings at age three years. In I. Bretherton & E. Waters (Eds.), Growing points in attachment theory and research (pp. 167–193). *Monographs of the Society for Research in Child Development, 50* (1–2, Serial No. 209).

Bayley, N. (1969). *Bayley Scales of Infant Development.* New York: Psychological Corporation.

Bellah, R. N., Madsen, R., Sullivan, W. M., Swidler, A., & Tipton, S. M. (1985). *Habits of the heart: Individualism and commitment in American life.* New York: Harper & Row.

Belsky, J. (1984). Two waves of day care research: Developmental effects and conditions of quality. In R. Ainslie (Ed.), *The child and the day care setting* (pp. 1–34). New York: Praeger.

Belsky, J. (1986). Infant day care: A cause for concern? *Zero to three: Bulletin of the National Center for Clinical Infant Studies, 6*, 1–7.

Belsky, J. (1988). The effects of infant day care reconsidered. *Early Childhood Research Quarterly, 3*, 235–272.

Belsky, J., Garduque, L., & Hrncir, E. (1984). Assessing performance, competence, and executive capacity in infant play: Relations to home environment and security of attachment. *Developmental Psychology, 20*, 406–417.

Belsky, J., & Rovine, M. (1988). Nonmaternal care in the first year of life and infant-parent attachment security. *Child Development, 59*, 157–167.

Belsky, J., & Steinberg, L. D. (1978). The effects of day care: A critical review. *Child Development, 49*, 929–949.

Belsky, J., Steinberg, L. D., & Walker, A. (1982). The ecology of day care. In M.E. Lamb (Ed.), *Nontraditional families* (pp. 71–116). Hillsdale, NJ: Lawrence Erlbaum Associates.

Belsky, J., & Walker, A. (1980). *Infant-toddler center spot observation system.* Unpublished manuscript, Pennsylvania State University, Department of Individual and Family Studies, University Park, PA.

Benn, R. (1985, April). *Factors associated with security of attachment in dual-career families.* Paper presented at the biennial meetings of the Society for Research in Child Development, Toronto.

Benn, R. (1986). Factors promoting secure attachment relationships between employed mothers and their sons. *Child Development, 57*, 1224–1231.

Berk, L. (1985). Relationships of educational attainment, child-oriented attitudes, job satisfaction, and career commitment to caregiver behavior toward children. *Child Care Quarterly, 14*, 103–129.

Berman, C. M. (1982). The ontogeny of social relationships with group companions among free-ranging infant rhesus monkeys: I. Social networks and differentiation. *Animal Behaviour, 30*, 149–162.

Berman, C. M. (1983). Influence of close female relatives on peer-peer rank acquisition. In R. A. Hinde (Ed.), *Primate social relationships: An integrated approach* (pp. 157–159). Sunderland, MA: Sinauer Associates.

Bermuda Bureau of Census. (1983). *Bermuda census report.* Hamilton, Bermuda: Government of Bermuda.

Berrueta-Clement, R. J., Schweinhart, L. J., Barnett, W. S., Epstein, A.S., & Weikart, D. P. (1984). Changed lives: The effects of the Perry Preschool Program on youths through age 19. *Monographs of the High/Scope Educational Research Foundation, 8.* Ypsilanti, MI: High/Scope Press.

Birch, T. L. (1985). Testimony in *Child care, the emerging crisis: Hearings before the Select Committee on Children, Youth, and Families*. 99th Cong., lst sess. Washington, DC.

Blank, H. (1983). *Children and federal child care cuts*. Washington, DC: Children's Defense Fund.

Blank, H. (1984). *Child care: The states' response. A survey of state child care policies 1983–1984*. Washington, DC: Children's Defense Fund.

Blehar, M. (1974). Anxious attachment and defensive reactions associated with day care. *Child Development, 45,* 683–692.

Block, J. H. (1976). Assessing sex differences: Issues, problems, and pitfalls. *Merrill-Palmer Quarterly, 22,* 285–308.

Block, J. H., & Block, J. (1980). The role of ego-control and ego-resiliency in the organization of behavior. In W.A. Collins (Ed.), *Minnesota symposium on child psychology* (Vol. 13, pp. 39–101). Hillsdale, NJ: Lawrence Erlbaum Associates.

BMF Marketing Insurance Services, Inc., a Bayly, Martin & Fay International Company (1986, August 18). Unpublished report of claims sampling, presented at meeting with Insurance for Child Care Project, Los Angeles.

Bookstein, F. L. (1986). The elements of latent variable models: A cautionary lecture. In M.E. Lamb, A.L. Brown, & B. Rogoff (Eds.), *Advances in developmental psychology* (Vol. 4, pp. 203–230). Hillsdale, NJ: Lawrence Erlbaum Associates.

Bowlby, J. (1969). *Attachment and loss: Vol. 1. Attachment*. New York: Basic Books.

Bowlby, J. (1973). *Attachment and loss: Vol. 2. Separation*. New York: Basic Books.

Bowlby, J. (1982). *Attachment and loss: Vol.1. Attachment* (2nd ed.). New York: Basic Books.

Boykin, A. W. (1978). Psychological/behavioral verve in academic task performance: Pretheoretical considerations. *Journal of Negro Education, 47,* 343–354.

Boykin, A. W. (1986). The triple quandary and the schooling of Afro-American children. In U. Meisser (Ed.), *The school achievement of minority children: New perspectives* (pp. 57–92). Hillsdale, NJ: Lawrence Erlbaum Associates.

Bredekamp, S. (1986). The reliability and validity of the Early Childhood Classroom Observation Scale for accrediting early childhood programs. *Early Childhood Research Quarterly, 1*(2), 103–118.

Bredekamp, S. (Ed.). (1987). *Developmentally appropriate practice in early childhood programs serving children from birth through age 8*. Washington, DC: National Association for the Education of Young Children.

Bredekamp, S., & Apple, P. (1986). How early childhood programs get accredited: An analysis of accreditation decisions. *Young Children, 42*(1), 34–37.

Bredekamp, S., & Berby, J. (1987). Maintaining quality: Accredited programs one year later. *Young Children, 43*(1), 13–15.

Bretherton, I. (1985). Attachment theory: Retrospect and prospect. In I. Bretherton & E. Waters (Eds.), Growing points in attachment theory and research (pp. 3–36). *Monographs of the Society for Research in Child Development, 50* (1–2, Serial No. 209).

Broberg, A., & Hwang, C.-P. (1987). *Barnomsorg i. Göteborg: En longitudinell studie [Child care in Göteborg: A longitudinal study].* Rapport no. 5: 1987. Göteborg, Sweden: Institut Psykologiska, Universität Göteborg.

Broberg, A., Lamb, M. E., Hwang, C.-P., & Bookstein, F. L. (1987). *Determinants of intellectual development in Swedish preschoolers.* Unpublished manuscript, University of Goteborg.

Bronfenbrenner, U., Belsky, J., & Steinberg, L. (1976). *Day care in context: An ecological perspective on research and public policy.* A report to the Department of Health, Education, and Welfare, Federal Interagency Day Care Requirements Committee, Washington, DC.

Bronfenbrenner, U., & Crouter, A. C. (1983). The evolution of environmental models in developmental research. In W. Kessen (Ed.), P. H. Mussen (Series Ed.), *The handbook of child psychology: Vol. 1. History, theory, and methods* (4th ed., pp. 357–414). New York: Wiley.

Brookhart, J., & Hock, E. (1976). The effects of experimental context and experiential background on infants' behavior toward their mothers and a stranger. *Child Development, 47,* 330–340.

Brunner, J. (1980). *Under five in Britain.* Ypsilanti, MI: High/Scope.

Bush, D. S., Steffen, S. L., Higley, J. D., & Suomi, S. J. (1987). Continuity of social separation responses in rhesus monkeys (*Macaca mulatta*) reared under different conditions. *American Journal of Primatology, 12,* 333.

Butler, R. A., & Harlow, H. F. (1954). Persistence of visual exploration in monkeys. *The Journal of Comparative and Physiological Psychology, 47,* 258–263.

Cain, L., Levine, S., & Elzey, E. (1963). *Cain-Levine Social Competency Scale.* Palo Alto, CA: Consulting Psychologists Press.

Caldwell, B. M. (1970). *Instruction manual: HOME inventory for infants.* Unpublished manuscript, University of Arkansas, Department of Early Childhood Education, Little Rock, AR.

Caldwell, B., & Bradley, R. H. (1984). *Home observation for measurement of the environment* (rev. ed.) Little Rock, AR: College of Education, University of Arkansas.

Caldwell, B., & Freyer, M. (1982). Day care and early education. In B. Spadek (Ed.), *Handbook of research in early childhood education* (pp. 21–43). New York: Free Press.

Caldwell, B., Wright, C., Honig, A., & Tannenbaum, J. (1970). Infant day care and attachment. *American Journal of Orthopsychiatry, 60*, 690–697.

California Assembly Office on Research. (1985). *Caring for tomorrow: A local government guide to child care.* Sacramento, CA.

California Department of Insurance, Joint Legislative Task Force on Child Care Liability. (1986a). *Child care insurance reporting survey.* San Francisco, CA: Author.

California Department of Insurance. (1986b). *Report of Department of Insurance joint investigative hearings on child care liability insurance.* San Francisco, CA: Author.

California Department of Insurance. (1987, Nov. 9). Hearings on a joint underwriting association for child care, Los Angeles, California Department of Insurance, Office of Counsel. San Francisco, CA: Author.

California Federation of Family Day Care Associations v. Mission Insurance Company, No. BO 16376, slip op. (Cal. Ct. App., 2d App. Dist., Nov. 7, 1985).

Candland, D., & Mason, W. (1968). Infant monkey heartrate: Habituation and the effects of social substitutes. *Developmental Psychology, 1*, 254–256.

Capitanio, J. P. (1986). Behavioral pathology. In G. Mitchell & J. Erwin (Eds.), *Comparative primate biology: Vol. 2, Part A. Behavior, conservation, and ecology* (pp. 411–454). New York: Alan R. Liss.

Cazden, C. (1970). The situation: A neglected source of social class differences in language use. *Journal of Social Issues, 26*(2), 35–60.

CDA National Credentialing Program. (1987). *Child development associate assessment system and competency standards: Preschool caregivers in center-based programs.* Washington, DC: Author.

Chamove, A., Harlow, H., & Mitchell, G. (1967). Sex differences in the infant-directed behavior of preadolescent rhesus monkeys. *Child Development, 38*, 329–335.

Chamove, A. S., Rosenblum, L. A., & Harlow, H. F. (1973). Monkeys (*Macaca mulatta*) raised only with peers: A pilot study. *Animal Behaviour, 21*, 316–325.

Champoux, M., Higley, J. D., Suomi, S. J., Hopkins, W., Marra, L., & Kreisler, M. C. (1982, August). *Redirection of filial attachment in infant rhesus macaques.* Paper presented at the annual meeting of the Animal Behavior Society, Duluth, MN.

Chase-Lansdale, L., & Owen, M. T. (1987). Maternal employment in a family context: Effects on infant-mother and infant-father attachments. *Child Development, 58,* 1505–1512.

Child Care Action Campaign. (1986). Unpublished news releases, January–April, 1986. Available from Child Care Action Campaign, 99 Hudson St., Rm. 1233, New York, NY 10013.

Children's Defense Fund. (1982). *The child care handbook.* Washington, DC: Author.

Children's Defense Fund. (1986). *School-age child care initiatives may often fail to help low-income families.* Washington, DC: Author.

Children's Defense Fund. (1987a). *A children's defense budget: FY 88.* Washington, DC: Author.

Children's Defense Fund. (1987b, June). *Testimony before Senate Subcommittee on Children, Families, Drugs and Alcoholism.* 100th Cong., lst sess. Washington, DC: Author.

Children's Defense Fund. (1987c). *1987 state child care fact book.* Washington, DC: Author.

Clarke-Stewart, K. A. (in press). The "effects" of infant day care reconsidered: Risks for parents, children and researchers. *Early Childhood Research Quarterly.*

Clarke-Stewart, K. A., & Fein, G. (1983). Early childhood programs. In M. M. Haith & J. J. Campos (Eds.), P. H. Mussen (Series Ed.), *Handbook of child psychology: Vol. 2. Infancy and developmental psychobiology* (pp. 917–999). New York: Wiley.

Class, N., & Orton, R. (1980). Day care regulation: The limits of licensing. *Young Children, 2,* 12–17.

Coalition for Consumer Justice. (1986). *Insurance reform campaign: Index of resources.* Washington, DC: Author

Cochran, M. (1977). A comparison of group day care and family child-rearing patterns in Sweden. *Child Development, 48,* 702–707.

Cochran, M., & Gunnarsson, L. (1985). A follow-up study of group day care and family-based childrearing patterns. *Journal of Marriage and the Family, 47,* 297–309.

Cohen, D., Dibble, E., & Grawe, J. (1977). Fathers' and mothers' perceptions of children's personality. *Archives of General Psychiatry, 34,* 482–487.

Cohen, J., & Cohen, P. (1983). *Applied multiple regression/correlation analysis for the behavioral sciences.* Hillsdale, NJ: Lawrence Erlbaum Associates.

Colletta, N. D., & Gregg, C. H. (1981). Adolescent mothers' vulnerability to stress. *Journal of Nervous and Mental Disease, 169,* 50–54.

Collins, R. C. (1983). Child care and the states: The comparative licensing study. *Young Children, 38*(5), 3–11.

Commission of the European Communities. (1984). *Day-care facilities and services for children under the age of three in the European community.* Luxembourg: Author.

Commission on California State Government Organizations and Economy. (1987). *Children's services study.* Sacramento, CA: Author.

Committee for Economic Development. (1987). *Children in need: Investment strategies for the educationally disadvantaged.* New York: Author.

Committee on Finance and Insurance, California Assembly. (1987, May 19). *Committee summary for bill AB 1201.* Sacramento, CA: Author.

Committee on Ways and Means, U.S. Congress, House. (1985). *Background material and data on programs within the jurisdiction of the Committee on Ways and Means.* 99th Cong., 1st sess. Washington, DC: Government Printing Office.

Congressional Budget Office. (1988). *Trends in family income.* Study prepared for the Senate Budget Committee and the Select Committee on Children, Youth, and Families, U.S. House of Representatives. Washington, DC.

Congressional Record. (1980). (S8033), June 30.

Congressional Record. (1985). (H12164), December 16.

Congressional Record. (1987). (S2423), February 26.

Cooper, M., Thomas, C., & Baer, D. M. (1970). The experimental modification of teacher attending behavior. *Journal of Applied Behavior Analysis, 3,* 153–157.

Cornbleth, C., & Korth, W. (1980). Teacher perceptions and teacher-student interaction in integrated classrooms. *Journal of Experimental Education, 48,* 259–263.

Crisis is over—but insurance will never be the same. (1987, May 25). *Business Week,* p. 122.

Crnick, K. A., Greenberg, M. T., & Ragozin, A. S. (1981). *The effects of stress and social support on maternal attitudes and the mother-infant relationship.* Paper presented at the biennial meetings of the Society for Research in Child Development, Boston.

Crnic, K. A., Greenberg, M. T., & Slough, N. M. (1986). Early stress and social support influences on mothers' and high-risk infants' functioning in late infancy. *Infant Mental Health Journal, 7,* 19–33.

Crockenberg, S. B. (1981). Infant irritability, mother responsiveness, and social support influences on the security of infant-mother attachment. *Child Development, 52,* 857–865.

Crockenberg, S. B. (1987). Support for adolescent mothers during the postnatal period: Theory and research. In F. Z. Boukydis (Ed.), *Research in support for parents and infants in the postnatal period,* (pp. 3–24). Norwood, NJ: Ablex.

Cummings, E. M., & Beagles-Ross, J. (1984). Toward a model of infant day care: Studies of factors influencing responding to separation in day care. In R. C. Ainslie (Ed.), *The child and the day care setting: Qualitative variations and development* (pp. 159–182). New York: Praeger.

Darlington, R., Royce, J., Snipper, A., Murray, H., & Lazar, I. (1980). Preschool programs and later school competence of children from low-income families. *Science, 208,* 202–204.

Davenport, R. K., & Menzel, E. W. (1963). Stereotyped behavior of the infant chimpanzee. *Archives of General Psychiatry, 8,* 115–120.

Dolhinow, P. (1980). An experimental study of mother loss in the Indian langur monkey (*Presbytis entellus*). *Folia Primatologica, 33,* 77–128.

Doyle, A. (1975). Infant development in day care. *Developmental Psychology, 4,* 655–656.

Doyle, A., & Sommers, K. (1978). The effects of group and family day care on infant attachment behaviors. *Canadian Journal of Behavioral Science, 10,* 38–45.

Drickamer, L. C. (1974). A ten-year summary of reproductive data for free-ranging *Macaca mulatta*. *Folia Primatologica, 21,* 61–80.

Dublin, M. D. (1984). The National Day Care Study and the Federal Interagency Day Care Requirements: A study in the limits of rationalization in the delivery of a complex social service. Unpublished doctoral dissertation, Harvard University. *Dissertation Abstracts International, 45,* 2060A.

DuBois, W. E. B. (1961). *The souls of black folk.* Greenwich, CT: Fawcett. (Originally published 1903)

Eastman, R. F., & Mason, W. A. (1975). Looking behavior in monkeys raised with mobile and stationary artificial mothers. *Developmental Psychobiology, 8,* 213–221.

Edelman, M. (1976). A political-legislative overview of federal child care proposals. In N. Talbot (Ed.), *Raising children in modern America* (pp. 304–318). Boston: Little, Brown.

Egeland, B. (1983). Comments on Kopp, Krakow, & Vaughn, Patterns of self-control in young handicapped children. In M. Perlmutter (Ed.), *Minnesota symposium in child psychology* (Vol. 16, pp. 117–128). Hillsdale, NJ: Lawrence Erlbaum Associates.

Elton, R. H., & Anderson, B. V. (1977). The behavior of a group of baboons (*Papio anubis*) under artificial crowding. *Primates, 18,* 225–234.

Equal Opportunities Commission (British). (1986). *Parental leave: The proposed E.C. directive. EOC study of the costs.* Manchester, England: Author.

Ergas, Y. (1987, December). *Child care policies in comparative perspective: An introductory discussion.* Background paper for the Conference of National Experts on Lone Parents: The Economic Challenge of Changing Family Structures. Paris: Organization of Economic Cooperation and Development.

Erickson, M., Sroufe, A., & Egeland, B. (1985). The relationship between quality of attachment and behavior problems in preschool in a high-risk sample. In I. Bretherton & E. Waters (Ed.), Growing points in attachment theory and research (pp 147–166). *Monographs of the Society for Research in Child Development, 50*, (1–2, Serial No. 209).

Everson, M., Sarnat, L., & Ambron, S. (1984). Day care and early socialization: The role of maternal attitude. In R. Ainslie (Ed.), *The child and the day care setting: Qualitative variations and development* (pp. 63–97). New York: Praeger.

Farran, D., & Ramey, C. (1977). Infant day care and attachment behaviors toward mothers and teachers. *Child Development, 48,* 1112–1116.

Fernandez, J. P. (1986). *Child care and corporate productivity.* Lexington, MA: Lexington Books.

Field, T. (1980). Preschool play: Effects of teacher:child ratio and the organization of classroom space. *Child Study Journal, 10,* 191–205.

Fiene, R., & Nixon, M. (1985). The instrument-based program monitoring information system and the indicator checklist for child care. *Child Care Quarterly, 14*(3), 198–214.

Finkelstein, N., Dent, C., Gallagher, K., & Ramey, C. (1978). Social behavior of infants and toddlers in a day care environment. *Developmental Psychology, 14,* 257–262.

Finkelstein, N., & Wilson, K. (1977, March). *The influence of day care on social behaviors towards peers and adults.* Paper presented at the biennial meetings of the Society for Research in Child Development, New Orleans.

Fishman, J., & Leuders-Salmon, E. (1972). What has sociology to say to the teacher? In C. B. Cazden, V. P. John, & D. Hymes (Eds.), *Functions of language in the classroom* (pp. 67–83). New York: Teachers College Press.

Flanagan, J. (1987, August 26). City thinks it's fine business to attract raiders. *Los Angeles Times,* Part IV, p. 1.

Floge, L. (1985). The dynamics of child-care use and some implications for women's employment. *Journal of Marriage and the Family, 47,* 143–154.

Fowler, W. (1974). *The comparative effects of group and home care on human development.* Paper presented at the annual meetings of the Canadian Psychological Association, Windsor, Ontario.

Fraiberg, S. (1977). *Every child's birthright: In defense of mothering.* New York: Basic Books.

Francis, P., & Self, P. (1982). Imitative responsiveness of young children in day care and home settings: The importance of the child to caregiver ratio. *Child Study Journal, 12,* 119–126.

Friedman, D. E. (1985). *Corporate financial assistance for child care.* Conference Board Research Bulletin 177. New York.

Frodi, A. M., Lamb, M. E., Hwang, C.-P., Frodi, M., Forsstrom, B., & Corry, T. (1982). Stability and change in parental attitudes following an infant's birth into traditional and nontraditional Swedish families. *Scandinavian Journal of Psychology, 23,* 53–62.

Galinsky, E., & Friedman, D. (1986). *Investing in quality child care: A report for AT&T.* Short Hills, NJ: AT&T.

Gallup Organization. (1985, February). *California child care: Final report* (GO 84229). Princeton, NJ: Author.

General Accounting Office. (1982). *Percentage distribution of child and dependent tax credit benefits claimed and received by income group for 1979* (Report no. IPE-82-7). Washington, DC: Author.

Gibber, J. R. (1981). *Infant-directed behaviors in male and female rhesus monkeys.* Unpublished doctoral dissertation, University of Wisconsin, Madison. *Dissertation Abstracts International, 42,* 2121B.

Goelman, H. (1988). A study of the relationships between structure and process variables in home and day care settings on children's language development. In A. Pence (Ed.), *The practice of ecological research: From concepts to methodology.* New York: Teachers College Press.

Goelman, H., & Pence, A. R. (1987). Some aspects of the relationships between family structure and child language development in three types of day care. In D. L. Peters & S. Kontos (Eds.), *Advances in applied developmental psychology: Vol. 2. Continuity and discontinuity of experience in child care.* Norwood, NJ: Ablex.

Goffman, E. (1963). *Stigma.* Englewood Cliffs, NJ: Prentice Hall.

Golden, M., Rosenbluth, L., Grossi, N. T., Policare, H. J., Freeman, H., & Brownlee, M. (1978). *The New York City infant day care project.* New York: Medical and Health Research Association of New York City.

Griffiths, R. (1954). *The abilities of babies.* London: University of London Press.

Griffiths, R. (1970). *The abilities of young children.* London: University of London Press.

Grotberg, E. H. (1980). The roles of the federal government in regulation and maintenance of quality in child care. In S. Kilmer (Ed.), *Advances in early education and day care: A research annual* (Vol. 1, pp. 14–46). Greenwich, CT: JAI Press.

Grubb, W. N., & Lazerson, M. (1982). *Broken promises: How Americans fail their children.* New York: Basic Books.

Gunnarsson, L. (1985). 117 modrar om vard, fostran och undervisning [117 mothers discuss socialization and childrearing]. In L. Gunnarsson (Ed.), *Symposiet vard forstram-undervisning: Del. 3. Relationen familj-in-*

stitutionem [Symposium on child socialization: Vol. 3. Relations between families and institutions]. Publikationer Nom. 18. Göteborg, Sweden: Institut for Pedagogik, Universität Göteborg.

Hale-Benson, J. (1986). Black children: Their roots, culture and learning styles. Baltimore: Johns Hopkins University Press.

Hansen, E. W. (1966). The development of maternal and infant behavior in the rhesus monkey. Behaviour, 27, 107–149.

Hare, B. (1987). Structural inequality and the endangered status of black youth. Journal of Negro Education, 56, 100–110.

Harlow, H. F. (1958). The nature of love. American Psychologist, 13, 673–685.

Harlow, H. F. (1962). The heterosexual affectional system in monkeys. American Psychologist, 17, 1–9.

Harlow, H. F., & Harlow, M. K. (1965). The affectional systems. In A. M. Schrier, H. F. Harlow, & F. Stollnitz (Eds.), Behavior of nonhuman primates: Vol. 2. Modern research trends (pp. 287–334). New York: Academic Press.

Harlow, H., Harlow, M., Dodsworth, R., & Arling, G. (1966). Maternal behavior of rhesus monkeys deprived of mothering and peer association in infancy. Proceedings of the American Philosophical Society, 110, 58–66.

Harlow, H. F., & Lauersdorf, H. E. (1974). Sex differences in passion and play. Perspectives in Biology and Medicine, 17, 348–360.

Harper, L. V., & Huie, K. S. (1985). The effects of prior group experience, age, and familiarity on the quality and organization of preschoolers' social relationships. Child Development, 56, 704–717.

Haskins, R. (1985). Public school aggression among children with varying day-care experience. Child Development, 56, 689–703.

Hauenstein, E., Scarr, S., & Abidin, R. (1987, April). Detecting children at risk for developmental delay: Efficacy of the Parenting Stress Index in a non-American culture. Paper presented at the biennial meetings of the Society for Research in Child Development, Baltimore.

Havighurst, R. J. (1976). The relative importance of social class and ethnicity in human development. Human Development, 19, 56–64.

Heckman, J. (1978). Statistical models for discrete panel data developed and applied to test the hypothesis of true state dependence against the hypothesis of spurious state dependence. Annales de L'Insee, 30–31, 227–270.

Henderson, D. H., & Washington, A. G. (1975). Cultural differences and the education of black children: An alternative model for program development. Journal of Negro Education, 44, 353–360.

Hess, R. D. (1970). Social class and ethnic influences upon socialization. In P. H. Mussen (Ed.), Carmichael's manual of child psychology (3rd ed., vol. 2, pp. 457–557). New York: Wiley.

Hess, R., Shipman, V., Brophy, J., & Bear, R. (1968). Administering and scoring the toy sorting task, Appendix H. *The cognitive environments of urban preschool children* (pp. 173–275). Chicago: University of Chicago Press.

Hiatt, A. (1982, November). Child care: A business responsibility. *Industry Week*, p. 13.

Higley, J. D., Hopkins, W. D., Suomi, S. J., Hirsch, R., & Orman, S. (1985). Peers as attachment sources to reduce separation distress. *American Journal of Primatology, 8,* 343.

Higley, J. D., & Suomi, S. J. (1986). Parental behavior in non-human primates. In W. Slackin & M. Herbert (Eds.), *Parental behavior* (pp. 152–207). Oxford, England: Basil Blackwell.

Higley, J. D., Suomi, S. J., Hopkins, W. J., & Bush, D. S. (1986). Early peer-only rearing produces deficits in rhesus monkeys that last into late childhood. *American Journal of Primatology, 10,* 407.

Hill-Scott, K. (1986). *Diversity: An approach to child care delivery.* Washington, DC: National Black Child Development Institute.

Hill-Scott, K. (in press). *The triple digit deficit: Child care needs in Los Angeles.* Inglewood, CA: Crystal Stairs.

Hill-Scott, K., & Pally, K. (1986, May). *Resource allocation plan for child care expansion.* Memorandum to State of California Department of Education, Child Development Division. (Available from author)

Hinde, R. A., & Spencer-Booth, Y. (1967). The behaviour of socially living rhesus monkeys in their first two and a half years. *Animal Behaviour, 15,* 169–196.

Hiraiwa, M. (1981). Maternal and alloparental care on a troop of free-ranging Japanese monkeys. *Primates, 22,* 309–329.

Hock, E., & Clinger, J. (1980). Behavior toward mother and stranger of infants who have experienced group day care, individual care, or exclusive maternal care. *Journal of Genetic Psychology, 134,* 49–61.

Hofferth, S. L. (1979). Day care in the next decade: 1980–1990. *Journal of Marriage and the Family, 41,* 649–658.

Hofferth, S. L. (1987). *Child care in the U.S.* Statement before the Select Committee on Children, Youth, and Families, U.S. House of Representatives. Washington, DC.

Hofferth, S. L., & Phillips, D. A. (1987). Child care in the United States, 1970 to 1995. *Journal of Marriage and the Family, 49,* 559–571.

Hofferth, S. L., & Phillips, D. A. (in press). Maternal labor force participation and child care: 1980 to 1995. *Journal of Marriage and the Family.*

Hoffman, L. (1984). Maternal employment and the child. In M. Perlmutter (Ed.), *Parent-child interaction and parent-child relations in development* (pp. 101–128). Hillsdale, NJ: Lawrence Erlbaum Associates.

Hollingshead, A. B. (1975). *The four factor index of social position.* Unpublished manuscript, Yale University, Department of Sociology, New Haven, CT.

Holloway, S. D., & Reichhart-Erickson, M. (1987, April). *The relationship of day care quality to children's social competence: Some effects of sex differences.* Paper presented to the biennial meetings of the Society for Research in Child Development, Baltimore.

Holloway, S. D., & Reichhart-Erickson, M. (in press). The relationship of day care quality to children's free play behavior and social problem solving skills. *Early Childhood Research Quarterly.*

Horler, V. (n.d.). *Guide to public debt financing in California.* Los Angeles: Rauscher Pierce Refsnes.

Hostetler, J., & Huntington, G. (1971). *Children in Amish society: Socialization and community education.* New York: Holt, Rinehart & Winston.

Howes, C. (1980). Peer play scale as an index of complexity of peer interaction. *Developmental Psychology, 16,* 371–372.

Howes, C. (1983). Caregiver behavior in center and family day care. *Journal of Applied Developmental Psychology, 4,* 99–107.

Howes, C., & Olenick, M. (1986). Family and child care influences on toddlers' compliance. *Child Development, 57,* 202–216.

Howes, C., Rodning, C., Galluzzo, D., & Myers, L. (in press). Attachment and child care: Relationships with mothers and caregivers. *Early Childhood Research Quarterly.*

Howes, C., & Rubenstein, J. (1985). Determinants of toddlers' experience in daycare: Age of entry and quality of setting. *Child Care Quarterly, 14,* 140–151.

Howes, C., & Stewart, P. (1987). Child's play with adults, toys, and peers: An examination of family and child-care influences. *Developmental Psychology, 23,* 423–430.

Hrdy, S. (1976). Care and exploitation of nonhuman primate infants by conspecifics other than mother. In J. S. Rosenblatt, R. A. Hinde, E. Shaw, & C. Beer (Eds.), *Advances in the study of behavior* (pp. 101–158). New York: Academic Press.

Insurance for Child Care Project. (1987). [Unpublished letters to Insurance for Child Care Project, P.O. Box 880433, San Diego, CA 92108.]

Insurance Information Institute. (1987). *Working toward a fairer civil justice system.* New York: Author.

Insurance Services Offices, Inc. (1986, June 25). [Written statement for public hearings by insurance commissioner and Legislative Task Force on Child Care Liability Insurance, San Francisco.]

Jacobsen, J., & Wille, D. (1984). Influence of attachment and separation experience on separation distress at 18 months. *Developmental Psychology, 20,* 477–484.

Joffe, C. E. (1977). *Friendly intruders: Childcare professionals and family life.* Berkeley, CA: University of California Press.

Joffee, L. (1981, April). *The quality of mother-infant attachment and its relationship to compliance with maternal commands and prohibitions.* Paper presented at the biennial meetings of the Society for Research in Child Development, Boston.

Joint Economic Committee, U.S. Congress. (1985). *Economic future of the baby boom.* 99th Cong., 1st sess., Washington, DC.

Joreskog, K. G., & Wold, H. (Eds.). (1982). *Systems under indirect observation: Causality, structure, prediction* (Vols. 1–2). Amsterdam: North Holland.

Kagan, J., Kearsley, R., & Zelazo, P. (1978). *Infancy: Its place in human development.* Cambridge, MA: Harvard University Press.

Kahn, A., & Kamerman, S. (1987). *Child care: Facing the hard choices.* Dover, MA: Auburn House.

Kalemkiarian, S. (1987, November 9). Testimony before California Department of Insurance hearings on Joint Underwriting Association for Child Care, Los Angeles, California Department of Insurance, Office of Counsel. San Francisco: California Department of Insurance.

Kamerman, S. (1983). Child care services: A national picture. *Monthly Labor Review, 106*(12), 35–39.

Kamerman, S. B. (1988). Maternity and parenting benefits: An international overview. In E. Zigler & M. Frank (Eds.), *The parental leave crisis: Towards a national policy* (pp. 235–244). New Haven, CT: Yale University Press.

Kamerman, S. B., & Kahn, A. J. (1981). *Child care, family benefits, and working parents.* New York: Columbia University Press.

Kamerman, S. B., & Kahn, A. J. (1984). Europe's innovative family policies. In U.S. House of Representatives, Select Committee on Children, Youth, and Families, *Child care: Beginning a national initiative.* Washington, DC: Government Printing Office.

Kamerman, S. B., & Kahn, A. J. (1987). *Mother-only families in western Europe.* (Report to the German Marshall Fund of the United States) New York: Columbia University School of Social Work.

Kamerman, S. B., & Kahn, A. J. (1988). Social policy and children in the United States and Europe. In J. L. Palmer, T. Smeeding, & B. B. Torrey (Eds.), *The vulnerable: America's young and old in the industrialized world* (pp. 351–380). Washington, DC: The Urban Institute.

Kaplan, M., & Conn, J. (1984). The effects of caregiver training on classroom setting and caregiver performance in eight community day care centers. *Child Study Journal, 14(2)*, 79–93.

Katz, L., Johnson, C., & Gelfand, S. (1972). Modifying the dispensing of reinforcers. *Behavior Therapy, 3*, 579–588.

Kearney, S. S. (1984). *Caring for our children: Day care issues facing the states* (Report No. PS01 5063). Lexington, KY: States Information Center, Council of State Governments. (ERIC Document Reproduction Service No. ED 256 472)

Keister, M. (1970). *A demonstration project: Group care of infants and toddlers.* Washington, DC: Department of Health, Education, and Welfare.

Kendall, E. D. (1983). Child care and disease: What is the link? *Young Children, 38(5)*, 68–77.

Kendall, E. D., Aronson, S., Goldberg, S., & Smith, H. (1987). Training for child day care staff and for licensing and regulatory personnel in the prevention of infectious disease transmission. In M. T. Osterholm, J. O. Klein, S. S. Aronson, & L. K. Pickering (Eds.), *Infectious diseases in child day care: Management and prevention* (pp. 139–144). Chicago: University of Chicago Press.

Kendall, E. D., & Walker, L. H. (1984). Day care licensing: The eroding regulations. *Child Care Quarterly, 13(4)*, 278–290.

Ketterlinus, R. D., Bookstein, F. L., Sampson, P. D., & Lamb, M. E. (1988). *Partial Least Squares analytic approaches as exemplified using data from the Swedish Day Care Study.* Unpublished manuscript, National Institutes of Child Health and Human Development, Bethesda, MD.

Kildee, D. (1987). *Kildee child care summary.* Washington, DC: Children's Defense Fund.

Klein, J. O. (1987). Infectious diseases and day care. In M. T. Osterholm, J. O. Klein, S. S. Aronson, & L. K. Pickering (Eds.), *Infectious diseases in child day care: Management and prevention* (pp. 9–14). Chicago: University of Chicago Press.

Klein, R. P. (1985). Caregiving arrangements by employed women with children under 1 year of age. *Developmental Psychology, 21*, 403–406.

Kontos, S. J. (1987, April). *Day care quality, family background, and children's development.* Paper presented at the biennial meetings of the Society for Research in Child Development, Baltimore.

Kontos, S. J., & Fiene, R. (1987). Predictors of quality and children's development in day care. In D. Phillips (Ed.), *Quality indicators of child care* (pp. 57–79). Washington, DC: National Association for the Education of Young Children.

Kontos, W., & Stremmel, A. J. (1987). Caregiver's perceptions of working conditions in a child care environment. *Early Childhood Research Quarterly, 3,* 100–121.

Labor and Human Resources Committee, U.S. Congress, Senate. (1979). *The coming decade: American women and human resources policies and programs.* 96th Cong., 1st sess., Washington, DC.

Labov, W. (1964). Stages in the acquisition of standard English. In R. Shuy (Ed.), *Social dialects and language learning* (pp. 77–104). Champaign, IL: National Council of Teachers of English.

LaFreniere, P., & Sroufe, L. A. (1985). Profiles of peer competence in the preschool: Interrelations between measures, influence of social ecology, and relation to attachment history. *Developmental Psychology, 21,* 56–68.

Lamb, M. E. (1982). Individual differences in infant sociability: Their origins and implications for cognitive development. In H. W. Reese & L. P. Lipsitt (Eds.), *Advances in child development and behavior* (Vol. 16, pp. 213–239). New York: Academic Press.

Lamb, M. E., Hwang, C.-P., Bookstein, F. L., Broberg, A., Hult, G., & Frodi, M. (1988). The development of social competence in Swedish preschoolers. *Developmental Psychology, 24,* 58–70.

Lamb, M. E., Hwang, C.-P., Broberg, A., & Bookstein, F. L. (in press). The effects of out-of-home care on the development of social competence in Sweden: A longitudinal study. *Early Childhood Research Quarterly.*

Lamb, M. E., Pleck, J. H., & Levine, J. A. (1985). The role of the father in child development: The effects of increased paternal involvement. In B. B. Lahey & A. E. Kazdin (Eds.), *Advances in clinical child psychology* (Vol. 8, pp. 229–266). New York: Plenum.

Lamb, M. E., & Sternberg, K. J. (in press). Day care. In H. Keller (Ed.), *Handbuch der kleinkind forschung.* Heidelberg: Springer-Verlag.

Lamb, M. E., Thompson, R. A., Gardner, W., & Charnov, E. L. (1985). *Infant-mother attachment.* Hillsdale, NJ: Lawrence Erlbaum Associates.

Lamb, M. E., Thompson, R. A., Gardner, W., Charnov, E. L., & Estes, D. (1984). Security of infantile attachment as assessed in the "Strange Situation": Its study and biological interpretation. *Behavioral and Brain Sciences, 7,* 127–147.

Lande, J. S., Higley, J. D., Snowdon, C. T., Goy, R. W., & Suomi, S. J. (1985). Elicitors of parental care in rhesus monkeys. *American Journal of Primatology, 8,* 349.

Lazar, I., Darlington, R., Murray, H., Royce, J., & Snipper, A. (1982). Lasting effects of early education. *Monographs of the Society for Research in Child Development, 47*(1–2, Serial No. 194). Chicago, IL: University of Chicago Press.

Lee, P. C. (1983a). Effects of the loss of the mother on social development. In R. A. Hinde (Ed.), *Primate social relationships: An integrated approach* (pp. 73–79). Sunderland, MA: Sinauer Associates.

Lee, P. C. (1983b). Effects of parturition on the mother's relationship with older offspring. In R. A. Hinde (Ed.), *Primate social relationships: An integrated approach* (pp. 134–139). Sunderland, MA: Sinauer Associates.

Lehrman, K., & Pace, J. (1985). *Day-care regulation: Serving children or bureaucrats?* (Cato Institute Policy Analysis No. 59). Washington, DC: Cato Institute. (ERIC Document Reproduction Service No. ED 263 985)

Lewis, M., Feiring, C., McGuffog, C., & Jaskir, J. (1984). Predicting psychopathology in six-year-olds from early social relations. *Child Development, 55,* 123–136.

Lindburg, D. (1971). The rhesus monkey in north India: An ecological and behavioral study. In L. A. Rosenblum (Ed.), *Primate behavior: Developments in field and laboratory research* (pp. 1–106). New York: Academic Press.

Londerville, S., & Main, M. (1981). Security, compliance, and maternal training methods in the second year of life. *Developmental Psychology, 17,* 289–299.

Lovejoy, C. O. (1981). The origin of man. *Science, 211,* 341–350.

MacDonald, K., & Parke, R. D. (1984). Bridging the gap: Parent-child play interaction and peer interactive competence. *Child Development, 55,* 1265–1277.

Main, M. (1973). *Play, exploration, and competence as related to child-adult attachment.* Unpublished doctoral dissertation, Johns Hopkins University, Baltimore, MD.

Main, M., & Weston, D. R. (1981). The quality of the toddler's relationship to mother and to father: Related to conflict behavior and the readiness to establish new relationships. *Child Development, 52,* 932–940.

Martinez, S. (1986). Child care and public policy. In N. Gunzenhauser & B. Caldwell (Eds.), *Group care for young children* (pp. 71–81). Skillman, NJ: Johnson & Johnson.

Maslin, L., & Bates, J. (1982, March). *Anxious attachment as a predictor of disharmony in the mother-toddler relationship.* Paper presented at the International Conference on Infant Studies, Austin, TX.

Mason, W. A. (1970). Motivational factors in psychosocial development. *Nebraska Symposium on Motivation, 18,* 35–67. Lincoln, NE: University of Nebraska Press.

Mason, W. A. (1978). Social experience and primate cognitive development. In G. M. Burghardt & M. Bekoff (Eds.), *The development of behavior: Comparative and evolutionary aspects* (pp. 233–251). New York: Garland Press.

Mason, W. A., & Berkson, G. (1975). Effects of maternal mobility on the development of rocking and other behaviors in rhesus monkeys: A study with artificial mothers. *Developmental Psychobiology, 8,* 197–211.

Matas, L., Arend, R. A., & Sroufe, L. A. (1978). Continuity of adaptation in the second year: The relationship between quality of attachment and later competence. *Child Development, 49,* 547–556.

McCartney, K. (1984). The effect of quality of day care environment upon children's language development. *Developmental Psychology, 20,* 244–260.

McCartney, K. (in press). Child care and attachment: A new frontier the second time around. *Journal of Orthopsychiatry.*

McCartney, K., & Phillips, D. (1988). Motherhood and child care. In B. Birns & D. Hay (Eds.), *Different faces of motherhood.* New York: Plenum Press.

McCartney, K., Scarr, S., Phillips, D., & Grajek, S. (1985). Day care as intervention: Comparisons of varying quality programs. *Journal of Applied Developmental Psychology, 6,* 247–260.

McCartney, K., Scarr, S., Phillips, D., Grajek, S., & Schwarz, J. C. (1982). Environmental differences among day care centers and their effects on children's development. In E. F. Zigler & E. W. Gordon (Eds.), *Day care: Scientific and social policy issues* (pp. 136–151). Boston: Auburn House.

McCulloch, T. (1939). The role of clasping activity in adaptive behavior of the infant chimpanzee: III. The mechanism of reinforcement. *Journal of Psychology, 7,* 305–316.

McDermott, R. (1987). Achieving school failure: An anthropological approach to literacy and social stratification. In G. Spindler (Ed.), *Education and cultural process: Anthropological approaches* (2nd ed., pp. 173–204). Prospect Heights, IL: Waveland Press.

Miller, R. E. (1967). Experimental approach to the physiological and behavioral concomitants of affective communication in rhesus monkeys. In S. A. Altmann (Ed.), *Social communication among primates* (pp. 125–134). Chicago: The University of Chicago Press.

Mineka, S., Davidson, M., Cook, M., Keir, R. (1984). Observational conditioning of snake fear in rhesus monkeys. *Journal of Abnormal Psychology, 93,* 355–372.

Mineka, S., Gunnar, M., Champoux, M. (1986). Control and early socioemotional development: Infant rhesus monkeys reared in controllable versus uncontrollable environments. *Child Development, 57,* 1241–1256.

Mineka, S., & Suomi, S. J. (1978). Social separation in monkeys. *Psychological Bulletin, 85,* 1376–1400.

Modigliani, K. (1986). But who will take care of the children? Childcare, women and devalued labor. *Journal of Education, 168,* 46–69.

Molnar, J., & Thompson, V. L. (1987, April). *Public education for four-year-olds: Policy issues.* Paper presented at the biennial meetings of the Society for Research in Child Development, Baltimore.

Morado, C. (1986). Public policy report: Prekindergarten programs for 4-year-olds: Some key issues. *Young Children, 41,* 61–65.

Morgan, G. (1979). Regulation: One approach to quality child care. *Young Children, 34,(6),* 22–27.

Morgan, G. (1984a). Change through regulation. In J. T. Greenman & R. W. Fuqua (Eds.), *Making day care better: Training, evaluation and the process of change* (pp. 163–184). New York: Teachers College Press.

Morgan, G. (1984b). *Public attention and concern about sexual abuse in child care.* New York: Child Care Action Campaign. (ERIC Document Reproduction Service No. ED 258 400)

Morgan, G. (1987). *The national state of child care regulation, 1986.* Watertown, MA: Work/Family Directions.

Morgan, G. G., Stevenson, C. S., Fiene, R., & Stephens, K. O. (1987). Gaps and excesses in the regulation of child day care. In M. T. Osterholm, J. O. Klein, S. S. Aronson, & L. K. Pickering (Eds.), *Infectious diseases in child day care: Management and prevention* (pp. 122–131). Chicago: University of Chicago Press.

Moskowitz, D., Schwarz, J., & Corsini, D. (1977). Initiating day care at three years of age: Effects on attachment. *Child Development, 48,* 1271–1276.

Moss, P. (1988). *Childcare and equality of opportunity: Consolidated report to the European Commission.* London: Commission of the European Community.

National Association for the Education of Young Children. (1984). *Accreditation Criteria and Procedures of the National Academy of Early Childhood Programs.* Washington, DC: Author.

National Association for the Education of Young Children. (1985). *The child care boom: Growth in licensed child care, 1977–1985.* Washington, DC: Author.

National Association for the Education of Young Children. (1986). *Child care liability insurance survey.* Washington, DC: Author.

National Association for the Education of Young Children. (1987). NAEYC position statement on licensing and other forms of regulation of early childhood programs in centers and family day care homes. Public Policy Report. *Young Children, 42(5),* 64–68.

National Black Child Development Institute. (1985). *Child care in the public schools: Incubator for inequality?* Washington, DC: Author.

National Black Child Development Institute. (1987). *Safeguards: Guidelines for establishing programs for four-year-olds in the public schools.* Washington, DC: Author.

National Center for Clinical Infant Programs. (1986). *Infants can't wait.* Washington, DC: Author.

National Commission on Excellence in Education. (1983). *A nation at risk.* Washington, DC: U.S. Department of Education.

National Commission on Working Women. (1986). *Women's work: Underpaid and undervalued,* fact sheet. Washington, DC: Author.

National Insurance Consumer Organization. (1986). *Insurance in California: A 1986 status report to the Assembly.* Alexandria, VA: Author.

National Opinion Research Council. (1978). *Occupational classification.* Chicago: University of Chicago Press.

Nixon, R. (1972). *Public papers of the presidents: Richard Nixon, 1971.* Washington, DC: Government Printing Office.

Nordberg, L., & Alin-Akerman, B. (1983). *Standardisering av Griffiths utvecklingsskala for åldrarna två till åtta år.* (Del rapport II). Stockholm: Resultat redovisning, Psykologiforlaget.

Norgren, J. (1981). In search of a national child care policy: Background and prospects. *Western Political Quarterly, 34,* 127–142.

O'Connell, J. (1985). A neo no-fault contract in lieu of tort: Preaccident guarantees of postaccident settlement offers. *California Law Review, 73,* 898–916.

Ogilvie, D. G. (1972). *Employer-subsidized child care.* Washington, DC: U. S. Department of Health, Education, and Welfare.

Olenick, M. R. (1986). The relationship between day care quality and selected social policy variables. (Doctoral dissertation, University of California, Los Angeles). *Dissertation Abstracts International, 47,* 3657A.

Oppenheim, O., Sagi, A., & Lamb, M. E. (1988). Infant-adult attachments on the kibbutz and their relation to socioemotional development four years later. *Developmental Psychology, 24,* 427–433.

Osterholm, M. T., Klein, J. O., Aronson, S. S., & Pickering, L. K. (Eds.). (1987). *Infectious diseases in child day care: Management and prevention.* Chicago: University of Chicago Press.

Owen, M., & Cox., M. (in press). Maternal employment and the transition to parenthood. In A. E. Gottfried & A. W. Gottfried (Eds.), *Maternal employment and children's development: Longitudinal studies.* New York: Plenum.

Parke, R. D., MacDonald, K. B., Beitel, A., & Bhavnagri, N. (in press). The role of the family in the development of peer relationships. In R. DeV. Peters & R. J. McMahon (Eds.), *Marriages and families: Behavioral treatments and processes.* New York: Brunner/Mazel.

Patterson, G. (1980). Mothers: The unacknowledged victims. *Monographs of the Society for Research in Child Development, 45,* (5, Serial No. 186).

Pedersen, F., Cain, R., Zaslow, M., & Anderson, B. (1983). Variation in infant experience associated with alternative family roles. In L. M. Laosa & I. E. Siegel (Eds.), *Families as learning environments for children* (pp. 121–138). New York: Plenum.

Pemberton, C. (1987, June 11). Testimony before the Senate Subcommittee on Children, Families, Drugs and Alcoholism. 100th Cong., 1st sess., Washington, DC.

Peters, D., & Kostelnik, M. (1981). Current research in day care personnel preparation. *Advances in Early Childhood Education and Day Care, 2,* 29–60.

Peters, D., & Sutton, R. (1984). The effects of CDA training on the beliefs, attitudes, and behaviors of Head Start personnel. *Child Care Quarterly, 13,* 251–261.

Peterson, P. (1987). The morning after. *The Atlantic, 260,* 43–50.

Phillips, D. (1984). Day care: Promoting collaboration between research and policymaking. *Journal of Applied Developmental Psychology, 5,* 91–113.

Phillips, D. (1986). The federal child care standards of 1985: Step in the right direction or hollow gesture? *American Journal of Orthopsychiatry, 56,* 56–64.

Phillips, D. (Ed.). (1987a). *Quality in child care: What does research tell us?* Washington, DC: National Association for the Education of Young Children.

Phillips, D. (1987b). Sparing the rod and escaping the regulators: Religious exemptions from child care regulations. *Child Care Information Exchange, 57,* 9–12.

Phillips, D. (1987c). Whither churches that mind the children? *Child Care Information Exchange, 55,* 35–38.

Phillips, D., & Howes, C. (1987). Indicators of quality in child care: Review of research. In D. Phillips (Ed.), *Quality in child care: What does research tell us?* (pp. 1–20). Washington, DC: National Association for the Education of Young Children.

Phillips, D., & McCartney, K. (in press). Child care quality: Its influence on children's socioemotional development. *Developmental Psychology.*

Phillips, D., McCartney, K., & Scarr, S. (1987). Child-care quality and children's social development. *Developmental Psychology, 23,* 537–543.

Phillips, D., McCartney, K., Scarr, S., & Howes, C. (1987). Selective review of infant day care research: A cause for concern. *Zero to three: Bulletin of the National Center for Clinical Infant Studies, 7,* 18–21.

Phillips, D., Scarr, S., & McCartney, K. (1987). Dimensions and effects of child care quality: The Bermuda study. In D. Phillips (Ed.), *Quality in child care: What does research tell us?* (pp. 43–57). Washington, DC: National Association for the Education of Young Children.

Phillips, D., & Whitebook, M. (1986). Who are child care workers? *Young Children, 41*, 14–20.

Phillips, D., & Whitebook, M. (in press). The child care provider: Pivotal player in the child's world. In S. Chehrazi (Ed.), *Day care: Psychological and developmental implications.* New York: American Psychiatric Press.

Phillips, D., & Zigler, E. (1987). The checkered history of federal child care regulation. In E. Rothkopf (Ed.), *Review of research in education* (Vol. 14, pp. 3–42). Washington, DC: American Educational Research Association.

Plimpton, E., & Rosenblum, L. (1983). The ecological context of infant maltreatment in primates. In M. Reite & N. G. Caine (Eds.), *Child abuse: The nonhuman primate data* (pp. 103–117). New York: Alan R. Liss.

Population Resource Center. (1984). *Child care and the public schools.* Washington, DC: Author.

Pratt, C. L. (1969). *The developmental consequences of variations in early social stimulation.* Unpublished doctoral dissertation, University of Wisconsin, Madison.

Rabinovich, B., Zaslow, M., Berman, P., & Heyman, R. (1987, April). *Employed and homemaker mothers' compliance behavior in the home.* Paper presented at the biennial meetings of the Society for Research in Child Development, Baltimore.

Radin, N. (1982). Primary caregiving and rolesharing fathers. In M. E. Lamb (Ed.), *Nontraditional families* (pp. 173–204). Hillsdale, NJ: Lawrence Erlbaum Associates.

Ramey, C., Bryant, D., & Suarez, T. (in press). Preschool compensatory education and the modifiability of intelligence: A critical review. In D. Detterman (Ed.), *Current topics in human intelligence.* Norwood, NJ: Ablex.

Ramey, C., & Campbell, F. A. (1979). Compensatory education for disadvantaged children. *Social Review, 87,* 171–189.

Ramey, C., & Farran, D. (1983). *Intervening with high-risk families via infant day care.* Paper presented at the biennial meetings of the Society for Research in Child Development, Detroit, MI.

Rashid, H. M. (1981). Early childhood education as a cultural transition for African-American children. *Educational Research Quarterly, 6*(3), 55–63.

Rawlins, R. G., & Kessler, M. J. (1986). *The Cayo Santiago macaques: History, behavior, and biology.* Albany: State University of New York Press.

Redican, W., & Mitchell, G. (1973). A longitudinal study of paternal behavior in adult male rhesus monkeys: I. Observations on the first dyad. *Developmental Psychology, 8,* 135–136.

Reuter, J., & Yunick, G. (1973). Social interaction in nursery schools. *Developmental Psychology, 9,* 319–325.

Ricciuti, H. N. (1974). Fear and the development of social attachments in the first year of life. In M. Lewis & L. A. Rosenblum (Eds.), *The origins of fear* (pp. 73–106). New York: Wiley.

Rist, J. (1970). Student social class and teacher expectations. *Harvard Educational Review, 40*, 411–451.

Ristau, C., Gardner, A., & Hodges, W. (1976). *West Virginia paraprofessional child care system.* Atlanta, GA: Family Training Centers.

Robins, P. K. (1988, January). *Federal financing of child care: Alternative approaches and economic implications.* Paper presented at Wingspread Conference, "Economic implications and benefits of child care," Racine, WI.

Roonwal, M. L., & Mohnot, S. M. (1977). *Primates of South Asia: Ecology, sociobiology, and behavior.* Cambridge: Harvard University Press.

Rosenblum, L. A., & Paully, G. S. (1984). The effects of varying environmental demands on maternal and infant behavior. *Child Development, 55*, 305–314.

Rothbart, M. (1981). Measurement of temperament in infancy. *Child Development, 52*, 569–578.

Rubenstein, J., & Howes, C. (1979). Caregiving and infant behavior in day care and in homes. *Developmental Psychology, 15*, 1–24.

Rubenstein, J., Howes, C., & Boyle, P. (1981). A two-year follow-up of infants in community-based day care. *Journal of Child Psychology and Psychiatry, 22*, 209–218.

Ruopp, R., Travers, J., Glantz, F., & Coelen, C. (1979). *Children at the center: Final report of the National Day Care Study* (Vol. 1). Cambridge, MA: Abt.

Ruppenthal, G. C., Arling, G. L., Harlow, H. F., Sackett, G. P., & Suomi, S. J. (1976). A 10-year perspective of motherless-mother monkey behavior. *Journal of Abnormal Psychology, 85*, 341–349.

Ruppenthal, G. C., Harlow, M. K., Eisele, C. D., Harlow, H. F., & Suomi, S. J. (1974). Development of peer interactions of monkeys reared in a nuclear-family environment. *Child Development, 45*, 670–682.

Rutter, M. (1981). Socioemotional consequences of day care for preschool children. *American Journal of Orthopsychiatry, 51*, 4–28.

Rutter, M., & Garmezy, N. (1983). Developmental psychopathology. In E. M. Hetherington (Ed.), P. H. Mussen (Series Ed.), *Handbook of child psychology: Vol. 4. Socialization, personality and social development* (pp. 775–912). New York: Wiley.

Sackett, G., Griffin, G. A., Pratt, C., Joslyn, W. D., & Ruppenthal, G. (1967). Mother-infant and adult female choice behavior in rhesus monkeys after various rearing experiences. *Journal of Comparative and Physiological Psychology, 63*(3), 376–381.

Sagi, N., Lamb, M. E., Lewkowicz, K. S., Shoham, R., Dvir, R., & Oter, D. (1985). Security of infant-mother-father and -metapelet attachments among kibbutz-reared Israeli children. In I. Bretherton & E. Waters (Eds.), Growing points in attachment theory and research (pp. 257–275). *Monographs of the Society for Research in Child Development, 50* (1–2, Serial No. 209).

Saraceno, C. (1984). The social construction of childhood: Child care and educational policies in Italy and the United States. *Social Problems,31*(3), 351–363.

Sarason, S. B. (1973). Jewishness, blackness, and the nature-nurture controversy. *American Psychologist, 28*, 962–971.

Sarich, V. (1985). A molecular approach to the question of human origins. In R. L. Ciochon & J. G. Fleagle (Eds.), *Primate evolution and human origins* (pp. 314–322). Menlo Park, CA: Benjamin Cummings.

Scarr, S. (1984). *Mother care/other care.* New York: Basic Books.

Scarr, S. (1985). Constructing psychology: Making facts and fables for our times. *American Psychologist, 40*, 499–512.

Scarr, S. (1986). Cultural lenses on mothers and children. In L.Friedrich-Cofer (Ed.), *Human nature and public policy: Scientific views of women, children, and families* (pp. 202–238). New York: Praeger.

Scarr, S., & McAvay, G. (1985). *Educational and occupational achievements, Part II: Predicting the occupational achievements of brothers and sisters in adoptive and biologically related families.* Unpublished manuscript, Yale University, New Haven, CT.

Scarr, S., & McCartney, K. (1988). Far from home: An experimental evaluation of the mother-child home program in Bermuda. *Child Development, 59*, 531–543.

Scarr, S., & Weinberg, R. A. (1976). IQ test performance of black children adopted by white families. *American Psychologist, 31*, 726–739.

Scarr, S., & Weinberg, R. (1986). The early childhood enterprise: Care and education of the young. *American Psychologist, 41*, 1140–1146.

Schindler, P. J., Moely, B. E., & Frank, A. L. (1987). Time in day care and social participation of young children. *Developmental Psychology, 23*, 255–261.

Schwartz, P. (1983). Length of day-care attendance and attachment behavior in eighteen-month-old infants. *Child Development,54*, 1073–1078.

Schwarz, J. C., Krolick, G., & Strickland, R. (1973). Effects of early day care on adjustment to a new environment. *American Journal of Orthopsychiatry,43*(3), 340–346.

Schwarz, J. C., Strickland, R. G., & Krolick, G. (1974). Infant day care: Behavioral effects at preschool age. *Developmental Psychology,10*, 502–506.

Schweinhart, L., & Weikart, D. (1983). The effects of the Perry Preschool Program on youths through age 15: A summary. In The Consortium for Longitudinal Studies (Eds.), *As the twig is bent....* Hillsdale, NJ: Lawrence Erlbaum Associates.

Sciarra, D. J., & Dorsey, A. G. (1979). *Developing and administering a child care center* (chap. 3: Licensing and certifying). Boston: Houghton Mifflin.

Select Committee on Children, Youth, and Families, U.S. House of Representatives. (1984). *Families and child care: Improving the options.* 98th Cong., 2nd sess., Washington, DC: Government Printing Office.

Select Committee on Children, Youth, and Families, U.S. House of Representatives. (1987a). *Federal programs affecting children.* 100th Cong., 1st sess., Washington, DC: Government Printing Office.

Select Committee on Children, Youth, and Families, U.S. House of Representatives. (1987b). *U.S. children and their families: Current conditions and recent trends.* 100th Cong., 1st sess., Washington, DC: Government Printing Office.

Select Committee on Children, Youth, and Families, U.S. House of Representatives. (1988). *Opportunities for success: Cost-effective programs, update 1988.* Washington, DC: Government Printing Office.

Simonds, P. (1965). The bonnet macaque in south India. In I. Devore (Ed.), *Primate behavior: Field studies of monkeys and apes* (pp. 175–195). New York: Holt, Rinehart & Winston.

Smith, P., & Connolly, K. (1981). *The behavioral ecology of the preschool.* Cambridge: Cambridge University Press.

Smith, R. E. (1979). The movement of women into the labor force. In R. E. Smith (Ed.), *The subtle revolution: Women at work* (pp. 1–30). Washington, DC: The Urban Institute.

Snowdon, C. T., & Suomi, S. J. (1982). Paternal behavior in primates. In H. E. Fitzgerald, J. A. Mullins, & P. Gage (Eds.), *Child nurturance* (Vol. 3, pp. 63–108). New York: Plenum Press.

Southwick, C. H., Beg, M. A., & Siddiqi, M. R. (1965). *Rhesus monkeys in north India.* New York: Holt, Rinehart & Winston.

Spindler, G. (1963). The transmission of American culture. In G. Spindler (Ed.), *Education and culture* (pp. 148–172). New York: Holt, Rinehart & Winston. (Originally published 1959)

Spivack, G., & Shure, M. (1974). *Social adjustment of young children: A cognitive approach to solving real-life problems.* San Francisco: Jossey-Bass.

Sroufe, L. A. (1979). The coherence of individual development. *American Psychologist, 34,* 834–841.

Sroufe, L. A. (1983). Infant-caregiver attachment and patterns of adaptation in preschool: The roots of maladaptation and competence. In M. Perlmutter (Ed.), *Minnesota symposium in child psychology* (Vol. 16, pp. 41–81). Hillsdale, NJ: Lawrence Erlbaum Associates.

Sroufe, L. A. (1985). Attachment classification from the perspective of infant-caregiver relationships and infant temperament. *Child Development, 56,* 1–14.

Sroufe, L. A., & Fleeson, J. (1986). Attachment and the construction of relationships. In W. Hartup & Z. Rubin (Eds.), *Relationships and development* (pp. 27–54). Hillsdale, NJ: Lawrence Erlbaum Associates.

Sroufe, L. A., Fox, N., & Pancake, V. (1983). Attachment and dependency in developmental perspective. *Child Development, 54,* 1615–1627.

Sroufe, L. A., & Waters, E. (1977). Attachment as an organizational construct. *Child Development, 48,* 1184–1199.

Steinberg, L., & Green, G. (1979). What parents seek in day care. *Human Ecology Forum, 10,* 13–14, 38–48.

Steinfels, M. O. (1973). *Who's minding the children? The history and politics of day care in America.* New York: Simon & Schuster.

Stephan, S. (1987, October). *Child day care: Issues and legislation in the 100th Congress.* Congressional Research Service Issue Brief. Washington, DC.

Stevenson, M. B., & Lamb, M. E. (1979). Effects of infant sociability and the caretaking environment on infant cognitive performance. *Child Development, 50,* 340–349.

Subcommittee on Child and Human Development, U.S. Congress, Senate Committee on Labor and Human Resources. (1978). *Hearings on child care and child development.* 95th Cong., 2d sess., Washington, DC.

Subcommittee on Child and Human Development, U.S. Congress, Senate Committee on Labor and Human Resources. (1979). *Hearings on S. 4, the proposed Child Care Act of 1979.* 96th Cong., 1st sess., Washington, DC.

Subcommittee on Children and Youth, U.S. Congress, Senate Committee on Labor and Public Welfare. (1976). *Background materials concerning the Child and Family Services Act, S. 626.* 94th Cong., 1st sess. Washington, DC.

Suomi, S. J. (1978). Maternal behavior by socially incompetent monkeys: Neglect and abuse of offspring. *Journal of Pediatric Psychology, 3,* 28–34.

Suomi, S. J. (1979). Peers, play, and primary prevention in primates. In M. W. Kent & J. E. Rolf (Eds.), *Primary prevention of psychopathology: Vol. 3. Social competence in children* (pp. 127–149). Hanover, NH: University Press of New England.

Suomi, S. J. (1982a). Abnormal behavior in nonhuman primates. In J. Forbes & J. King (Eds.), *Primate behavior* (pp. 171–215). New York: Academic Press.

Suomi, S. J. (1982b). The development of social competence by rhesus monkeys. *Annali Dell Instituto Superiore Di Sanita, 18,* 193–202.

Suomi, S. J. (1983). Social development in rhesus monkeys: Consideration of individual differences. In A. Oliverio & M. Zappella (Eds.), *The behavior of human infants* (pp. 71–92). New York: Plenum Press.

Suomi, S. J. (in press). Genetic and maternal contribution to individual differences in rhesus monkeys' biobehavioral development. In N. Krasnegor (Ed.), *Psychobiological aspects of biobehavioral development.* New York: Academic Press.

Suomi, S. J., & Harlow, H. F. (1975). The role and reason of peer relationships in rhesus monkeys. In M. Lewis & L. A. Rosenblum (Eds.), *Friendship and peer relations* (pp. 153–185). New York: Wiley.

Suomi, S. J., & Ripp, C. (1983). A history of motherless mother monkey mothering at the University of Wisconsin Primate Laboratory. In M. Reite & N. Caine (Eds.), *Child abuse: The nonhuman primate data* (pp. 50–78). New York: Alan R. Liss.

Suwalsky, J., Zaslow, M., Klein, R., & Rabinovich, B. (1986, August). *Continuity of substitute care in relation to infant-mother attachment.* Paper presented at the annual meetings of the American Psychological Association, Washington, DC.

Terman, L., & Merrill, M. (1972). *Stanford-Binet Intelligence Scale.* Boston, MA: Houghton Mifflin.

Terpstra, J. (1985). Program licensing and you. *Child Care Quarterly, 14*(4), 283–286.

Thomas, A., Chess, S., Birch, H., Hertzig, M. E., & Korn, S. (1963). *Behavioral individuality in early childhood.* New York: New York University Press.

Thompson, R. (in press). The effects of infant day care through the prism of attachment theory: A critical appraisal. In A. Fein & N. Fox (Eds.), *Early childhood research quarterly.* Norwood, NJ: Ablex.

Thompson, R. A., & Lamb, M. E. (1983). Security of attachment and stranger sociability in infancy. *Developmental Psychology, 19,* 184–191.

Thompson, W. W., Higley, J. D., Byrne, E. A., Scanlan, J. M., & Suomi, S. J. (1986, November). *Behavioral inhibition in nonhuman primates: Psychobiological corrrelates and continuity over time.* Paper presented at the meeting of the International Society for Developmental Psychobiology, Annapolis, MD.

Tizard, B., Philps, J., & Plewis, E. (1976). Play in the preschool centres. *Journal of Child Orthopsychiatry, 17,* 251–274.

Tobias, A. (1982). *The invisible bankers.* New York: Simon & Schuster.

Travers, J., & Goodson, B. (1979). *Research results of the National Day Care Home Study.* Cambridge, MA: Abt.

Trotter, R. J. (1987, December). Project day-care. *Psychology Today,* pp. 32–38.

Unco, Inc. (1975). *National Day Care Consumer Study: 1975* (Vols 1–4). Arlington, VA: Author.

U.S. Bureau of Census. (1982). Trends in child care arrangements of working mothers. *Current population reports,* ser. P-23, no. 117. Washington, DC: Government Printing Office.

U.S. Bureau of Census. (1984, May). *1980 Census of the population: Vol. 2. Earnings by occupation and education.* (Subject reports, Number PC80-2-8B). Washington, DC: Government Printing Office.

U.S. Bureau of Census. (1986). Women in the American economy. *Current population reports,* ser. P-23, no. 146. Washington, DC: Government Printing Office.

U.S. Bureau of Census. (1987a). After school care of school-age children: December 1984. *Current population reports,* Special studies, ser. P-23, no. 149. Washington, DC: Government Printing Office.

U.S. Bureau of Census. (1987b). Who's minding the kids? Child care arrangements: Winter 1984-85. *Current population reports,* ser. P-70, no. 9. Washington, DC: Government Printing Office.

U.S. Department of Health, Education, and Welfare. (1966, May). *Proceedings of the National Conference on Day-Care Services.* (Children's Bureau Publication No. 438-1966). Washington, DC: Government Printing Office.

U.S. Department of Health and Human Services. (1982). *Comparative licensing study: Profiles of state day care licensing requirements.* Washington, DC: Government Printing Office.

U.S.D.L. See U.S. Department of Labor.

U.S. Department of Labor. (1967, June 1). *Report of a consultation on working women and child care needs.* Washington, DC.

U.S. Department of Labor, Bureau of Labor Statistics. (1985a). [Current population survey of 1984, unpublished data.] Washington, DC.

U.S. Department of Labor, Bureau of Labor Statistics. (1985b, January). *Employment and earnings* (annual report for 1984). Washington, DC.

U.S. Department of Labor, Bureau of Labor Statistics. (1986, August 20). Half of mothers with children under 3 now in labor force. *News.* Washington, DC.

U.S. Department of Labor, Bureau of Labor Statistics. (1987). Current population survey of March 1987, unpublished data. Washington, DC.

U.S. Department of Labor, Office of Information, Publications, and Reports. (1987, August). Over half of mothers with children one year or under in labor force in March 1987. *Women and Work.* Washington, DC.

U.S. Department of Labor, Women's Bureau. (1980). *Child care centers sponsored by employers and labor unions in the United States.* Washington, DC.

U.S. Department of Labor, Women's Bureau. (1985). *The United Nations Decade for Women, 1976-1985: Employment in the U.S.* Washington, DC.

U.S. Department of Labor, Women's Bureau. (1986). *Fact sheet no. 86–2: Women who maintain families.* Washington, DC.

U.S. teachers can expect more four-year-old faces. (1987, December 10). *Atlanta Journal,* p. C3.

Vandell, D. L., & Corasaniti, M. (1988). *Variations in early child care: Do they predict subsequent social, emotional, and cognitive differences?* Unpublished manuscript, University of Texas at Dallas, Richardson, TX.

Vandell, D. L., Henderson, U. K., & Wilson, K. W. (1987, April). *A follow-up study of children in excellent, moderate, and poor quality day care.* Paper presented at the biennial meetings of the Society for Research in Child Development, Baltimore.

Vaughn, B. E., Gove, F. L., & Egeland, B. (1980). The relationship between out-of-home care and the quality of infant-mother attachment in an economically disadvantaged population. *Child Development, 51,* 971–975.

Volling, B., & Belsky, J. (1987). *Demographic, maternal and infant factors associated with maternal employment in the infant's first year of life.* Unpublished manuscript, The Pennsylvania State University.

Wechsler, D. (1955). *Wechsler adult intelligence scale.* New York: Psychological Corporation.

Weintraub, K. S., & Furman, L. N. (in press). Child care: Quality, regulation, and research [Special issue]. *Social Policy Report,* Society for Research in Child Development.

Whitebook, M. (1984, June 18). Testimony before the Select Committee on Children, Youth and Families, U.S. House of Representatives, San Francisco, CA. 98th Cong., 2d sess.

Whitebook, M., Howes, C., Friedman, J., & Darrah, R. (1982). Caring for the caregivers: Burn-out in child care. In L. Katz (Ed.), *Current topics in early childhood education* (Vol. 4, pp. 211–235). Norwood, NJ: Ablex.

Wille, D., & Jacobsen, J. (1984, April). *The influence of maternal employment, attachment pattern, extrafamilial child care, and previous experience with peers on early peer interaction.* Paper presented at the International Conference on Infant Studies, New York.

Wold, H. (1975). Path models with latent variables: The NIPALS approach. In H. M. Blalock, F. M. Borodkin, R. Boudon, & V. Capecchi (Eds.), *Quantitative sociology: International perspectives on mathematical and statistical modeling* (pp. 307–357). New York: Academic Press.

Yaeger, K. (1979). *Modal choice in child care demand: The effects of costs, convenience and quality.* Menlo Park, CA: Stanford Research Institute International.

Zigler, E. (1987a). *Day care for children of working mothers.* Invited presentation at the biennial meetings of the Society for Research in Child Development, Baltimore.

Zigler, E. (1987b, September 18). *A solution to the nation's child care crisis: The school of the twenty-first century.* Paper presented at the 10th anniversary of the Bush Center in Child Development and Social Policy, New Haven, Ct.

Zigler, E., & Muenchow, S. (1987). Infectious diseases in day care: Parallels between psychologically and physically healthy care. In M. T. Osterholm, J. O. Klein, S. S. Aronson, & L. K. Pickering (Eds.), *Infectious diseases in child day care: Management and prevention* (pp. 2–8). Chicago: University of Chicago Press.

Author Index

Subject Index